Letters of
Emily Dickinson

Emily Dickinson

Letters of
Emily Dickinson

EMILY DICKINSON

Edited by
Mabel Loomis Todd

DOVER PUBLICATIONS, INC.
Mineola, New York

Bibliographical Note

This Dover edition, first published in 2003, contains the unabridged text of *Letters of Emily Dickinson,* edited by Mabel Loomis Todd, as published by the World Publishing Company, Cleveland, in 1951. The original edition of the work was first published by Roberts Brothers, Boston, in 1894.

Library of Congress Cataloging-in-Publication Data

Dickinson, Emily, 1830–1886.
    Letters of Emily Dickinson / Emily Dickinson ; edited by Mabel Loomis Todd.
      p. cm.
    Originally published: Boston: Roberts Brothers, 1894.
    Includes index.
    ISBN 0-486-42858-3 (pbk.)
      1. Dickinson, Emily, 1830–1886—Correspondence. 2. Poets, American—19th century—Correspondence. I. Todd, Mabel Loomis, 1856–1932. II. Title.

PS1541.Z5 A4 2003
811'.4—dc21

                              2002072875

Manufactured in the United States of America
Dover Publications, Inc., 31 East 2nd Street, Mineola, N.Y. 11501

THE LOVERS of Emily Dickinson's poems have been so eager for her prose that her sister has gathered these letters, and committed their preparation to me.

Emily Dickinson's verses, often but the reflection of a passing mood, do not always completely represent herself, —rarely, indeed, showing the dainty humor, the frolicsome gayety, which continually bubbled over in her daily life. The sombre and even weird outlook upon this world and the next, characteristic of many of the poems, was by no means a prevailing condition of mind; for, while fully apprehending all the tragic elements in life, enthusiasm and bright joyousness were yet her normal qualities, and stimulating moral heights her native dwelling-place. All this may be glimpsed in her letters, no less full of charm, it is believed, to the general reader, than to Emily Dickinson's personal friends. As she kept no journal, the letters are the more interesting because they contain all the prose which she is known to have written.

It was with something almost like dread that I approached the task of arranging these letters, lest the deep revelations of a peculiarly shy inner life might so pervade them that in true loyalty to their writer none could be publicly used. But with few exceptions they have been read and prepared with entire relief from that feeling, and with unshrinking pleasure; the sanctities were not invaded. Emily kept her little reserves, and bared her soul but seldom, even in intimate correspondence. It was not so much that she was always on spiritual guard, as that she sported with her varying moods, and tested them upon her friends with apparent delight in the effect, as airy and playful as it was half unconscious.

So large is the number of letters to each of several correspondents, that it has seemed best to place these sets in separate chapters. The continuity is perhaps more perfectly preserved in this way than by the usual method of mere chronological succession; especially as, in a life singularly uneventful, no marked periods of travel or achievement serve otherwise to classify them. On this plan a certain order has been possible, too; the opening letters in each chapter are always later than the first of the preceding, although the last letters of one reach a date beyond the beginning of the next. The less remarkable writing, of course, fills the first chapters; but even this shows her love of study, of Nature, and a devotion to home almost as intense as in strange Emily Brontë.

Nothing is perhaps more marked than the change of style between the diffuseness of girlhood and the brilliant sententiousness of late middle life, often startlingly unexpected. And yet suggestions of future picturesque and epigrammatic power occasionally flash through the long, youthful correspondence. Lowell once wrote of the first letters of Carlyle, "The man . . . is all there in the earliest of his writing that we have (potentially there, in character wholly there)." It is chiefly for these "potential" promises that Emily Dickinson's girlish letters are included, all the variations in the evolution of a style having hardly less

interest for the student of human nature than of literature. Village life, even in a college town, was very democratic in the early days when the first of these letters were
written, and they suggest a refreshing atmosphere of homely
simplicity.

Unusual difficulties have been encountered in arranging the letters with definite reference to years, as none but
the very earliest were dated. The change in handwriting,
of which specimens are given in facsimile, was no less no-
ticeable than Emily Dickinson's development in literary
style; and this alone has been a general guide. The thoughtfulness of a few correspondents in recording the time of
the letters' reception has been a farther and most welcome
assistance; while occasionally the kind of postage-stamp and
the postmark helped to indicate when they were written,
although generally the envelopes had not been preserved.
But the larger part have been placed by searching out the
dates of contemporaneous incidents mentioned,—for instance, numerous births, marriages, and deaths; any epoch
in the life of a friend was an event to Emily Dickinson,
always noticed by a bit of flashing verse, or a graceful, if
mystically expressed, note of comfort or congratulation. If
errors are found in assignment to the proper time, it will
not be from lack of having interrogated all available sources
of information.

In more recent years, dashes instead of punctuation, and
capitals for all important words, together with the quaint
handwriting, give to the actual manuscript an individual
fascination quite irresistible. But the coldness of print de-
stroys that elusive charm, so that dashes and capitals have
been restored to their conventional use.

In her later years, Emily Dickinson rarely addressed the
envelopes: it seemed as if her sensitive nature shrank from

the publicity which even her handwriting would undergo, in the observation of indifferent eyes. Various expedients were resorted to,—obliging friends frequently performed this office for her; sometimes a printed newspaper label was pasted upon the envelope; but the actual strokes of her own pencil were, so far as possible, reserved exclusively for friendly eyes.

Emily Dickinson's great disinclination for an exposition of the theology current during her girlhood is matter for small wonder. While her fathers were men of recognized originality and force, they did not question the religious teaching of the time; they were leaders in town and church, even strict and uncompromising in their piety. Reverence for accepted ways and forms, merely as such, seems entirely to have been left out of Emily's constitution. To her, God was not a far-away and dreary Power to be daily addressed,—the great "Eclipse" of which she wrote,—but He was near and familiar and pervasive. Her garden was full of His brightness and glory; the birds sang and the sky glowed because of Him. To shut herself out of the sunshine in a church, dark, chilly, restricted, was rather to shut herself away from Him; almost pathetically she wrote, "I believe the love of God may be taught not to seem like bears."

In essence, no real irreverence mars her poems or her letters. Of malice aforethought,—an intentional irreverence,—she is never once guilty. The old interpretation of the biblical estimate of life was cause to her for gentle, wide-eyed astonishment. No one knew better the phrases which had become cant, and which seemed always to misrepresent the Father Whom she knew with personal directness and without necessity for human intervention. It was a theologically misconceived idea of a "jealous God," for which she had a profound contempt; and the fact that those ideas were still held by the stricter New England people of her day made not the slightest difference in her expression of disapproval. Fearless and daring, she had biblical quotation at her finger-tips; and even if she sometimes used it in a way which might shock a conventionalist, she had in her heart too profound an adoration for the great, ever-living, and present Father to hold a shadow of real irreverence toward Him, so peculiarly near. No soul in which dwelt not a very noble and actual love and respect for the essentials could have written as she did of real triumph, of truth, of aspiration.

> "We never know how high we are,
>   Till we are called to rise;
> And then, if we are true to plan,
>   Our statures touch the skies.
>
> "The heroism we recite
>   Would be a daily thing
> Did not ourselves the cubits warp,
>   For fear to be a king."

Must not one who wrote that have had her ever-open shrine, her reverenced tribunal?

The whims and pretences of society, its forms and unrealities, seemed to her thin and unworthy. Conventionalities, while they amused, exasperated her also; and the little poem beginning,

> "The show is not the show,
>   But they that go,"

expresses in large measure her attitude toward society, when she lived in the midst of it. Real life, on the other hand, seemed vast and inexpressibly solemn. Petty trivialities had no part in her constitution, and she came to despise them more and more,—so much, indeed, that with her increasing shyness, she gradually gave up all journeys, and finally retired completely from even the simple life of a New England college town.

As has been said of Emily Brontë, "To this natural isolation of spirit we are in a great measure indebted for that passionate love of Nature which gives such a vivid reality and exquisite simplicity to her descriptions." Emily Dickinson's letters, almost as much as the poems, exhibit her elf-like intimacy with Nature. She sees and apprehends the great mother's processes, and shares the rapture of all created things under the wide sky. The letters speak of flowers, of pines and autumnal colors; but no natural sight or sound or incident seems to have escaped her delicate apprehension.

Bird songs, crickets, frost, and winter winds, even the toad and snake, mushrooms and bats, have an indescribable charm for her, which she in turn brings to us. March, "that month of proclamation," was especially dear; and among her still unpublished verses is a characteristic greeting to the windy month. In all its aspects "Nature became the unique charm and consolation of her life, and as such she has written of it."

Warm thanks are due the friends who have generously lent letters for reproduction. That they were friends of Emily Dickinson, and willing to share her words with the larger outside circle, waiting and appreciative, entitles them to the gratitude, not merely of the Editor, but of all who make up the world that Emily "never saw," but to which, nevertheless, she sent a "message."

MABEL LOOMIS TODD

AMHERST, MASSACHUSETTS
October 1894

❧ *CONTENTS* ☙

INTRODUCTION TO THE FIRST EDITION   vii

I. TO *Mrs. A. P. Strong* (1845-1853)   3

II. TO *Mr. W. A. Dickinson* (1847-1854)   55

III. TO *Mrs. Gordon L. Ford, Mr. Bowdoin, Mrs. Anthon, and Miss Lavinia Dickinson* (1848-1865)   104

IV. TO *Dr. and Mrs. J. G. Holland* (1853-1883)   129

V. TO *Mr. and Mrs. Samuel Bowles* (1858-1881)   158

VI. TO *the Misses* ——— (1859-1885)   193

VII. TO *Mr. T. W. Higginson* (1862-1884)   252

VIII. TO *Mr. Perez D. Cowan, Miss Maria Whitney, Mr. Bowles, Mr. F. D. Clark, and Mr. C. H. Clark* (1870-1885)   280

IX. TO *Mr. and Mrs. Jenkins, Mrs. Read, Mrs. W. A. Stearns, Mrs. Edward Tuckerman, Mrs. Cooper, Mrs. Davis, Mrs. Hills, Mrs. Jameson, Mr. Emerson, Maggie Maher, Mr. and Mrs. Montague, Mrs. W. F. Stearns, Mr. J. K. Chickering, Mrs. Sweetser, Mr. Niles, Mrs. Carmichael, Dr. and Mrs. Field, Mr.*

CONTENTS

Holland, "H.H.," Miss Hall, Mrs. Crowell,
and Mrs. J. C. Greenough (1872-1885)   310

x. TO Mrs. Todd, Mrs. Tuckerman, the
Misses ——, Mr. Clark, and Mrs. Currier   367

INDEX   377

ILLUSTRATIONS

CHILD PORTRAIT OF EMILY DICKINSON   Frontispiece

LETTER TO DR. AND MRS. HOLLAND, *facsimile*   132

LETTER TO MR. SAMUEL BOWLES, *facsimile*   183

LETTER TO MR. C. H. CLARK, *facsimile*   300

Letters of
Emily Dickinson

i

TO *Mrs. A. P. Strong*

THE LETTERS *in this chapter were written to a schoolmate and early friend. The first is one of the oldest yet found, dated when Emily Dickinson had but recently passed her fourteenth birthday.*

Before the era of outer envelopes, it is quaintly written on a large square sheet, and so folded that the fourth page forms a cover bearing the address. Most of the remaining letters to Mrs. Strong are thus folded, and sealed either with wax or wafers,—occasionally with little rectangular or diamond papers bearing mottoes stamped in gold. The handwriting is almost microscopic, the pages entirely filled. Merely personal items have been generally omitted.

It will be seen that the name "Emilie E. Dickinson" is sometimes used. The ie was a youthful vagary, and the second initial, E., stood for Elizabeth, a "middle name" entirely discarded in later years.

AMHERST, *Feb.* 23, 1845

DEAR A.,—After receiving the smitings of conscience for a long time, I have at length succeeded in stifling the voice of that faithful monitor by a promise of a long letter to you; so leave everything and sit down prepared for a long siege in the shape of a bundle of nonsense from friend E.

. . . I keep your lock of hair as precious as gold and a great deal more so. I often look at it when I go to my little lot of treasures, and wish the owner of that glossy lock were here. Old Time wags on pretty much as usual at Amherst, and I know of nothing that has occurred to break the silence; however, the reduction of the postage has excited my risibles somewhat. Only think! We can send a letter before long for five little coppers only, filled with the thoughts and advice of dear friends. But I will not get into a philosophizing strain just yet. There is time enough for that upon another page of this mammoth sheet. . . . Your *beau idéal* D. I have not seen lately. I presume he was changed into a star some night while gazing at them, and placed in the constellation Orion between Bellatrix and Betelgeux. I doubt not if he was here he would wish to be kindly remembered to you. What delightful weather we have had for a week! It seems more like smiling May crowned with flowers than cold, arctic February wading through snowdrifts. I have heard some sweet little birds sing, but I fear we shall have more cold weather and their little bills will be frozen up before their songs are finished. My plants look beautifully. Old King Frost has not had the pleasure of snatching any of them in his cold embrace as yet, and I hope will not. Our little pussy has made out to live. I believe you know what a fatality attends our little kitties, all of them, having had six die one right after the other. Do you love your little niece J. as well as ever? Your soliloquy on the year that is past and gone was not unheeded by me. Would that we might spend the year which is now fleeting so swiftly by to better advantage than the one which we have not the power to recall! Now I know you will laugh, and say I wonder what makes Emily so sentimental. But I don't care if you do, for I sha'n't hear you. What are you doing this winter? I am about everything. I am now working a pair of slippers to adorn my father's feet. I wish you would come and help me finish them. . . . Although it is late in the day, I am going to wish you a happy New Year,—not but what I think your New Year will pass just as happily without it, but to make a little return for your kind wish, which so far in a good many respects has been granted, probably because you wished that it might be so. . . . I go to singing-school Sabbath evenings to improve my voice. Don't you envy me? . . .

I wish you would come and make me a long visit. If you will, I will entertain you to the best of my abilities, which you know are neither few nor small. Why can't you persuade your father and mother to let you come here to school next term, and keep me company, as I am going? Miss ——, I presume you can guess who I mean, is going to finish her education next summer. The finishing stroke is to be put on at Newton. She will then have learned all that we poor foot-travellers are toiling up the hill of knowledge to acquire. Wonderful thought! Her horse has carried her along so swiftly that she has nearly gained the summit, and we are plodding along on foot after her. Well said and sufficient this. We'll finish an education sometime, won't we? You may then be Plato, and I will be Socrates, provided you won't be wiser than I am. Lavinia just now interrupted my flow of thought by saying give my love to A. I presume you will be glad to have some one break off this epistle. All the girls send much love to you. And please accept a large share for yourself.

From your beloved
EMILY E. DICKINSON

Please send me a copy of that Romance you were writing at Amherst. I am in a fever to read it. I expect it will be against my Whig feelings.

After this postscript many others follow, across the top, down the edges, tucked in wherever space will allow. There are also a few lines from each of three girl friends to "dear A."

AMHERST, *May* ·7, 1845

DEAR A.,—It seems almost an age since I have seen you, and it is indeed an age for friends to be separated. I was delighted to receive a paper from you, and I also was much pleased with the news it contained, especially that you are taking lessons on the "piny," as you always call it. But remember not to get on ahead of me. Father intends to have a piano very soon. How happy I shall be when I have one of my own! Old Father Time has wrought many changes here since your last short visit. Miss S. T. and Miss N. M. have both taken the marriage vows upon themselves. Dr. Hitchcock has moved into his new house, and Mr. Tyler across the way from our house has moved into President Hitchcock's old house. Mr. C. is going to move into Mr. T.'s former house, but the worst thing old Time has done here is he has walked so fast as to overtake H. M. and carry her to Hartford on last week Saturday. I was so vexed with him for it that I ran after him and made out to get near enough to him to put some salt on his tail, when he fled and left me to run home alone. . . . Viny went to Boston this morning with father, to be gone a fortnight, and I am left alone in all my glory. I suppose she has got there before this time, and is probably staring with mouth and eyes wide open at the wonders of the city. I have been to walk to-night, and got some very choice wild flowers. I wish you had some of them. Viny and I both go to school this term. We have a very fine school. There are 63 scholars. I have four studies. They are Mental Philosophy, Geology, Latin, and Botany. How large they sound, don't they? I don't believe you have such big studies. . . . My plants look finely now. I am going to send you a little geranium leaf in this letter, which you must press for me. Have you made you an herbarium yet? I hope you will if you have not, it would be such a treasure to you; 'most all the girls are making one. If you do, perhaps I can make some additions to it from flowers growing around here. How do you enjoy your school this term? Are the teachers as pleasant as our old school-teachers? I expect you have a great many prim, starched up young ladies there, who, I doubt not, are perfect models of propriety and good behavior. If they are, don't let your free spirit be chained by them. I don't know as there [are] any in school of this stamp. But there 'most always are a few, whom the teachers look up to and regard as their satellites. I am growing handsome very fast indeed! I expect I shall be the belle of Amherst when I reach my 17th year. I don't doubt that I shall have perfect crowds of admirers at that age. Then how I shall delight to make them await my bidding, and with what delight shall I witness their suspense while I make my final decision. But away with my nonsense. I have written one composition this term, and I need not assure you it was exceedingly edifying to myself as well as everybody else. Don't you want to see it? I really wish you could have a chance. We are obliged to write compositions once in a fortnight, and select a piece to read from some interesting book the week that we don't write compositions.

We really have some most charming young women in school this term. I sha'n't call them anything but women, for women they are in every sense of the word. I must, however, describe one, and while I describe her I wish Imagination, who is ever present with you, to make a little picture of this self-same young lady in your mind, and by her aid see if you cannot conceive how she looks. Well, to begin. . . . Then just imagine her as she is, and a huge string of gold beads encircling her neck, and don't she present a lively picture; and then she is so bustling, she is always whizzing about, and whenever I come in contact with her I really think I am in a hornet's nest. I can't help thinking every time I see this singular piece of humanity of Shakespeare's description of a tempest in a teapot. But I must not laugh about her, for I verily believe she has a good heart, and that is the principal thing now-a-days. Don't you hope I shall become wiser in the company of such virtuosos? It would certainly be desirable. Have you noticed how beautifully the trees look now? They seem to be completely covered with fragrant blossoms. . . . I had so many things to do for Viny, as she was going away, that very much against my wishes I deferred writing you until now, but forgive and forget, dear A., and I will promise to do better in future. Do write me soon, and let it be a long, long letter; and when you can't get time to write, send a paper, so as to let me know you think of me still, though we are separated by hill and stream. All the girls send much love to you. Don't forget to let me receive a letter from you soon. I can say no more now as my paper is all filled up.

Your affectionate friend,
EMILY E. DICKINSON

Written in 1845; *postmarked* AMHERST, *August* 4
Sabbath Eve

DEAR A.,—I have now sat down to write you a long, long letter. My writing apparatus is upon a stand before me, and all things are ready. I have no flowers before me as you had to inspire you. But then you know I can imagine myself inspired by them, and perhaps that will do as well. You cannot imagine how delighted I was to receive your letter. It was so full, and everything in it was interesting to me because it came from you. I presume you did not doubt my gratitude for it, on account of my delaying so long to answer it, for you know I have had no leisure for anything. When I tell you that our term has been eleven weeks long, and that I have had four studies and taken music lessons, you can imagine a little how my time has been taken up lately. I will try to be more punctual in such matters for the future. How are you now? I am very sorry to hear that you are unable to remain in your school on account of your health, it must be such a disappointment to you. But I presume you are enjoying yourself much to be at home again. You asked me in your last letter if old Father Time wagged on in Amherst pretty much as ever. For my part, I see no particular change in his movements unless it be that he goes on a swifter pace than formerly, and that he wields his sickle more sternly than ever. How do you like taking music lessons? I presume you are delighted with it. I am taking lessons this term of Aunt S——, who is spending the summer with us. I never enjoyed myself more than I have this summer; for we have had such a delightful school and such pleasant teachers, and besides I have had a piano of my own. Our examination is to come off next week on Monday. I wish you could be here at that time. Why can't you come? If you will, you can come and practise on my piano as much as you wish to. I am already gasping in view of our examination; and although I am determined not to dread it I know it is so foolish, yet in spite of my heroic resolutions, I cannot avoid a few misgivings when I think of those tall, stern trustees, and when I know that I shall lose my character if I don't recite as precisely as the laws of the Medes and Persians. But what matter will that be a hundred years hence? I will distress you no longer with my fears, for you know well enough what they are without my entering into any explanations. Are you practising now you are at home? I hope you are, for if you are not you would be likely to forget what you have learnt. I want very much to hear you play. I have the same instruction book that you have, Bertini, and I am getting along in it very well. Aunt S—— says she sha'n't let me have many tunes now, for she wants I should get over in the book a good ways first. Oh, A., if Sarah G——, H——, and yourself were only here this summer, what times we should have! I wish if we can't be together all the time that we could meet once in a while at least. I wish you would all come to our house, and such times as we would have would be a caution. I want to see you all so much that it seems as if I could not wait. Have you heard anything from Miss Adams, our dear teacher? How much I would give to see her once more, but I am afraid I never shall. She is so far away. You asked me in your letter to tell you all the news worth telling, and although there is not much, yet I will endeavor to think of everything that will be new to you. In the first place, Mrs. J. and Mrs. S. M. have both of them a little daughter. Very promising children, I understand. I don't doubt if they live they will be ornaments to society. I think they are both to be considered as embryos of future usefulness. Mrs. W. M. has now two grand-daughters. Isn't she to be envied? . . . I am sorry that you are laying up H.'s sins against her. I think you had better heap coals of fire upon her head by writing to her constantly until you get an answer. I have some patience with these "school marms." They have so many trials. I hope you will decide to blot out her iniquities against her. I don't know about this Mr. E. giving you concert tickets. I think for my part it looks rather suspicious. He is a young man, I suppose. These music teachers are always such high-souled beings that I think they would exactly suit your fancy. My garden looks beautifully now. I wish you could see it. I would send you a bouquet if I could get a good opportunity. My house plants look very finely, too. You wished me to give you some account of S. P. She is attending school this term and studying Latin and Algebra. She is very well and happy and sends much love to you. All the girls send much love to you, and wish you to write to them. I have been working a beautiful book-mark to give to one of our school-girls. Perhaps you have seen it. It is an arrow with a beautiful wreath around it. Have you altered any since I have seen you? Isn't it a funny question for one friend to ask another? I haven't altered any, I think, except that I have my hair done up, and that makes me look different. I can imagine just how you look now. I wonder what you are doing this moment. I have got an idea that you are knitting edging. Are you? Won't you tell me when you answer my letter whether I guessed right or not? . . . You gave me a compliment in your letter in regard to my being a faithful correspondent. I must say I think I deserve it. I have been learning several beautiful pieces lately. The "Grave of Bonaparte" is one, "Lancers Quickstep," and "Maiden, weep no more," which is a sweet little song. I wish much to see you and hear you play. I hope you will come to A. before long. Why can't you pass commencement here? I do wish you would. . . . I have looked my letter over, and find I have written nothing worth reading. . . . Accept much love from your affectionate friend,

                                        EMILY E. D.

                                Thursday, Sept. 26, 1845

DEAREST A.,—As I just glanced at the clock and saw how smoothly the little hands glide over the surface, I could scarcely believe that those selfsame little hands had eloped with so many of my precious moments since I received your affectionate letter, and it was still harder for me to believe that I, who am always boasting of being so faithful a correspondent, should have been guilty of negligence in so long delaying to answer it. . . . I am very glad to hear that you are better than you have been, and I hope in future disease will not be as neighborly as he has been heretofore to either of us. I long to see you, dear A., and speak with you face to face; but so long as a bodily interview is denied us, we must make letters answer, though it is hard for friends to be separated. I really believe you would have been frightened to have heard me scold when Sabra informed me that you had decided not to visit Amherst this fall. But as I could find no one upon whom to vent my spleen for your decision, I thought it best to be calm, and therefore have at length resigned myself to my cruel fate, though with not a very good grace. I think you do well to inquire whether anything has been heard from H. I really don't know what has become of her, unless procrastination has carried her off. I think that must be the case. I think you have given quite a novel description of the wedding. Are you quite sure Mr. F., the minister, told them to stand up and he would tie them in a great bow-knot? But I beg pardon for speaking so lightly of so solemn a ceremony. You asked me in your letter if I did not think you partial in your admiration of Miss Helen H., ditto Mrs. P. I answer, Not in the least. She was universally beloved in Amherst. She made us quite a visit in June, and we regretted more than ever that she was going where we could not see her as often as we had been ac-customed. She seemed very happy in her prospects, and seemed to think distance nothing in comparison to a home with the one of her choice. I hope she will be happy, and of course she will. I wished much to see her once more, but was denied the privilege. . . . You asked me if I was attending school now. I am not. Mother thinks me not able to confine myself to school this term. She had rather I would exercise, and I can assure you I get plenty of that article by staying at home. I am going to learn to make bread to-morrow. So you may imagine me with my sleeves rolled up, mixing flour, milk, saleratus, etc., with a deal of grace. I advise you if you don't know how to make the staff of life to learn with dispatch. I think I could keep house very comfortably if I knew how to cook. But as long as I don't, my knowledge of housekeeping is about of as much use as faith without works, which you know we are told is dead. Excuse my quoting from Scripture, dear A., for it was so handy in this case I couldn't get along very well without it. Since I wrote you last, the summer is past and gone, and autumn with the sere and yellow leaf is already upon us. I never knew the time to pass so swiftly, it seems to me, as the past summer. I really think some one must have oiled his chariot wheels, for I don't recollect of hearing him pass, and I am sure I should if something had not prevented his chariot wheels from creaking as usual. But I will not expatiate upon him any longer, for I know it is wicked to trifle with so revered a personage, and I fear he will make me a call in person to inquire as to the remarks which I have made concerning him. Therefore I will let him alone for the present. . . . How are you getting on with your music? Well, I hope and trust. I am taking lessons and am getting along very well, and now I have a piano, I am very happy. I feel much honored at having even a doll named for me. I believe I shall have to give it a silver cup, as that is the custom among old ladies when a child is named for them. . . . Have you any flowers now? I have had a beautiful flower-garden this summer; but they are nearly gone now. It is very cold to-night, and I mean to pick the prettiest ones before I go to bed, and cheat Jack Frost of so many of *the treasures* he calculates to rob to-night. Won't it be a capital idea to put him at defiance, for once at least, if no more? I would love to send you a bouquet if I had an opportunity, and you could press it and write under it, The last flowers of summer. Wouldn't it be poetical, and you know that is what young ladies aim to be now-a-days. . . . I expect I have altered a good deal since I have seen you, dear A. I have grown tall a good deal, and wear my golden tresses done up in a net-cap. Modesty, you know, forbids me to mention whether my personal appearance has altered. I leave that for others to judge.

But my [word omitted] has not changed, nor will it in time to come. I shall always remain the same old sixpence. . . . I can say no more now, as it is after ten, and everybody has gone to bed but me. Don't forget your affectionate friend,

EMILY E. D.

AMHERST, *Jan.* 12, 1846

A., MY DEAR,—Since I received your precious letter another year has commenced its course, and the old year has gone never to return. How sad it makes one feel to sit down quietly and think of the flight of the old year, and the unceremonious obtrusion of the new year upon our notice! How many things we have omitted to do which might have cheered a human heart, or whispered hope in the ear of the sorrowful, and how many things have we done over which the dark mantle of regret will ever fall! How many good resolutions did I make at the commencement of the year now flown, merely to break them and to feel more than ever convinced of the weakness of my own resolutions! The New Year's day was unusually gloomy to me, I know not why, and perhaps for that reason a host of unpleasant reflections forced themselves upon me which I found not easy to throw off. But I will no longer sentimentalize upon the past, for I cannot recall it. I will, after inquiring for the health of my dear A., relapse into a more lively strain. I can hardly have patience to write, for I have not seen you for so long that I have worlds of things to tell you, and my pen is not swift enough to answer my purpose at all. However, I will try to make it communicate as much information as possible and wait to see your own dear self once more before I relate all my thoughts which have come and gone since I last saw you. I suppose from your letter that you are enjoying yourself finely this winter at Miss C.'s school. I would give a great deal if I was there with you. I don't go to school this winter except to a recitation in German. Mr. C. has a very large class, and father thought I might never have another opportunity to study it. It takes about an hour and a half to recite. Then I take music lessons and practise two hours in a day, and besides these two I have a large stand of plants to cultivate. This is the principal round of my occupation this winter. . . . I have just seen a funeral procession go by of a negro baby, so if my ideas are rather dark you need not marvel. . . . Old Santa Claus was very polite to me the last Christmas. I hung up my stocking on the bedpost as usual. I had a perfume bag and a bottle of otto of rose to go with it, a sheet of music, a china mug with *Forget me not* upon it, from S. S.,—who, by the way, is as handsome, entertaining, and as fine a piano player as in former times,—a toilet cushion, a watch case, a fortuneteller, and an amaranthine stock of pin-cushions and needlebooks, which in ingenuity and art would rival the works of Scripture Dorcas. I found abundance of candy in my stocking, which I do not think has had the anticipated effect upon my disposition, in case it was to sweeten it, also two hearts at the bottom of all, which I thought looked rather ominous; but I will not enter into any more details, for they take up more room than I can spare.

Haven't we had delightful weather for a week or two? It seems as if Old Winter had forgotten himself. Don't you believe he is absent-minded? It has been bad weather for colds, however. I have had a severe cold for a few days, and can sympathize with you, though I have been delivered from a stiff neck. I think you must belong to the tribe of Israel, for you know in the Bible the prophet calls them a stiff-necked generation. I have lately come to the conclusion that I am Eve, alias Mrs. Adam. You know there is no account of her death in the Bible, and why am not I Eve? If you find any statements which you think likely to prove the truth of the case, I wish you would send them to me without delay.

Have you heard a word from H. M. or S. T.? I consider them lost sheep. I send them a paper every week on Monday, but I never get one in return. I am almost a mind to take a hand-car and go around to hunt them up. I can't think that they have forgotten us, and I know of no reason unless they are sick why they should delay so long to show any signs of remembrance. Do write me soon a very long letter, and tell me all about your school and yourself too.

> Your affectionate friend,
> EMILY E. DICKINSON

Friday Eve [summer], 1846

MY DEAR A.,—Though it is a long time since I received your affectionate epistle, yet when I give you my reasons for my long delay, I know you will freely forgive and forget all past offences.

It seems to me that time has never flown so swiftly with me as it has the last spring. I have been busy every minute, and not only so, but hurried all the time. So you may imagine that I have not had a spare moment, much though my heart has longed for it, to commune with an absent friend. . . . I presume you will be wondering by this time what I am doing to be in so much haste as I have declared myself to be. Well, I will tell you. I am fitting to go to South Hadley Seminary, and expect if my health is good to enter that institution a year from next fall. Are you not astonished to hear such news? You cannot imagine how much I am anticipating in entering there. It has been in my thought by day, and my dreams by night, ever since I heard of South Hadley Seminary. I fear I am anticipating too much, and that some freak of fortune may overturn all my airy schemes for future happiness. But it is my nature always to anticipate more than I realize. . . . Have you not heard that Miss Adams—dear Miss Adams—is here this term? Oh, you cannot imagine how natural it seems to see her happy face in school once more. But it needs Harriet, Sarah, and your own dear self to complete the ancient picture. I hope we shall get you all back before Miss Adams goes away again. Have you yet heard a word from that prodigal,—H.? . . .

Your affectionate friend,
EMILY E. D.

I send you a memento in the form of a pressed flower, which you must keep.

A converted Jew has been lecturing here for the last week. His lectures were free, and they were on the present condition of the Jews. Dr. Scudder, a returned missionary, is here now, and he is lecturing also. Have you seen a beautiful piece of poetry which has been going through the papers lately? *Are we almost there?* is the title of it. . . . I have two hours to practise daily now I am in school. I have been learning a beautiful thing, which I long to have you hear. . . .

BOSTON, *Sept.* 8, 1846

MY DEAR FRIEND A.,—It is a long, long time since I received your welcome letter, and it becomes me to sue for forgiveness, which I am sure your affectionate heart will not refuse to grant. But many and unforeseen circumstances have caused my long delay. . . . Father and mother thought a journey would be of service to me, and accordingly I left home for Boston week before last. I had a delightful ride in the cars, and am now getting settled down, if there can be such a state in the city. I am visiting in my aunt's family, and am happy. Happy! did I say? No; not happy, but contented. I have been here a fortnight to-day, and in that time I have both seen and heard a great many wonderful things. Perhaps you might like to know how I have spent the time here. I have been to Mount Auburn, to the Chinese Museum, to Bunker Hill; I have attended two concerts and one Horticultural Exhibition. I have been upon the top of the State House, and almost everywhere that you can imagine. Have you ever been to Mount Auburn? If not, you can form but slight conception of this "City of the Dead." It seems as if nature had formed this spot with a distinct idea in view of its being a resting-place for her children, where, wearied and disappointed, they might stretch themselves beneath the spreading cypress, and close their eyes "calmly as to a night's repose, or flowers at set of sun."

The Chinese Museum is a great curiosity. There are an endless variety of wax figures made to resemble the Chinese, and dressed in their costume. Also articles of Chinese manufacture of an innumerable variety deck the rooms. Two of the Chinese go with this exhibition. One of them is a professor of music in China, and the other is teacher of a writing-school at home. They were both wealthy, and not obliged to labor, but they were also opium-eaters; and fearing to continue the practice lest it destroy their lives, yet unable to break the "rigid chain of habit" in their own land, they left their families, and came to this country. They have now entirely overcome the practice. There is something peculiarly interesting to me in their self-denial. The musician played upon two of his instruments, and accompanied them with his voice. It needed great command over my risible faculties to enable me to keep sober as this amateur was performing; yet he was so very polite to give us some of his native music that we could not do otherwise than to express ourselves highly edified with his performances. The writing-master is constantly occupied in writing the names of visitors who request it, upon cards in the Chinese language, for which he charges 12½ cents apiece. He never fails to give his card besides to the persons who wish it. I obtained one of his cards for Viny and myself, and I consider them very precious. Are you still in Norwich, and attending to music? I am not now taking lessons, but I expect to when I return home.

Does it seem as though September had come? How swiftly summer has fled, and what report has it borne to heaven of misspent time and wasted hours? Eternity only will answer. The ceaseless flight of the seasons is to me a very solemn thought; and yet why do we not strive to make a better improvement of them? With how much emphasis the poet has said, "We take no note of time but from its loss. 'Twere wise in man to give it then a tongue. Pay no moment but in just purchase of its worth, and what its worth ask death-beds. They can tell. Part with it as with life reluctantly." Then we have higher authority than that of man for the improvement of our time. For God has said, "Work while the day lasts, for the night is coming in the which no man can work." Let us strive together to part with time more reluctantly, to watch the pinions of the fleeting moment until they are dim in the distance, and the new-coming moment claims our attention. I have perfect confidence in God and His promises, and yet I know not why I feel that the world holds a predominant place in my affections. . . . Your affectionate friend,

Emily E. D.

Numerous postscripts are appended, as usually:—

I have really suffered from the heat the last week. I think it remarkable that we should have such weather in September. There were over one hundred deaths in Boston last week, a great many of them owing to the heat. Mr. Taylor, our old teacher, was in Amherst at Commencement time. Oh, I do love Mr. Taylor. It seems so like old times to meet Miss Adams and Mr. Taylor together again. I could hardly refrain from singing, "Auld Lang Syne." It seemed so very *à propos*. Have you forgotten the memorable ride we all took with Mr. Taylor, "Long, long ago"? . . . Austin entered college last Commencement. Only think! I have a brother who has the honor to be a Freshman! Will you not promise me that you will come to Commencement when he graduates? Do! Please! I have altered very much since you were here. I am now very tall, and wear long dresses nearly. Do you believe we shall know each other when we meet? Don't forget to write soon.

E.

Sabbath Eve, 1846

My dear A.,—When I last wrote you I was in Boston, where I spent a delightful visit of four weeks. I returned home about the middle of September in very good health and spirits, for which it seems to me I cannot be sufficiently grateful to the Giver of all mercies. I expected to go into the Academy upon my return home, but as I stayed longer than I expected to, and as the school had already commenced, I made up my mind to remain at home during the fall term and pursue my studies the winter term, which commences a week after Thanksgiving. I kept my good resolution for once in my life, and have been sewing, practising upon the piano, and assisting mother in household affairs. I am anticipating the commencement of the next term with a great deal of pleasure, for I have been an exile from school two terms on account of my health, and you know what it is to "love school." Miss Adams is with us now, and will remain through the winter, and we have an excellent Principal in the person of Mr. Leonard Humphrey, who was the last valedictorian. We now have a fine school. I thank you a thousand times for your long and affectionate letter. . . . I found a quantity of sewing waiting with open arms to embrace me, or rather for me to embrace it, and I could hardly give myself up to "Nature's sweet restorer," for the ghosts of out-of-order garments crying for vengeance upon my defenceless head. However, I am happy to inform you, my dear friend, that I have nearly finished my sewing for winter, and will answer all the letters which you shall deem worthy to send so naughty a girl as myself, at short notice. . . .

Write soon. Your affectionate

EMILY E. D.

March 15, 1847
Sabbath Eve

EVER DEAR A.,— . . . We have spent our vacation of a fortnight, and school has commenced again since you wrote me. I go this term, and am studying Algebra, Euclid, Ecclesiastical History, and reviewing Arithmetic again to be upon the safe side of things next autumn. We have a delightful school this term under the instruction of our former principals, and Miss R. Woodbridge, daughter of Rev. Dr. W. of Hadley, for preceptress. We all love her very much. Perhaps a slight description of her might be interesting to my dear A. She is tall and rather slender, but finely proportioned, has a most witching pair of blue eyes, rich brown hair, delicate complexion, cheeks which vie with the opening rose-bud, teeth like pearls, dimples which come and go like the ripples in yonder little merry brook, and then she is so affectionate and lovely. Forgive my glowing description, for you know I am always in love with my teachers. Yet, much as we love her, it seems lonely and strange without "our dear Miss Adams." I suppose you know that she has left Amherst, not again to return as a teacher. It is indeed true that she is to be married. Are you not astonished? Nothing was known but that she was to return to the school, until a few days before she left for Syracuse, where she has gone to make her "wedding gear." She is to be married the first of next April, to a very respectable lawyer in Conway, Massachusetts. She seemed to be very happy in anticipation of her future prospects, and I hope she will realize all her fond hopes. I cannot bear to think that she will never more wield the sceptre and sit upon the throne in our venerable schoolhouse, and yet I am glad she is going to have a home of her own, and a kind companion to take life's journey with her. I am delighted that she is to live so near us, for we can ride up and see her often. You cannot imagine how much I enjoyed your description of your Christmas fête at Miss Campbell's. How magnificent the "Christmas tree" must have been, and what a grand time you must have had, so many of you! Oh! !

I had a great many presents, Christmas and New Year's holidays, both, but we had no such celebration of the former which you describe. . . . Do write me soon—a long letter—and tell me how soon you are coming, and how long we can keep you when you come. Your affectionate

EMILY E. DICKINSON

MT. HOLYOKE SEMINARY, *Nov.* 6, 1847

MY DEAR A.,—I am really at Mount Holyoke Seminary, and this is to be my home for a long year. Your affectionate letter was joyfully received, and I wish that this might make you as happy as yours did me. It has been nearly six weeks since I left home, and that is a longer time than I was ever away from home before now. I was very homesick for a few days, and it seemed to me I could not live here. But I am now contented and quite happy, if I can be happy when absent from my dear home and friends. You may laugh at the idea that I cannot be happy when away from home, but you must remember that I have a very dear home and that this is my first trial in the way of absence for any length of time in my life. As you desire it, I will give you a full account of myself since I first left the paternal roof. I came to South Hadley six weeks ago next Thursday. I was much fatigued with the ride, and had a severe cold besides, which prevented me from commencing my examinations until the next day, when I began. I finished them in three days, and found them about what I had anticipated, though the old scholars say they are more strict than they ever have been before. As you can easily imagine, I was much delighted to finish without failures, and I came to the conclusion then, that I should not be at all homesick, but the reaction left me as homesick a girl as it is not usual to see. I am now quite contented and am very much occupied in reviewing the Junior studies, as I wish to enter the middle class. The school is very large, and though quite a number have left, on account of finding the examinations more difficult than they anticipated, yet there are nearly 300 now. Perhaps you know that Miss Lyon is raising her standard of scholarship a good deal, on account of the number of applicants this year, and she makes the examinations more severe than usual.

You cannot imagine how trying they are, because if we cannot go through them all in a specified time, we are sent home. I cannot be too thankful that I got through as soon as I did, and I am sure that I never would endure the suspense which I endured during those three days again for all the treasures of the world.

I room with my cousin Emily, who is a Senior. She is an excellent room-mate, and does all in her power to make me happy. You can imagine how pleasant a good room-mate is, for you have been away to school so much. Everything is pleasant and happy here, and I think I could be no happier at any other school away from home. Things seem much more like home than I anticipated, and the teachers are all very kind and affectionate to us. They call on us frequently and urge us to return their calls, and when we do, we always receive a cordial welcome from them. I will tell you my order of time for the day, as you were so kind as to give me yours. At 6 o'clock we all rise. We breakfast at 7. Our study hours begin at 8. At 9 we all meet in Seminary Hall for devotions. At 10¼ I recite a review of Ancient History, in connection with which we read Goldsmith and Grimshaw. At 11, I recite a lesson in Pope's *Essay on Man,* which is merely transposition. At 12 I practise calisthenics, and at 12¼ read until dinner, which is at 12½, and after dinner, from 1½ until 2, I sing in Seminary Hall. From 2¾ until 3¾ I practise upon the piano. At 3¾ I go to Sections, where we give in all our accounts for the day, including absence, tardiness, communications, breaking silent study hours, receiving company in our rooms, and ten thousand other things which I will not take time or place to mention. At 4½ we go into Seminary Hall and receive advice from Miss Lyon in the form of a lecture. We have supper at 6, and silent study hours from then until the retiring bell, which rings at 8¾, but the tardy bell does not ring until 9¾, so that we don't often obey the first warning to retire. Unless we have a good and reasonable excuse for failure upon any of the items that I mentioned above, they are recorded and a *black mark* stands against our names. As you can easily imagine, we do not like very well to get 'exceptions,' as they are called scientifically here.

My domestic work is not difficult and consists in carrying the knives from the first tier of tables at morning and noon, and at night washing and wiping the same quantity of knives. I am quite well and hope to be able to spend the year here, free from sickness. You have probably heard many reports of the food here; and if so, I can tell you that I have yet seen nothing corresponding to my ideas on that point from what I have heard. Everything is wholesome and abundant and much nicer than I should imagine could be provided for almost 300 girls. We have also a great variety upon our tables and frequent changes. One thing is certain, and that is, that Miss Lyon and all the teachers seem to consult our comfort and happiness in everything they do, and you know that is pleasant. When I left home I did not think I should find a companion or a dear friend in all the multitude. I expected to find rough and uncultivated manners, and, to be sure, I have found some of that stamp, but on the whole, there is an ease and grace, a desire to make one another happy, which delights and at the same time surprises me very much. I find no Abby nor Abiah nor Mary, but I love many of the girls. Austin came to see me when I had been here about two weeks, and brought Viny and A. I need not tell you how delighted I was to see them all, nor how happy it made me to hear them say that "they were *so lonely*." It is a sweet feeling to know that you are missed and that your memory is precious at home. This week, on Wednesday, I was at my window, when I happened to look towards the hotel and saw father and mother, walking over here as dignified as you please. I need not tell you that I danced and clapped my hands, and flew to meet them, for you can imagine how I felt. I will only ask you, do you love your parents? They wanted to surprise me, and for that reason did not let me know they were coming. I could not bear to have them go, but go they must, and so I submitted in sadness. Only to think that in 2½ weeks I shall be at my *own dear home* again. You will probably go home at Thanksgiving time, and we can rejoice with each other.

You don't [know] how I laughed at your description of your introduction to Daniel Webster, and I read that part of your letter to cousin Emily. You must feel quite proud of the acquaintance, and will not, I hope, be vain in consequence. However, you don't know Governor Briggs, and I do, so you are no better off than I. . . . A., you must write me often, and I shall write you as often as I have time. . . .

From your affectionate
EMILY E. D.

MT. HOLYOKE FEMALE SEMINARY, *Jan.* 17, 1848

MY DEAR A.,—Your welcome epistle found me upon the eve of going home, and it is needless to say very happy. We all went home on Wednesday before Thanksgiving, and a stormy day it was, but the storm must not be in our way, so we tried to make the best of it and look as cheerful as we could. Many of the girls went very early in the morning in order to reach home the same day, and when we all sat down to the breakfast table, it seemed lonely enough to see so many places vacant. After breakfast, as we were not required to keep all the family rules, a number of us met together at one of the windows in the Hall to watch for our friends, whom we were constantly expecting. No morning of my life ever passed so slowly to me, and it really seemed to me they never were coming, so impatiently did I wait their arrival. At last, almost tired out, I spied a carriage in the distance, and surely Austin was in it. You, who have been away so much, can easily imagine my delight and will not laugh, when I tell you how I dashed downstairs and almost frightened my dignified brother out of his senses. All was ready in a moment or less than a moment, and cousin Emily and myself, not forgetting the driver, were far on our way towards home. The rain fell in torrents and the wind howled around the sides of the mountain over our heads, and the brooks below, filled by the rain, rushed along their pebbly beds almost frightfully, yet nothing daunted, we rode swiftly along, and soon the colleges and the spire of our venerable meeting-house rose to my delighted vision.

Never did Amherst look more lovely to me, and gratitude rose in my heart to God, for granting me such a safe return to my *own dear home.* Soon the carriage stopped in front of our own house, and all were at the door to welcome the returned one, from mother, with tears in her eyes, down to pussy, who tried to look as gracious as was becoming her dignity. Oh, A., it was the first meeting, as it had been the first separation, and it was a joyful one to all of us. The storm did not at all subside that night, but in the morning I was waked by the glorious sunshine [it] self, staring full in my face. We went to church in the morning and listened to an excellent sermon from our own minister, Mr. Colton. At noon we returned and had a nice dinner, which, you well know, cannot be dispensed with on Thanksgiving day. We had several calls in the afternoon, and had four invitations out for the evening. Of course we could not accept them all, much to my sorrow, but decided to make two visits. At about 7 o'clock father, mother, Austin, Viny, cousin Emily, and myself to bring up the rear, went down to Professor Warner's, where we spent an hour delightfully with a few friends, and then bidding them good eve, we young folks went down to Mrs. S. M.'s, accompanied by *sister Mary.* There was quite a company of young people assembled when we arrived, and after we had played many games we had, in familiar terms, a "candy scrape." We enjoyed the evening much, and returned not until the clock pealed out, "Remember ten o'clock, my dear, remember ten o'clock." After our return, father wishing to hear the piano, I, like an obedient daughter, played and sang a few tunes, much to his apparent gratification. We then retired, and the next day and the next were as happily spent as the eventful Thanksgiving day itself.

You will probably think me foolish thus to give you an inventory of my time while at home, but I did enjoy so much in those short four days that I wanted you to know and enjoy it too. Monday came so soon, and with it came a carriage to our door, and amidst tears falling thick and fast away I went again. Slowly and sadly dragged a few of the days after my return to the Seminary, and I was very homesick, but "after a storm there comes a calm," and so it was in my case. My sorrows were soon lost in study, and I again felt happy, if happiness there can be away from "home, sweet home."

Our term closes this week on Thursday, and Friday I hope to see home and friends once more. I have studied hard this term, and aside from my delight at going home, there is a sweetness in approaching rest to me. This term is the longest in the year, and I would not wish to live it over again, I can assure you. I love this Seminary, and all the teachers are bound strongly to my heart by ties of affection. There are many sweet girls here, and dearly do I love some new faces, but I have not yet found the place of a *few* dear ones filled, nor would I wish it to be here. I am now studying Silliman's Chemistry and Cutter's Physiology, in both of which I am much interested. We finish Physiology before this term closes, and are to be examined in it at the spring examinations, about five weeks after the commencement of the next term. I already begin to dread that time, for an examination in Mount Holyoke Seminary is rather more public than in our old academy, and a failure would be more disgraceful then, I opine; but I hope, to use my father's own words, "that I shall not disgrace myself." What are you studying now? You did not mention that item in your last letters to me, and consequently I am quite in the dark as regards your progress in those affairs. All I can say is, that I hope you will not leave poor me far behind. . . .

Your affectionate *sister*,

EMILY E. DICKINSON

P. S. Our Section have commenced reading compositions, and we read once in a month, during which time we write two.

Intellectual brilliancy of an individual type was already at seventeen her distinguishing characteristic, and nothing of the recluse was yet apparent. Traditions of extraordinary compositions still remain; and it is certain that each was an epoch for those who heard, whether teachers or pupils. An old friend and schoolmate of Emily tells me that she was always surrounded by a group of girls at recess, to hear her strange and intensely funny stories, invented upon the spot.

MT. HOLYOKE FEMALE SEMINARY, *May* 16, 1848

MY DEAR A.,—You must forgive me, indeed you must, that I have so long delayed to write you, and I doubt not you will when I give you all my reasons for so doing. You know it is customary for the first page to be occupied with apologies, and I must not depart from the beaten track for one of my own imagining. . . . I had not been very well all winter, but had not written home about it, lest the folks should take me home. During the week following examinations, a friend from Amherst came over and spent a week with me, and when that friend returned home, father and mother were duly notified of the state of my health. Have you so treacherous a friend?

Not knowing that I was to be reported at home, you can imagine my amazement and consternation when Saturday of the same week Austin arrived in full sail, with orders from head-quarters to bring me home at all events. At first I had recourse to words, and a desperate battle with those weapons was waged for a few moments, between my *Sophomore* brother and myself. Finding words of no avail, I next resorted to tears. But woman's tears are of little avail, and I am sure mine flowed in vain. As you can imagine, Austin was victorious, and poor, defeated I was led off in triumph. You must not imbibe the idea from what I have said that I do not love home—far from it. But I could not bear to leave teachers and companions before the close of the term and go home to be dosed and receive the physician daily, and take warm drinks and be condoled with on the state of health in general by all the old ladies in town.

Haven't I given a ludicrous account of going home sick from a boarding-school? Father is quite a hand to give medicine, especially if it is not desirable to the patient, and I was dosed for about a month after my return home, without any mercy, till at last out of mere pity my cough went away, and I had quite a season of peace. Thus I remained at home until the close of the term, comforting my parents by my presence, and instilling many a lesson of wisdom into the budding intellect of my only sister. I had almost forgotten to tell you that I went on with my studies at home, and kept up with my class. Last Thursday our vacation closed, and on Friday morn, midst the weeping of friends, crowing of roosters, and singing of birds, I again took my departure from home. Five days have now passed since we returned to Holyoke, and they have passed very slowly. Thoughts of home and friends "come crowding thick and fast, like lightnings from the mountain cloud," and it seems very desolate.

Father has decided not to send me to Holyoke another year, so this is my *last term*. Can it be possible that I have been here almost a year? It startles me when I really think of the advantages I have had, and I fear I have not improved them as I ought. But many an hour has fled with its report to heaven, and what has been the tale of me? . . . How glad I am that spring has come, and how it calms my mind when wearied with study to walk out in the green fields and beside the pleasant streams in which South Hadley is rich! There are not many wild flowers near, for the girls have driven them to a distance, and we are obliged to walk quite a distance to find them, but they repay us by their sweet smiles and fragrance.

The older I grow, the more do I love spring and spring flowers. Is it so with you? While at home there were several pleasure parties of which I was a member, and in our rambles we found many and beautiful children of spring, which I will mention and see if you have found them,—the trailing arbutus, adder's tongue, yellow violets, liver-leaf, bloodroot, and many other smaller flowers.

What are you reading now? I have little time to read when I am here, but while at home I had a feast in the reading line, I can assure you. Two or three of them I will mention: *Evangeline, The Princess, The Maiden Aunt, The Epicurean,* and *The Twins and Heart* by Tupper, complete the list. Am not I a pedant for telling you what I have been reading? Have you forgotten your visit to Amherst last summer, and what delightful times we had? I have not, and I hope you will come and make another and a longer, when I get home from Holyoke. Father wishes to have me at home a year, and then he will probably send me away again, where I know not. . . .

Ever your own affectionate
EMILIE E. DICKINSON

P. S. My studies for this series are Astronomy and Rhetoric, which take me through to the Senior studies. What are you studying now, if you are in school, and do you attend to music? I practise only one hour a day this term.

Although nearly two years elapse between the last letter and the following, the handwriting is quite unaltered, being still exceedingly small and clear, and averaging twenty words to a line.

AMHERST, *Jan.* 29, 1850

VERY DEAR A.,—The folks have all gone away; they thought that they left me alone, and contrived things to amuse me should they stay long, and *I* be lonely. Lonely, indeed,—they didn't look, and they couldn't have seen if they had, who should bear me company. *Three* here, instead of *one*, wouldn't it scare them? A curious trio, part earthly and part spiritual two of us, the other, all heaven, and no earth. *God* is sitting here, looking into my very soul to see if I think right thoughts. Yet I am not afraid, for I try to be right and good; and He knows every one of my struggles. He looks very gloriously, and everything bright seems dull beside Him; and I don't dare to look directly at Him for fear I shall die. Then *you* are here, dressed in that quiet black gown and cap,—that funny little cap I used to laugh at you about,—and you don't

34

appear to be thinking about anything in particular,—not in one of your *breaking-dish* moods, I take it. You seem aware that I'm writing you, and are amused, I should think, at any such friendly manifestation when you are already present. *Success,* however, even in making a fool of myself, isn't to be despised; so I shall persist in writing, and you may in laughing at me,—if you are fully aware of the value of time as regards your immortal spirit. I can't say that I advise you to laugh; but if you are punished, and I warned you, that can be no business of mine. So I fold up my arms, and leave you to fate—may it deal very kindly with you! The trinity winds up with me, as you may have surmised, and I certainly wouldn't be at the fag-end but for civility to you. This self-sacrificing spirit will be the ruin of me!

I am occupied principally with a cold just now, and the dear creature *will* have so much attention that my time slips away amazingly. It has heard *so* much of New Englanders, of their kind attentions to strangers, that it's come all the way from the Alps to determine the truth of the tale. It says the half wasn't told it, and I begin to be afraid it wasn't. Only think—came all the way from that distant Switzerland to find what was the truth! Neither husband, protector, nor friend accompanied it, and so utter a state of loneliness gives friends if nothing else. You are dying of curiosity; let me arrange that pillow to make your exit easier. I stayed at home all Saturday afternoon, and treated some disagreeable people who insisted upon calling here as tolerably as I could; when evening shades began to fall, I turned upon my heel, and walked. Attracted by the gayety visible in the street, I still kept walking till a little creature pounced upon a thin shawl I wore, and commenced riding. I stopped, and begged the creature to alight, as I was fatigued already, and quite unable to assist others. It wouldn't get down, and commenced talking to itself: "Can't be New England—must have made some mistake— disappointed in my reception—don't agree with accounts. Oh, what a world of deception and fraud! Marm, will you tell me the name of this country—it's Asia Minor, isn't it? I intended to stop in New England." By this time I was so completely exhausted that I made no further effort to rid me of my load, and travelled home at a moderate jog, pay- ing no attention whatever to it, got into the house, threw off both bonnet and shawl, and out flew my tormentor, and putting both arms around my neck, began to kiss me immoderately, and express so much love it completely bewildered me. Since then it has slept in my bed, eaten from my plate, lived with me everywhere, and will tag me through life for all I know. I think I'll wake first, and get out of bed, and leave it; but early or late, it is dressed before me, and sits on the side of the bed looking right into my face with such a comical expression it almost makes me laugh in spite of myself. I can't call it interesting, but it certainly *is* curious, has two peculiarities which would quite win your heart,—a huge pocket-handkerchief and a very red nose. The first seems so very *abundant,* it gives you the idea of independence and prosperity in business. The last brings up the "jovial bowl, my boys," and such an association's worth the having. If it *ever* gets tired of *me,* I will forward it to *you*—you would love it for *my* sake, if not for its own; it will tell you some queer stories about me, —how I sneezed so loud one night that the family thought the last trump was sounding, and climbed into the cur- rant-bushes to get out of the way; how the rest of the people, arrayed in long night-gowns, folded their arms, and were waiting; but this is a wicked story,—it can tell some better ones. Now, my dear friend, let me tell you that these last thoughts are fictions,—vain imaginations to lead astray foolish young women. They are flowers of speech; they both make and tell deliberate falsehoods; avoid them as the snake, and turn aside as from the rattle-snake, and I don't *think* you will be harmed. Honestly, though, a snake-bite is a serious matter, and there can't be too much said or done about it. The big serpent bites the deepest; and we get so accustomed to its bites that we don't mind about them. "Verily I say unto you, fear *him*." Won't you read some work upon snakes?—I have a real anxiety for you. *I* love those little green ones that slide around by your shoes in the grass, and make it rustle with their elbows; they are rather my favorites on the whole; but I wouldn't influence *you* for the world. There is an air of misanthropy about the striped snake that will commend itself at once to your taste,—there is no monotony about it—but we will more of this again. Something besides severe colds and serpents, and we will try to find *that* something. It can't be a garden, can it? or a strawberry-bed, which rather belongs to a garden; nor it can't be a schoolhouse, nor an attorney-at-law. Oh, dear! I don't know what it is. Love for the absent don't *sound* like it; but try it, and see how it goes.

I miss you very much indeed; think of you at night when the world's nodding, nid, nid, nodding—think of you in the daytime when the cares of the world, and its toils, and its continual vexations choke up the love for friends in some of our hearts; remember your warnings sometimes—try to do as you told me sometimes—and sometimes conclude it's no use to try; then my heart says it *is*, and new trial is followed by disappointment again. I wondered, when you had gone, why we didn't talk more,—it wasn't for want of a subject; it never *could be* for *that*. Too many, perhaps,—such a crowd of people that nobody heard the speaker, and all went away discontented. You astonished me in the outset, perplexed me in the continuance, and wound up in a grand snarl I shall be all my pilgrimage unravelling. Rather a dismal prospect certainly; but "it's always the darkest the hour before day," and this earlier sunset promises an earlier rise—a sun in splendor—and glory, flying out of its purple nest. Wouldn't you love to see God's bird, when it first tries its wings? If you were here I would tell you something—several somethings—which have happened since you went away; but time and space, as usual, oppose themselves, and I put my treasures away till "we two meet again." The hope that I shall continue in love towards you, and *vice versa*, will sustain me till then. If you are thinking soon to go away, and to show your face no more, just inform me, will you? I would have the "long, lingering look," which you cast behind,—it would be an invaluable addition to my treasures, and "keep your memory green." "Lord, keep all our memories green," and help on our affection, and tie the "link that doth us bind" in a tight bow-knot that will keep it from separation, and stop us from growing old; if that is impossible, make old age pleasant to us, put its arms around us kindly, and when we go home, let that home be called heaven.

Your very sincere and *wicked* friend,
EMILY E. DICKINSON

I haven't thanked you for your letter yet, but not for want of gratitude. I will do so *now* most sincerely, most heartily—gladly and gratefully. You will write me another soon, that I may have *four right* feelings again! They don't come for the asking. I have been introducing you to me in this letter so far; we will traffic in "joys" and "sorrows" some other day. Colds make one very carnal, and the spirit is always afraid of them. You will excuse all mistakes in view of ignorance; all sin, in view of "the fall"; all want of friendly affection, in the sight of the verse, "The deepest stream the stillest runs"; and other general deficiencies, on the ground of universal incapacity! Here is surely room for charity, and the heavenly visitor wouldn't have come but for these faults. "No loss without a gain." I called to see your cousins an evening since; they were well, and evidently delighted to see one another—and us.

When your letter came, I had two Western cousins— now at South Hadley Seminary—staying their vacation with me. They took an unbounded delight in a sentence I read them; and to pay for it, send you their love.

In the following letter appear farther traces of the later and almost invariable custom of using dashes, instead of conventional punctuation. These, however, will not be given generally. In printing her poems it was found necessary to employ usual punctuation, in order that the meaning should be more easily apprehended; and in the letters the same system, often for the same reason, has been adopted.

AMHERST, *May* 7, 1850

DEAR REMEMBERED,—The circumstances under which I write you this morning are at once glorious, afflicting, and beneficial,—glorious in *ends*, afflicting in *means*, and beneficial, I trust, in *both*. Twin loaves of bread have just been born into the world under my auspices,—fine children, the image of their mother; and here, my dear friend, is the *glory*.

On the lounge, asleep, lies my sick mother, suffering

39

intensely from acute neuralgia, except at a moment like this, when kind sleep draws near, and beguiles her,—here is the *affliction.*

I need not draw the beneficial inference,—the good I myself derive, the winning the spirit of patience, the genial housekeeping influence stealing over my mind and soul,— you know all these things I would say, and will seem to suppose they are written, when indeed they are only thought.

On Sunday my mother was taken, had been perfectly well before, and could remember no possible imprudence which should have induced the disease. Everything has been done, and though we think her gradually throwing it off, she still has much suffering. I have always neglected the culinary arts, but attend to them now from necessity, and from a desire to make everything pleasant for father and Austin. Sickness makes desolation, and the day is dark and dreary; but health will come back, I hope, and light hearts and smiling faces. We are sick hardly ever at home, and don't know what to do when it comes,—wrinkle our little brows, and stamp with our little feet, and our tiny souls get angry, and command it to go away. Mrs. Brown will be glad to see it,—old ladies expect to die; "as for *us,* the young and active, with all longings 'for the strife,' *we* to perish by the roadside, weary with the 'march of life'— no, no, my dear 'Father Mortality,' get out of the way if you please; we will call if we ever want you. Good-morning, sir! ah, good-morning!"

When I am not at work, I sit by the side of mother, provide for her little wants, and try to cheer and encourage her. I ought to be glad and grateful that I *can* do anything now, but I do feel so very lonely, and so anxious to have her cured. I haven't repined but once, and you shall know all the why. At noon . . . I heard a well-known rap, and a friend I love *so* dearly came and asked me to ride in the woods, the sweet, still woods,—and I wanted to exceedingly. I told him I could not go, and he said he was disappointed, he wanted me very much. Then the tears came into my eyes, though I tried to choke them back, and he said I *could* and *should* go, and it seemed to me unjust. Oh, I struggled with great temptation, and it cost me much of denial; but I think in the end I conquered,—not a glorious victory, where you hear the rolling drum, but a kind of a helpless victory, where triumph would come of itself, faintest music, weary soldiers, nor a waving flag, nor a long, loud shout. I had read of Christ's temptations, and how they were like our own, only he didn't sin; I wondered if *one* was like mine, and whether it made him angry. I couldn't make up my mind; do you think he ever did?

I went cheerfully round my work, humming a little air till mother had gone to sleep, then cried with all my might —seemed to think I was much abused—that this wicked world was unworthy such devoted and terrible suffering— and came to my various senses in great dudgeon at life, and time, and love for affliction and anguish.

What shall we do, my darling, when trial grows more and more, when the dim, lone light expires, and it's dark, so very dark, and we wander, and know not where, and cannot get out of the forest—whose is the hand to help us, and to lead, and forever guide us; they talk of a "Jesus of Nazareth"— will you tell me if it be he? . . .

It's Friday, my dear A., and that in another week, yet my mission is unfulfilled—and you so sadly neglected, and don't know the reason why. Where do you think I've strayed, and from what new errand returned? I have come from "to and fro, and walking up and down" the same place that Satan hailed from, when God asked him where he'd been;

but not to illustrate further, I tell you I have been dreaming, dreaming a *golden* dream, with eyes all the while wide open, and I guess it's almost morning; and besides, I have been at work, providing the "food that perisheth," scaring the timorous dust, and being obedient and kind. I am yet the Queen of the Court, if regalia be dust and dirt, have three loyal subjects, whom I'd rather relieve from service. Mother is still an invalid, though a partially restored one; father and Austin still clamor for food; and I, like a martyr, am feeding them. Wouldn't you love to see me in these bonds of great despair, looking around my kitchen, and praying for kind deliverance, and declaring by "Omai's beard" I never was in such plight? *My* kitchen, I think I called it—God forbid that it was, or shall be, my own—God keep me from what they call *households*, except that bright one of "faith"!

Don't be afraid of my imprecations—they never did any one harm, and they make me feel so cool, and so very much more comfortable! . . . I presume you are loving your mother, and loving the stranger and wanderer—visiting the poor and afflicted, and reaping whole fields of blessings—save me a little sheaf, only a very little one! Remember and care for me sometimes, and scatter a fragrant flower in this wilderness life of mine by writing me, and by not forgetting, and by lingering longer in prayer, that the Father may bless one more!

Your affectionate friend,
EMILY

Mr. Humphrey, spoken of in the following letter, is the same friend of whom Emily had already written (page 22); he graduated from Amherst as valedictorian in 1846, being subsequently Principal of the well-known Amherst Acad-

emy, and still later a theological student at Andover, and tutor in Amherst College. His sudden death, November 30, 1850, caused much grief to his many friends, who admired his polished scholarship and lovable personality.

AMHERST, *January* 2, 1851
Tuesday Evening

I write A. to-night, because it is cool and quiet, and I can forget the toil and care of the feverish day, and then I am *selfish* too, because I am feeling lonely; some of my friends are gone, and some of my friends are sleeping—sleeping the churchyard sleep—the hour of evening is sad—it was once my study hour—my master has gone to rest, and the open leaf of the book, and the scholar at school *alone*, make the tears come, and I cannot brush them away; I would not if I could, for they are the only tribute I can pay the departed Humphrey.

You have stood by the grave before; I have walked there sweet summer evenings and read the names on the stones, and wondered who would come and give me the same memorial; but I never have laid my friends there, and forgot that they too must die; this is my first affliction, and indeed 'tis hard to bear it. To those bereaved so often that home is no more here, and whose communion with friends is had only in prayers, there must be much to hope for, but when the unreconciled spirit has nothing left but God, that spirit is lone indeed. I don't think there will be any sunshine, or any singing-birds in the spring that's coming. . . . I will try not to say any more—my rebellious thoughts are many, and the friend I love and trust in has much *now* to forgive. I wish I were somebody else—I would pray the prayer of the "Pharisee," but I am a poor little "Publican." "Son of David," look down on me!

'Twas a great while ago when you wrote me, I remember the leaves were falling—and *now* there are falling snows; who maketh the two to differ—are not leaves the brethren of snows?

Then it *can't* be a great while since then, though I verily thought it *was;* we are not so young as we once were, and time seems to be growing long. I dream of being a grandame, and banding my silver hairs, and I seem to be quite submissive to the thought of growing old; no doubt you ride rocking-horses in your present as in young sleeps—quite a pretty contrast indeed, of me braiding my own gray hairs, and my friend at play with her childhood, a pair of decayed old ladies! Where *are* you, my *antique* friend, or my very dear and young one—just as you please to please—it *may* seem quite a presumption that I address you at all, knowing not if you habit here, or if my "bird has flown" in which world her wing is folded. When I think of the friends I love, and the little while we may dwell here, and then "we go away," I have a yearning feeling, a desire eager and anxious lest any be stolen away, so that I cannot behold them. I would have you here, all here, where I can *see* you, and *hear* you, and where I can say "Oh, no," if the "Son of Man" ever "cometh"!

It is not enough, now and then, at long and uncertain intervals to hear you're alive and well. I do not care for the body, I love the timid soul, the blushing, shrinking soul; it hides, for it is afraid, and the bold, obtrusive body— Pray, marm, did you call *me?* We are very small, A.—I think we grow still smaller—this tiny, insect life the portal to another; it seems strange—strange indeed. I'm afraid we are all unworthy, yet we shall "enter in."

I can think of no other way than for you, my dear girl, to come here—we are growing away from each other, and talk even now like strangers. To forget the "meum and teum," *dearest* friends must meet sometimes, and then comes the "bond of the spirit" which, if I am correct, is "unity."

. . . You are growing wiser than I am, and nipping in the bud fancies which I let blossom—perchance to bear no fruit, or if plucked, I may find it bitter. The shore is safer, A., but I love to buffet the sea—I can count the bitter wrecks here in these pleasant waters, and hear the murmuring winds, but oh, I love the danger! You are learning control and firmness. Christ Jesus will love you more. I'm afraid he don't love me *any*! . . . Write when you *will*, my friend, and forget all amiss herein, for as these few imperfect words to the full communion of spirits, so this small giddy life to the *better*, the life eternal, and that *we* may live this life, and be filled with this true communion, I shall not cease to pray.

E.

August, 1851
Tuesday Evening

"Yet a little while I am with you, and again a little while and I am *not* with you," because you go to your mother! . . . But the virtue of the text consists in this, my dear, that "if I *go*, I come again, and ye shall be with me where I am"; that is to say, that if you come in November, you shall be mine, and I shall be thine, and so on, *vice versa*, until *ad infinitum*, which isn't a great way off. While I think of it, my dear friend, and we are upon these subjects, allow me to remark that you have the funniest manner of popping into town, and the most lamentable manner of popping out again, of any one I know. It really becomes to me a matter of serious moment, this propensity of yours concerning your female friends—the "morning cloud and the early dew" are not more evanescent.

I think it was Tuesday evening that we were so amused by the oratorical feats of three or four young gentlemen. I remember I sat by you and took great satisfaction in such seat and society—I remember further our mutual good-nights, our promises to meet again, to tell each other tales of our own heart and life, to seek and find each other after so long a time of distant separation. I can hardly realize that these are recollections, that our happy to-day joins the great band of yesterdays and marches on to the dead—too quickly flown, my bird, for me to satisfy me that you *did* sit and sing beneath my chamber window! I only went out once after the time I saw you—the morning of Mr. Beecher I looked for you in vain. I discovered your Palmer cousins, but if you indeed were there, it must have been in a form to my gross sense impalpable. I was disappointed. I had been hoping much a little visit from you; when will the hour be that we shall sit together and talk of what we were and what we are and may be—with the shutters closed, dear A., and the balmiest little breeze stealing in at the window? I love those little fancies, yet I would love them more were they not quite so fanciful as they have seemed to be. I have fancied so many times, and so many times gone home to find it was *only* fancy, that I am half afraid to hope for what I long for. It would seem, my dear A., that out of all the moments crowding this little world, a *few* might be vouchsafed to spend with those we love— a separated hour, an hour more pure and true than ordinary hours, when we could pause a moment, before we journey on. We had a pleasant time talking the other morning—had I known it was all my portion, mayhap I'd improved it more, but it never'll come back again to try, whether or no. Don't you think sometimes these brief, imperfect meetings have a tale to tell—perhaps but for the sorrow which accompanies them we should not be reminded of brevity and change, and should build the dwelling earthward whose site is in the skies—perhaps the treasure here would be too dear a treasure couldn't "the moth corrupt, and the thief break through and steal"; and this makes me think how I found a little moth in my stores the other day, a very subtle moth that had, in ways and manners to me and mine unknown—contrived to hide itself in a favorite worsted basket—how long my little treasure-house had furnished an arena for its destroying labors it is not mine to tell; it had an errand there—I trust it fulfilled its mission; it taught me, dear A., to have no treasure here, or rather it tried to tell me in its little mothy way of another enduring treasure the robber cannot steal, nor time waste away. How many a lesson learned from lips of such tiny teachers—don't it make you think of the Bible, "not many mighty, nor wise"?

You met our dear Sarah T. after I saw you here. Her sweet face is the same as in those happy school-days—and in vain I search for wrinkles brought on by many cares; we all love Sarah dearly, and shall try to do all in our power to make her visit happy. Isn't it very remarkable that in so many years Sarah has changed so little—not that she has stood still, but has made such *peaceful* progress—her thoughts, though they are older, have all the charm of youth—have not yet lost their freshness, their innocence and peace; she seems so pure in heart, so sunny and serene, like some sweet lark or robin, ever soaring and singing. I have not seen her much—I want to see her more—she speaks often of *you,* and with a warm affection. I hope no change or time shall blight those loves of ours, I would bear them all in my arms to my home in the glorious heaven and say, "Here am I, my Father, and those whom thou hast given me." If the life which is to come is better than dwelling *here,* and angels are there and our friends are glorified and are singing there and praising there, need we fear to go when spirits beyond wait for us? I was meaning to see you more and talk about such things with you—I want to know your views and your eternal feelings—how things beyond are to you—oh, there is much to speak of in meeting one you love, and it always seems to me that I might have spoken more, and I almost always think that what we found to say might have been left unspoken.

Shall it *always* be so, A.? Is there no longer day given for our communion with the spirits of our love? Writing is brief and fleeting—conversation will come again, yet if it *will,* it hastes and must be on its way. Earth is short, but Paradise is long—there must be many moments in an eternal day; then sometime we shall tarry while time and tide roll on, and till then *vale.*

Your own dear

EMILIE

Written from Amherst between January 1, and the middle of June, 1852
Sunday Evening

MY VERY DEAR A.,—I love to sit here alone, writing a letter to you, and whether your joy in reading will amount to as much or more, or even less than mine in penning it to you, becomes to me just now a very important problem—and I will tax each power to solve the same for

me; if as happy, indeed, I have every occasion for gratitude—more so, my absent friend, I may not hope to make
you, but I do hope most earnestly it may not give you
less. Oh, I do know it will not, if school-day hearts are
warm and school-day memories precious! As I told you, it
is Sunday to-day, so I find myself quite curtailed in the
selection of subjects, being myself quite vain, and naturally
adverting to many worldly things which would doubtless
grieve and distress you: much more will I be restrained
by the fact that such stormy Sundays I always remain
at home, and have not those opportunities for hoarding
up great truths which I would have otherwise. In view
of these things, A., your kind heart will be lenient, for-
giving all empty words and unsatisfying feelings on the
Sabbath-day ground which we have just alluded to. I rejoice in one theme appropriate to every place and time—
indeed it cannot intrude in the hour most unseemly for
every other thought and every other feeling; and sure I
am to-day, howe'er it may be holy. I shall not break or
reproach by speaking of the links which bind us to each
other, and make the very thought of you, and time when
I last saw you, a sacred thing to me. And I have many
memories, and many thoughts beside, which by some
strange entwining, circle you round and round; if you
please, a vine of fancies, towards which dear A. sustains the
part of oak, and as up each sturdy branch there climbs a
little tendril so full of faith and confidence and the most
holy trust, so let the hearts do also, of the dear "estray";
then the farther we may be from home and from each
other, the nearer by that faith which "overcometh all
things" and bringeth us to itself.

Amherst and Philadelphia, separate indeed, and yet how
near, bridged by a thousand trusts and a "thousand times

ten thousand" the travellers who cross, whom you and I may not see, nor hear the trip of their feet, yet faith tells us they are there, ever crossing and re-crossing. Very likely, A., you fancy me at home in my own little chamber, writing you a letter, but you are greatly mistaken. I am on the blue Susquehanna paddling down to you; I am not much of a sailor, so I get along rather slowly, and I am not much of a mermaid, though I verily think I shall be, if the tide overtakes me at my present jog. Hard-hearted girl! I don't believe you care, if you did you would come quickly and help me out of this sea; but if I drown, A., and go down to dwell in the seaweed forever and forever, I will not forget your name, nor all the wrong you did me!

Why did you go away and not come to see me? I felt so sure you would come, because you promised me, that I watched and waited for you, and bestowed a tear or two upon my absentee. How very sad it is to have a confiding nature, one's hopes and feelings are quite at the mercy of all who come along; and how very desirable to be a stolid individual, whose hopes and aspirations are safe in one's waistcoat pocket, and *that* a pocket indeed, and one not to be picked!

Notwithstanding your faithlessness I should have come to see you, but for that furious snow-storm; I did attempt in spite of it, but it conquered in spite of me, and I doffed my hood and shawl, and felt very crestfallen the remainder of the day. I did want one more kiss, one sweet and sad good-by, before you had flown away; perhaps, my dear A., it is well that I go without it; it might have added anguish to our long separation, or made the miles still longer which keep a friend away. I always try to think in any disappointment that had I been gratified, it had been sadder still, and I weave from such supposition, *at times*, considerable consolation; consolation upside down as I am pleased to call it.

. . . Shall I have a letter soon—oh, may I very soon, for "some days are dark and dreary, and the wind is never weary."

EMILY E.

Also written before the middle of June, 1852
Sabbath Day

I love to link you, A. and E., I love to put you together and look at you side by side—the picture pleases me, and I should love to watch it until the sun goes down, did I not call to mind a very precious letter for which I have not as yet rendered a single farthing, so let me thank you that midst your many friends and cares and influenzas, you yet found time for me, and loved me. You remarked that I had written you more affectionately than wont—I have thought that word over and over, and it puzzles me now; whether our few last years have been cooler than our first ones, or whether I write indifferently when I truly know it not, the query troubles me. I do believe sincerely, that the friendship formed at school was no warmer than now, nay more, that *this* is warmest—they differ indeed to me as morning differs from noon—one may be fresher, cheerier, but the other fails not.

You and I have grown older since school-days, and our years have made us soberer—I mean have made *me* so, for you were always dignified, e'en when a little girl, and I used, now and then, to cut a timid caper. That makes me think of you the very first time I saw you, and I can't repress a smile, not to say a hearty laugh, at your little girl expense. I have roused your curiosity, so I will e'en tell you that one Wednesday afternoon, in the days of

51

that dear old Academy, I went in to be entertained by the rhetoric of the gentlemen and the milder form of the girls—I had hardly recovered myself from the dismay attendant upon entering august assemblies, when with the utmost equanimity you ascended the stairs, bedecked with dandelions, arranged, it seemed, for curls. I shall never forget that scene, if I live to have gray hairs, nor the very remarkable fancies it gave me then of you, and it comes over me now with the strangest bygone funniness, and I laugh merrily. Oh, A., you and the early flower are forever linked to me; as soon as the first green grass comes, up from a chink in the stones peeps the little flower, precious "leontodon," and my heart fills toward you with a warm and childlike fulness! Nor do I laugh now; far from it, I rather bless the flower which sweetly, slyly too, makes me come nearer you.

But, my dear, I can't give the dandelion the privilege due to you, so good-by, little one!

I would love to see you, A., I would rather than write to you, might I with equal ease, for the weather is very warm, and my head aches a little, and my heart a little more, so taking me *collectively*, I seem quite miserable, but I'll give you the sunny corners, and you mustn't look at the shade. You were happy when you wrote me; I hope so now, though I would you were in the country, and could reach the hills and fields. I can reach them, carry them home, which I do in my arms daily, and when they drop and fade, I have only to gather fresh ones. Your joy would indeed be full, could you sit as I, at my window, and hear the boundless birds, and every little while feel the breath of some new flower! Oh, do you love the spring, and isn't it brothers and sisters, and blessed, ministering spirits unto you and me, and us all?

I often see A.—oftener than at sometimes when friendship drooped a little. Did you ever know that a flower, once withered and freshened again, became an immortal flower, —that is, that it rises again? I think resurrections here are sweeter, it may be, than the longer and lasting one—for you expect the one, and only hope for the other. . . . I will show you the *sunset* if you will sit by me, but I cannot bring it there, for so much gold is heavy. Can you see it in Philadelphia?

A rather long interval seems to have elapsed between the preceding letter and the next, which was written about July 26, probably of 1853. The hand-writing is quite different from the earlier letters, more resembling that middle period of which an illustration is given (page 182), yet still somewhat smaller.

The delicate and sunshiny sarcasm in this note may be the more fully appreciated by recalling that Emily Dickinson was not yet twenty-two years old.

Tuesday Evening

MY DEAR CHILD,—Thank you for that sweet note which came so long ago, and thank you for asking me to come and visit you, and thank you for loving me, long ago, and to-day, and too for all the sweetness, and all the gentleness, and all the tenderness with which you remember me,— your quaint, old-fashioned friend.

I wanted very much to write you sooner, and I tried frequently, but till now in vain, and as I write to-night, it is with haste, and fear lest something still detain me. You know, my dear A., that the summer has been warm, that at this pleasant season we have much company, that this irresolute body refuses to serve sometimes, and the indignant tenant can only hold its peace,—all this you know, for I have often told you, and yet I say it again, if mayhap it persuades you that I do love you indeed, and have not done neglectfully. . . . I think it was in June that your note reached here, and I did snatch a moment to call upon your friend. Yet I went in the dusk, and it was Saturday evening, so even then, A., you see how cares pursued me. I found her very lovely in what she said to me, and I fancied in her face so, although the gentle dusk would draw her curtain close, and I didn't see her clearly. We talked the most of you,—a theme we surely loved, or we had not discussed it in preference to all. I would love to meet her again, and give my love to her, for your sake. You asked me to come and see you—I must speak of that. I thank you, A., but I don't go from home, unless emergency leads me by the hand, and then I do it obstinately, and draw back if I can. Should I ever leave home, which is improbable, I will, with much delight, accept your invitation; till then, my dear A., my warmest thanks are yours, but don't expect me. I'm so old-fashioned, darling, that all your friends would stare. I should have to bring my workbag, and my big spectacles, and I half forgot my grandchildren, and my pincushion, and puss—why, think of it seriously, A.,—do you think it my *duty* to leave? Will you write me again? Mother and Vinnie send their love, and here's a kiss from me.

Good-night, from

EMILY

T O *Mr. William Austin Dickinson*

THE FOLLOWING *letters were written to Emily Dickinson's brother between the years* 1847 *and* 1854, *the earlier ones being sent from South Hadley, while he was a student in Amherst College. Later ones were written at Amherst, and sent to Boston, where he had charge of a school after graduation,* 1851 *and* 1852; *while the latest were addressed to Cambridge during her brother's studies at the Harvard Law School,* 1853 *and* 1854. *During these last two years their father, the Hon. Edward Dickinson, was in Congress at Washington.*

SOUTH HADLEY, *Autumn,* 1847
Thursday Noon

MY DEAR BROTHER AUSTIN,—I have not really a moment of time in which to write you, and I am taking time from "silent study hours"; but I am determined not to break my promise again, and I generally carry my resolutions into effect. I watched you until you were out of sight Saturday evening, and then went to my room and looked over my treasures; and surely no miser ever counted his heaps of gold with more satisfaction than I gazed upon the presents from home. . . .

I can't tell you now how much good your visit did me. My spirits have wonderfully lightened since then. I had a great mind to be homesick after you went home, but I concluded not to, and therefore gave up all homesick feelings. Was not that a wise determination? . . .

There has been a menagerie here this week. Miss Lyon provided "Daddy Hawks" as a beau for all the Seminary girls who wished to see the bears and monkeys, and your sister, not caring to go, was obliged to decline the gallantry of said gentleman,—which I fear I may never have another opportunity to avail myself of. The whole company stopped in front of the Seminary and played for about a quarter of an hour, for the purpose of getting custom in the afternoon, I opine. Almost all the girls went; and I enjoyed the solitude finely.

I want to know when you are coming to see me again, for I want to see you as much as I did before. I went to see Miss F. in her room yesterday. . . . I love her very much, and think I shall love all the teachers when I become better acquainted with them and find out their ways, which, I can assure you, are almost "past finding out."

I had almost forgotten to tell you of a dream which I dreamed last night, and I would like to have you turn Daniel and interpret it to me; or if you don't care about going through all the perils which he did, I will allow you to interpret it without, provided you will try to tell no lies about it. Well, I dreamed a dream, and lo! father had failed, and mother said that "our rye-field, which she and I planted, was mortgaged to Seth Nims." I hope it is not true; but do write soon and tell me, for you know I should expire of mortification to have our rye-field mortgaged, to say nothing of its falling into the merciless hands of a loco!

Won't you please to tell me when you answer my letter who the candidate for President is? I have been trying to find out ever since I came here, and have not yet succeeded. I don't know anything more about affairs in the world than if I were in a trance, and you must imagine with all your "Sophomoric discernment" that it is but little and very faint. Has the Mexican War terminated yet, and how? Are we beaten? Do you know of any nation about to besiege South Hadley? If so, do inform me of it, for I would be glad of a chance to escape, if we are to be stormed. I suppose Miss Lyon would furnish us all with daggers and order us to fight for our lives in case such perils should befall us. . . . Miss F. told me if I was writing to Amherst to send her love. Not specifying to whom, you may deal it out as your good sense and discretion prompt. Be a good boy and mind me!

SOUTH HADLEY, *November 2, 1847*
Tuesday Noon

MY DEAR BROTHER AUSTIN,—I have this moment finished my recitation in history, and have a few minutes which I shall occupy in answering your short but welcome letter. You probably heard that I was alive and well yesterday, unless Mr. E. Dickinson was robbed of a note whose contents were to that effect. But as robbers are not very plenty now-a-days, I will have no forebodings on that score, for the present. How do you get along without me now, and does "it seem any more like a funeral" than it did before your visit to your humble servant in this place? Answer me! I want much to see you all at home, and expect to three weeks from to-morrow if nothing unusual, like a famine or a pestilence, occurs to prevent my going home. I am anticipating much in seeing you on this week Saturday, and you had better not disappoint me! for if you do, I will harness the "furies," and pursue you with "a whip of scorpions," which is even worse, you will find, than the "long oat" which you may remember. . . . Tell father I am obliged to him much for his offers of pecuniary assistance, but do not need any. We are furnished with an account-book here, and obliged to put down every mill which we spend, and what we spend it for, and show it to Miss Whitman every Saturday; so you perceive your sister is learning accounts in addition to the other branches of her education. I am getting along nicely in my studies, and am happy, quite, for me.

Do write a long letter to

Your affectionate sister,

EMILY

Enclosed with this was a delicately written "bill of fare" for one of the Seminary dinners.

SOUTH HADLEY SEMINARY

Nov. 2d, 1847

BILL OF FARE

ROAST VEAL

POTATOES

SQUASH

GRAVY

WHEAT AND BROWN BREAD

BUTTER

PEPPER AND SALT

Dessert
APPLE DUMPLING
SAUCE

WATER

Isn't that a dinner fit to set before a king?

SOUTH HADLEY, *December* 11, 1847
Saturday, P.M.

MY DEAR BROTHER AUSTIN,— . . . I finished my examination in Euclid last evening, and without a failure at any time. You can easily imagine how glad I am to get through with four books, for you have finished the whole forever. . . . How are you all at home, and what are you doing this vacation? You are reading *Arabian Nights,* according to Viny's statement. I hope you have derived much benefit from their perusal, and presume your powers of imagining will vastly increase thereby. But I must give you a word of advice too. Cultivate your other powers in proportion as you allow imagination to captivate you. Am not I a very wise young lady?

I had almost forgotten to tell you what my studies are now—"better late than never." They are Chemistry, Physiology, and quarter course in Algebra. I have completed four studies already, and am getting along well. Did you think that it was my birthday yesterday? I don't believe I am *seventeen!* . . .

From your affectionate sister,

EMILY

SOUTH HADLEY, *about February* 14, 1848
Thursday Morn

MY DEAR AUSTIN,—You will perhaps imagine from my date that I am quite at leisure, and can do what I please

even in the forenoon, but one of our teachers, who is engaged, received a visit from her intended quite unexpectedly yesterday afternoon, and she has gone to her home
to show him, I opine, and will be absent until Saturday.
As I happen to recite to her in one of my studies, her absence gives me a little time in which to write.

Your welcome letter found me all engrossed in the study
of sulphuric acid! I deliberated for a few moments after its
reception on the propriety of carrying it to Miss Whitman,
your friend. The result of my deliberation was a conclusion to open it with moderation, peruse its contents with
sobriety becoming my station, and if after a close investigation of its contents I found nothing which savored of rebellion or an unsubdued will, I would lay it away in my
folio, and forget I had received it. Are you not gratified
that I am so rapidly gaining correct ideas of female propriety
and sedate deportment? After the proposed examination,
finding it concealed no dangerous sentiments, I with great
gravity deposited it with my other letters, and the impression that I once had such a letter is entirely obliterated by
the waves of time.

I have been quite lonely since I came back, but cheered
by the thought that I am not to return another year, I take
comfort, and still hope on. My visit at home was happy,
very happy to me; and had the idea of in so short a time
returning been constantly in my dreams by night and day,
I could not have been happier. "There is no rose without
a thorn" to me. Home was always dear to me, and dearer
still the friends around it; but never did it seem so dear as
now. All, all are kind to me, but their tones fall strangely
on my ear, and their countenances meet mine not like
home-faces, I can assure you most sincerely. Then when
tempted to feel sad, I think of the blazing fire and the

cheerful meal and the chair empty now I am gone. I can hear the cheerful voices and the merry laugh, and a desolate feeling comes home to my heart, to think I am alone. But my good angel only waits to see the tears coming and then whispers, "Only this year! only twenty-two weeks more, and then home again you will be to stay." To you, all busy and excited, I suppose the time flies faster; but to me slowly, very slowly, so that I can see his chariot wheels when they roll along, and himself is often visible. But I will no longer imagine, for your brain is full of *Arabian Nights'* fancies, and it will not do to pour fuel on your already kindled imagination. . . .

I suppose you have written a few and received a quantity of valentines this week. Every night have I looked, and yet in vain, for one of Cupid's messengers. Many of the girls have received very beautiful ones; and I have not quite done hoping for one. Surely my friend *Thomas* has not lost all his former affection for me! I entreat you to tell him I am pining for a valentine. I am sure I shall not very soon forget last Valentine week, nor any the sooner the fun I had at that time. . . . Monday afternoon Mistress Lyon arose in the hall, and forbade our sending "any of those foolish notes called valentines." But those who were here last year, knowing her opinions, were sufficiently cunning to write and give them into the care of D. during the vacation; so that about 150 were despatched on Valentine morn, before orders should be put down to the contrary effect. Hearing of this act, Miss Whitman, by and with the advice and consent of the other teachers, with frowning brow, sallied over to the Post Office to ascertain, if possible, the number of the valentines, and worse still, the names of the offenders. Nothing has yet been heard as to the amount of her information, but as D. is a good hand

61

to help the girls, and no one has yet received sentence, we begin to think her mission unsuccessful. I have not written one, nor do I intend to.

Your injunction to pile on the wood has not been unheeded, for we have been obliged to obey it to keep from freezing up. . . . We cannot have much more cold weather, I am sure, for spring is near. . . . Professor Smith preached here last Sabbath, and such sermons I never heard in my life. We were all charmed with him, and dreaded to have him close. . . .

Your affectionate sister,

EMILY

SOUTH HADLEY, *late May*, 1848
Monday Morn

MY DEAR AUSTIN,—I received a letter from home on Saturday by Mr. G—— S——, and father wrote in it that he intended to send for cousin Emily and myself on Saturday of this week to spend the Sabbath at home. I went to Miss Whitman, after receiving the letter, and asked her if we could go if you decided to come for us. She seemed stunned by my request, and could not find utterance to an answer for some time. At length she said, "Did you not know it was contrary to the rules of the Seminary to ask to be absent on the Sabbath?" I told her I did not. She then took a Catalogue from her table, and showed me the law in full at the last part of it. She closed by saying that we could not go, and I returned to my room without farther ado. So you see I shall be deprived of the pleasure of a visit home, and you that of seeing me, if I may have the presumption to call it a pleasure! The teachers are not willing to let the girls go home this term as it is the last one, and as I have only nine weeks more to spend here, we had better be contented to obey the commands. We shall only be the more glad to see one another after a longer absence, that will be all. I was highly edified with your imaginative note to me, and think your flights of fancy indeed wonderful at your age! When are you coming to see me—it would be very pleasant to us to receive a visit from your highness if you can be absent from home long enough for such a purpose. . . . I can't write longer.

Your affectionate sister,
EMILIE

The next letter was written three years later, and sent to Boston.

AMHERST, early in 1851
Sunday Evening

It might not come amiss, dear Austin, to have a tiding or two concerning our state and feelings, particularly when we remember that "Jamie has gone awa'."

Our state is pretty comfortable, and our feelings are somewhat solemn, which we account for satisfactorily by calling to mind the fact that it is the Sabbath day. Whether a certain passenger in a certain yesterday's stage has any sombre effect on our once merry household or the reverse, "I dinna choose to tell," but be the case as it may, we are rather a crestfallen company, to make the best of us, and what with the sighing wind, the sobbing rain, and the whining of Nature generally, we can hardly contain ourselves, and I only hope and trust that your this-evening's-lot is cast in far more cheery places than the ones you leave behind.

We are enjoying this evening what is called a "northeast storm"—a little north of east in case you are pretty definite. Father thinks it's "amazin' raw," and I'm half disposed to think that he's in the right about it, though I keep pretty dark and don't say much about it! Vinnie is at the instrument, humming a pensive air concerning a young lady who thought she was "almost there." Vinnie seems much grieved, and I really suppose *I* ought to betake myself to weeping; I'm pretty sure that I *shall* if she don't abate her singing.

Father's just got home from meeting and Mr. Boltwood's, found the last quite comfortable and the first not quite so well. . . . There has been not much stirring since when you went away—I should venture to say prudently that matters had come to a stand—unless something new "turns up," I cannot see anything to prevent a quiet season. Father takes care of the doors and mother of the windows, and Vinnie and I are secure against all outward attacks. If we can get our hearts "under," I don't have much to fear—I've got all but three feelings down, if I can only keep them! . . .

I shall think of you to-morrow with four and twenty Irish boys all in a row. I miss you very much—I put on my bonnet to-night, opened the gate very desperately, and for a little while the suspense was terrible—I think I was held in check by some invisible agent, for I returned to the house without having done any harm!

If I hadn't been afraid that you would "poke fun" at my feelings, I had written a sincere letter, but since "the world is hollow, and dollie's stuffed with sawdust," I really do not think we had better expose our feelings. . . .

Your dear sister,
Emily

AMHERST, 1851
Sunday Evening

I received your letter, Austin, permit me to thank you
for it and to request some more as soon as it's convenient—
permit me to accord with your discreet opinion concerning
Swedish Jennie, and to commend the heart brave enough
to express it—combating the opinion of two civilized worlds
and New York into the bargain must need considerable
daring—indeed, it had never occurred to me that amidst
the hallelujahs one tongue would dare be dumb, and much
less, I assure you, that this dissenting one should be my
romantic brother! For I had looked for delight and a very
high style of rapture in such a youth as you. . . .

We have all been rather piqued at Jennie's singing so
well, and this first calumnious whisper pleases us so well,
we rejoice that we didn't come—our visit is yet before us.
. . . You haven't told us yet as you promised about your
home—what kind of people they are—whether you find
them pleasant—whether those timid gentlemen have yet
"found tongues to say." Do you find the life and living any
more annoying than you at first expected—do you light
upon any friends to help the time away—have you whipped
any more bad boys—all these are solemn questions, pray
give them proper heed!

Two weeks of your time are gone; I can't help wondering sometimes if you would love to see us, and come to this
still home. . . . A Senior levee was held at Professor and
Mrs. Haven's on Tuesday of last week—Vinnie played
pretty well. There's another at the President's this next
Friday evening. *Clarum et venerabile* Seniors!

AMHERST, *March*, 1851
Sunday Afternoon

. . . It's a glorious afternoon—the sky is blue and warm—the wind blows just enough to keep the clouds sailing, and the sunshine—oh *such* sunshine! It isn't like gold, for gold is dim beside it; it isn't like anything which you or I have seen! It seems to me "Ik Marvel" was born on such a day; I only wish you were here. Such days were made on purpose for you and me; then what in the world are you gone for? Oh, dear, I do not know, but this I do know, that if wishing would bring you home, you were here to-day. Is it pleasant in Boston? Of *course* it isn't, though. I might have known more than to make such an inquiry. No doubt the streets are muddy, and the sky some dingy hue, and I can think just how everything bangs and rattles, and goes rumbling along through stones and plank and clay! I don't feel as if I could have you there, possibly, another day. I'm afraid you'll turn into a bank, or a Pearl Street counting-room, if you have not already assumed some monstrous shape, living in such a place.

Let me see—April; three weeks until April—the very first of April—well, perhaps that will do, only be sure of the week, the *whole* week, and nothing but the week. If they make new arrangements, give my respects to them, and tell them old arrangements are good enough for you, and you will have them; then if they raise the wind, why, let it blow—there's nothing more excellent than a breeze now and then!

What a time we shall have Fast day, after we get home from meeting—why, it makes me dance to think of it; and Austin, if I dance so many days beforehand, what will become of me when the hour really arrives? I don't know, I'm sure; and I don't care, much, for that or for anything else but get you home. . . . Much love from mother and Vinnie; we are now pretty well, and our hearts are set on April, the *very first* of April!

EMILIE

AMHERST, late March, 1851
Thursday Night

DEAR AUSTIN,— . . . I have read *Ellen Middleton.* I needn't tell you I like it, nor need I tell you more, for you know already.

I thank you more and more for all the pleasures you give me—I can give you nothing, Austin, but a warm and grateful heart that is yours now and always. Love from all.

EMILIE

Only think, you are coming Saturday! I don't know why it is that it's always *Sunday* immediately you get home. I will arrange it differently. If it wasn't twelve o'clock I would stay longer.

AMHERST, June 16, 1851
Sunday Evening

. . . I'm glad you are so well pleased, I'm glad you are *not* delighted. I would not that foreign places should wear the smile of home. We are quite alarmed for the *boys*— hope you won't kill or pack away any of 'em—so near Dr Webster's bones 'tis not strange you have had temptations! . . . The country's still just now, and the severities alluded to will have a salutary influence in waking the people up. Speaking of *getting up*, how early are metropolitans expected to wake up, especially young men—more especially school-masters? I miss my "department" mornings. I lay it quite to heart that I've no one to wake up. *Your* room looks lonely enough, I do not love to go in there; whenever I pass through I find I 'gin to whistle, as we read that little boys are wont to do in the graveyard. I am going to set out crickets as soon as I find time, that they by their shrill singing shall help disperse the gloom; will they grow if I transplant them?

You importune me for news; I am very sorry to say "Vanity of vanities" there's no such thing as news—it is almost time for the cholera, and then things will take a start! . . . All of the folks send love.

Your affectionate

EMILY

July 5, 1851

Sunday Afternoon

I have just come in from church very hot and faded. . . . Our church grows interesting—Zion lifts her head—I overhear remarks signifying Jerusalem,—I do not feel at liberty to say any more to-day!

. . . I wanted to write you Friday, the night of Jennie Lind, but reaching home past midnight, and my room sometime after, encountering several perils starting and on the way, among which a kicking horse, an inexperienced driver, a number of Jove's thunderbolts, and a very terrible rain, are worthy to have record. All of us went—just four—add an absent individual and that will make full five. The concert commenced at eight, but knowing the world was *hollow* we thought we'd start at six, and come up with everybody that meant to come up with us; we had proceeded some steps when one of the beasts showed symptoms; and just by the blacksmith's shop exercises commenced, consisting of kicking and plunging on the part of the horse, and whips and moral suasion from the gentleman who drove—the horse refused to proceed, and your respected family with much chagrin dismounted, advanced to the hotel, and for a season halted; another horse procured, we were politely invited to take our seats, and proceed, which we refused to do till the animal was warranted. About half through our journey thunder was said to be heard, and a suspicious cloud came travelling up the sky. What words express our horror when rain began to fall, in drops, sheets, cataracts—what fancy conceive of drippings and of drenchings which we met on the way; how the stage and its mourning captives drew up at Warner's Hotel; how all of us alighted, and were conducted in,— how the rain did not abate,—how we walked in silence to the old Edwards church[1] and took our seats in the same— how Jennie came out like a child and sang and sang again—how bouquets fell in showers, and the roof was rent with applause—how it thundered outside, and inside with the thunder of God and of men—judge ye which was the loudest; how we all loved Jennie Lind, but not accustomed oft to her manner of singing didn't fancy *that* so well as we did *her*. No doubt it was very fine, but take some notes from her *Echo,* the bird sounds from the *Bird Song,* and some of her curious trills, and I'd rather have a Yankee.

Herself and not her music was what we seemed to love —she has an air of exile in her mild blue eyes, and a something sweet and touching in her native accent which charms her many friends. *Give me my thatched cottage* as she sang she grew so earnest she seemed half lost in song, and for a transient time I fancied she *had* found it and would be seen "na mair"; and then her foreign accent

[1] Evidently a slip of the pen, as Jenny Lind sang in the old First Church at Northampton on that occasion.

made her again a wanderer—we will talk about her sometime when you come. Father sat all the evening looking
mad, and yet so much amused you would have *died* a-laughing. . . . It wasn't sarcasm exactly, nor it wasn't disdain,
it was infinitely funnier than either of those virtues, as if
old Abraham had come to see the show, and thought it was
all very well, but a little excess of *monkey*! She took $4,000
for tickets at Northampton aside from all expenses. . . .

About our coming to Boston—we think we shall probably come—we want to see our friends, yourself and Aunt
L.'s family. We don't care a fig for the Museum, the still-
ness, or Jennie Lind. . . . Love from us all.

Your affectionate sister,

EMILY

Late July, 1851

Sunday Evening

. . . Oh how I wish I could see your world and its little
kingdoms, and I wish I could see the king—Stranger! he
was my brother! I fancy little boys of several little sizes,
some of them clothed in blue cloth, some of them clad in
gray—I seat them round on benches in the school-room
of my mind—then I set them all to shaking—on peril of
their lives that they move their lips or whisper; then I
clothe you with authority and empower you to punish, and
to enforce the law, I call you "Rabbi, Master," and the picture is complete! It would seem very funny, say for Vinnie and me to come round as Committee—we should enjoy
the terrors of fifty little boys, and any specimens of disci-
pline in your way would be a rare treat for us. I should love
to know how you managed—whether government as a
science is laid down and executed, or whether you *cuff*
and *thrash* as the occasion dictates; whether you use *pure*

law as in the case of commanding, or whether you enforce it by means of sticks and stones as in the case of agents. I suppose you have authority bounded but by their lives. . . . I should think you'd be tired of school and teaching and such hot weather. I really wish you were here, and the Endicott school where you found it. Whenever we go to ride in our beautiful family carriage we think if "wishes were horses" we four "beggars would ride." We shall enjoy brimful everything now but half full, and to have you home once more will be like living again.

We are having a pleasant summer—without one of the five it is yet a lonely one. Vinnie says sometimes—Didn't we have a brother—it seems to me we did, his name was Austin—we call but he answers not again—echo, Where is Austin? laughing, "Where *is* Austin?" . . . I wish they need not exhibit just for once in the year, and give you up on Saturday instead of the next week Wednesday; but keep your courage up and show forth those Emerald Isles till school committees and mayors are blinded with the dazzling! Wouldn't I love to be there! . . .

Our apples are ripening fast. I am fully convinced that with your approbation they will not only pick themselves, but arrange one another in baskets and present themselves to be eaten.

Love from all.
EMILIE

August, 1851
Sunday Afternoon

At my old stand again, dear Austin, and happy as a queen to know that while I speak those whom I love are listening, and I am happier still if I shall make them happy.

I have just finished reading your letter which was

brought in since church. I like it grandly—very—because
it is so long, and also it's *so* funny—we have all been laughing till the old house rung again at your delineation of men,
women, and things. I feel quite like retiring in presence
of one so grand, and casting my small lot among small
birds and fishes; you say you don't comprehend me, you
want a simpler style—gratitude indeed for all my fine
philosophy! I strove to be exalted, thinking I might reach
you, and while I pant and struggle and climb the nearest
cloud, you walk out very leisurely in your slippers from
Empyrean, and without the slightest notice, request me
to get down! As simple as you please, the simplest sort of
simple—I'll be a little ninny, a little pussy catty, a little
Red Riding Hood; I'll wear a bee in my bonnet, and a rose-
bud in my hair, and what remains to do you shall be told
hereafter.

Your letters are richest treats, send them always just
such warm days—they are worth a score of fans and many
refrigerators—the only difficulty they are so *queer*, and
laughing such hot weather is anything but amusing. A
little more of earnest, and a little less of jest until we are out
of August, and then you may joke as freely as the father
of rogues himself, and we will banish care, and daily die
a-laughing!

It is very hot here now; I don't believe it's any hotter in
Boston than it is here. . . . Vinnie suggests that she may
sometimes occur to mind when you would like more collars
made. I told her I wouldn't tell you—I haven't, however,
decided whether I will or not.

I often put on five knives and forks, and another tumbler,
forgetting for the moment that "we are not all here." It
occurs to me, however, and I remove the extra, and brush
a tear away in memory of my brother.

We miss you now and always. When God bestows but three, and one of those is withdrawn, the others are left alone. . . . Father is as uneasy when you are gone away as if you catch a trout and put him in Sahara. When you first went away he came home very frequently—walked gravely towards the barn, and returned looking very stately—then strode away down street as if the foe was coming; *now* he is more resigned—contents himself by fancying that "we shall hear to-day," and then when we do not hear, he wags his head profound, and thinks without a doubt there will be news "to-morrow." "Once one is two," once one will be two—ah, I have it here!

I wish you could have some cherries—if there was any way we would send you a basket of them—they are very large and delicious, and are just ripening now. Little Austin Grout comes every day to pick them, and mother takes great comfort in calling him by name, from vague association with her departed boy. Austin, to tell the truth, it is very still and lonely—I do wish you were here. . . . The railroad is "a-workin'." My love to all my friends. I am on my way downstairs to put the tea-kettle boiling—writing and taking tea cannot sympathize. If you forget me now, your right hand *shall* its cunning.

EMILIE

Written after a visit of the sisters in Boston. AMHERST, *September* 24, 1851
Tuesday Evening

We have got home, dear Austin. It is very lonely here —I have tried to make up my mind which was better, home and parents and country, or city and smoke and dust shared with the only being whom I can call my brother. The scales *don't* poise very evenly, but so far as I can judge, the balance is in your favor. The folks are much more lonely than while we were away—they say they seemed to feel that we were straying together and together would return, and the unattended sisters seemed very sad to them. . . . They have had a number of friends to call and visit with them. Mother never was busier than while we were away —what with fruit and plants and chickens and sympathizing friends she really was so hurried she hardly knew what to do.

Vinnie and I came safely, and met with no mishap— the bouquet was not withered nor was the bottle cracked. It was fortunate for the freight car that Vinnie and I were there, ours being the only baggage passing along the line. The folks looked very funny who travelled with us that day—they were dim and faded, like folks passed away— the conductor seemed so grand with about half a dozen tickets which he dispersed and demanded in a very small space of time—I judged that the minority were travelling that day, and couldn't hardly help smiling at our ticket friend, however sorry I was at the small amount of people passing along his way. He looked as if he wanted to make an apology for not having more travellers to keep him company.

The route and the cars seemed strangely—there were no boys with fruit, there were no boys with pamphlets; one fearful little fellow ventured into the car with what appeared to be publications and tracts; he offered them to no one, and no one inquired for them, and he seemed greatly relieved that no one wanted to buy them. . . . Mother sends much love, and Vinnie.

Your lonely sister,

EMILY

AMHERST, *Autumn,* 1851
Saturday Morn

DEAR AUSTIN,—I've been trying to think this morning how many weeks it was since you went away—I fail in calculations; it seems so long to me since you went back to school that I set down days for years, and weeks for a score of years—not reckoning time by minutes, I don't know what to think of such great discrepancies between the actual hours and those which "seem to be." It may seem long to you since you returned to Boston—how I wish you would stay and never go back again. Everything is so still here, and the clouds are cold and gray—I think it will rain soon. Oh, I am so lonely! . . . You had a windy evening going back to Boston, and we thought of you many times and hoped you would not be cold. Our fire burned so cheerfully I couldn't help thinking of how many were here, and how many were away, and I wished so many times during that long evening that the door would open and you come walking in. Home is a holy thing,—nothing of doubt or distrust can enter its blessed portals. I feel it more and more as the great world goes on, and one and another forsake in whom you place your trust, here seems indeed to be a bit of Eden which not the sin of any can utterly destroy,—smaller it is indeed, and it may be less fair, but fairer it is and brighter than all the world beside.

I hope this year in Boston will not impair your health, and I hope you will be as happy as you used to be before. I don't wonder it makes you sober to leave this blessed air —if it were in my power I would on every morning transmit its purest breaths fragrant and cool to you. How I wish you could have it—a thousand little winds waft it to me this morning, fragrant with forest leaves and bright autumnal berries. I would be willing to give you my portion for to-day, and take the salt sea's breath in its bright, bounding stead. . . .

Your affectionate
EMILY

. . . Mother sends her love and your waistcoat, thinking you'll like the one, and quite likely need the other.

AMHERST, October 2, 1851
Wednesday Noon

We are just through dinner, Austin, I want to write so much that I omit digestion, and a dyspepsia will probably be the result. . . . I received your letter yesterday. . . . You say we mustn't trouble to send you any fruit, also your clothes must give us no uneasiness. I don't ever want to have you say any more such things. They make me feel like crying. If you'd only teased us for it, and declared that you would have it, I shouldn't have cared so much that we could find no way to send you any, but you resign so cheerfully your birthright of purple grapes, and do not so much as murmur at the departing peaches, that I hardly can taste the one or drink the juice of the other. They are so beautiful, Austin,—we have such an abundance "while you perish with hunger."

I do hope some one will make up a mind to go before our peaches are quite gone. The world is full of people travelling everywhere, until it occurs to you that you will send an errand, and then by "hook or crook" you can't find any traveller who, for money or love, can be induced to go and carry the opprobrious package. It's a very selfish age, that is all I can say about it. Mr. Storekeeper S——

has been "almost persuaded" to go, but I believe he has put it off "till a more convenient season," so to show my disapprobation I sha'n't buy any more gloves at Mr. S——'s store! Don't you think it will seem very cutting to see me pass by his goods and purchase at Mr. K——'s? I don't think I shall retract should he regret his course and decide to go to-morrow, because it is the principle of disappointing people which I disapprove! . . .

The peaches are very large—one side a rosy cheek, and the other a golden, and that peculiar coat of velvet and of down which makes a peach so beautiful. The grapes, too, are fine, juicy, and *such* a purple—I fancy the robes of kings are not a tint more royal. The vine looks like a kingdom, with ripe round grapes for kings, and hungry mouths for subjects—the first instance on record of subjects devouring kings! You *shall* have some grapes, dear Austin, if I have to come on foot in order to bring them to you.

The apples are very fine—it isn't quite time to pick them—the cider is almost done—we shall have some I guess by Saturday, at any rate Sunday noon. The vegetables are not gathered, but will be before very long. The horse is doing nicely; he travels "like a bird" to use a favorite phrase of your delighted mother's. You ask about the leaves—shall I say they are falling? They had begun to fall before Vinnie and I came home, and we walked up the steps through little brown ones rustling. . . .

Vinnie tells me she has detailed the news—she reserved the deaths for me, thinking I might fall short of my usual letter somewhere. In accordance with her wishes I acquaint you with the decease of your aged friend Deacon——. He had no disease that we know of, but gradually went out. . . . Monday evening we were all startled by a violent church-bell ringing, and thinking of nothing but fire, rushed out in the street to see. The sky was a beautiful red, bordering on a crimson, and rays of a gold pink color were constantly shooting off from a kind of sun in the centre. People were alarmed at this beautiful phenomenon, supposing that fires somewhere were coloring the sky. The exhibition lasted for nearly fifteen minutes, and the streets were full of people wondering and admiring. Father happened to see it among the very first, and rang the bell himself to call attention to it. You will have a full account from the pen of Mr. Trumbull, who, I have not a doubt, was seen with a long lead pencil a-noting down the sky at the time of its highest glory. . . . You will be here now so soon—we are impatient for it—we want to see you, Austin, how much I cannot say here.

Your affectionate
EMILY

AMHERST, *early October*, 1851
Friday Morning

DEAR AUSTIN,— . . . I would not spend much strength upon those little school-boys—you will need it all for something better and braver after you get away. It would rejoice my heart if on some pleasant morning you'd turn the schoolroom key on Irish boys, nurse and all, and walk away to freedom and the sunshine here at home. Father says all Boston wouldn't be a temptation to you another year—I wish it would not tempt you to stay another day. Oh, Austin, it is wrong to tantalize you so while you are braving all things in trying to fulfil duty. Duty is black and brown—home is bright and shining, "and the spirit and the bride say come, and let him that" wandereth come, for "behold all things are ready." We are having such lovely weather—the air is as sweet and still—now and then a gay leaf falling—the crickets sing all day long—high in a crimson tree a belated bird is singing—a thousand little painters are tingeing hill and dale. I admit now, Austin, that autumn is *most* beautiful, and spring is but the least, yet they "differ as stars" in their distinctive glories. How happy if you were here to share these pleasures with us— the fruit should be more sweet, and the dying day more golden—merrier the falling nut if with you we gathered it and hid it down deep in the abyss of basket; but you complain not, wherefore do we?

Tuesday evening we had a beautiful time reading and talking of the good times of last summer, and we anticipated—boasted ourselves of to-morrow—of the future we created, and all of us went to ride in an air-bubble for a carriage. We cherish all the past, we glide a-down the present, awake yet dreaming; but the future of ours together —there the bird sings loudest, and the sun shines always there. . . .

I had a dissertation from E. C. a day or two ago—don't know which was the author, Plato or Socrates—rather think Jove had a finger in it. . . . They all send their love. Vinnie sends hers. How soon you will be here! Days, flee away—"lest with a whip of scorpions I overtake your lingering." I am in a hurry—this pen is too slow for me—"it hath done what it could."

Your affectionate

EMILY

AMHERST, *"before Cattle Show,"* 1851
Friday Morning
. . . The breakfast is so warm, and pussy is here a-singing, and the tea-kettle sings too, as if to see which was loudest, and I am so afraid lest kitty should be beaten—yet a shadow

falls upon my morning picture—where is the youth so bold, the bravest of our fold—a seat is empty here—spectres sit in your chair, and now and then nudge father with their long, bony elbows. I wish you were here, dear Austin; the dust falls on the bureau in your deserted room, and gay, frivolous spiders spin away in the corners. I don't go there after dark whenever I can help it, for the twilight seems to pause there, and I am half afraid; and if ever I have to go, I hurry with all my might, and never look behind me, for I know who I should see.

Before next Tuesday—oh, before the coming stage, will I not brighten and brush it, and open the long-closed blinds, and with a sweeping broom will I not bring each spider down from its home so high, and tell it it may come back again when master has gone—and oh, I will bid it to be a tardy spider, to tarry on the way; and I will think my eye is fuller than sometimes, though *why* I cannot tell, when it shall rap on the window and come to live again. I am so happy when I know how soon you are coming that I put away my sewing and go out in the yard to think. I have tried to delay the frosts, I have coaxed the fading flowers, I thought I *could* detain a few of the crimson leaves until you had smiled upon them; but their companions call them, and they cannot stay away.

You will find the blue hills, Austin, with the autumnal shadows silently sleeping on them, and there will be a glory lingering round the day, so you'll know autumn has been here; and the setting sun will tell you, if you don't get home till evening. . . . I thank you for such a long letter, and yet if I might choose, the next should be a longer. I think a letter just about three days long would make me happier than any other kind of one, if you please,—dated at Boston, but thanks be to our Father you may conclude it here. Everything has changed since my other letter,—the doors are shut this morning, and all the kitchen wall is covered with chilly flies who are trying to warm themselves, —poor things, they do not understand that there are no summer mornings remaining to them and me, and they have a bewildered air which is really very droll, didn't one feel sorry for them. You would say 'twas a gloomy morning if you were sitting here,—the frost has been severe, and the few lingering leaves seem anxious to be going, and wrap their faded cloaks more closely about them as if to shield them from the chilly northeast wind. The earth looks like some poor old lady who by dint of pains has bloomed e'en till now, yet in a forgetful moment a few silver hairs from out her cap come stealing, and she tucks them back so hastily and thinks nobody sees. The cows are going to pasture, and little boys with their hands in their pockets are whistling to try to keep warm. Don't think that the sky will frown so the day when you come home! She will smile and look happy, and be full of sunshine then, and even should she frown upon her child returning, there is another sky, ever serene and fair, and there is another sunshine, though it be darkness there; never mind faded forests, Austin, never mind silent fields—*here* is a little forest, whose leaf is ever green; here is a brighter garden, where not a frost has been; in its unfading flowers I hear the bright bee hum; prithee, my brother, into *my* garden come!

Your very affectionate sister.

November, 1851
Thursday Evening

DEAR AUSTIN,—Something seems to whisper "He is thinking of home this evening," perhaps because it rains, perhaps because it's evening and the orchestra of winds perform their strange, sad music. I wouldn't wonder if home were thinking of him; and it seems so natural for one to think of the other, perhaps it is no superstition or omen of this evening,—no omen "at all, at all," as Mrs. Mack would say.

Father is staying at home this evening it is so inclement —Vinnie diverts his mind with little snatches of music; and mother mends a garment to make it snugger for you— and what do you think *I* do among this family circle? I am thinking of you with all my might, and it just occurs to me to note a few of my thoughts for your own inspection. "Keeping a diary" is not familiar to me as to your sister Vinnie, but her own bright example is quite a comfort to me, so I'll try.

I waked up this morning thinking for all the world I had had a letter from you—just as the seal was breaking, father rapped at my door. I was sadly disappointed not to go on and read; but when the four black horses came trotting into town, and their load was none the heavier by a tiding for me—I was not disappointed then, it was harder to me than had I been disappointed. . . . I found I had made no provision for any such time as that. . . . The weather has been unpleasant ever since you went away— Monday morning we waked up in the midst of a furious snow-storm—the snow was the depth of an inch; oh, it looked so wintry! By-and-by the sun came out, but the wind blew violently and it grew so cold that we gathered all the quinces, put up the stove in the sitting-room, and bade the world good-by. Kind clouds came over at evening; still the sinking thermometer gave terrible signs of what would be on the morning. At last the morning came, laden with mild south winds, and the winds have brought the rains, so here we are. . . . Your very hasty letter just at your return rejoiced us—that you were "better—happier —heartier." What made you think of such beautiful words to tell us how you were, and how cheerful you were feeling? It did us a world of good. How little the scribe thinks of the value of his line—how many eager eyes will search its every meaning, how much swifter the strokes of "the little mystic clock, no human eye hath seen, which ticketh on and ticketh on, from morning until e'en." If it were not that I could write you, you could not go away; therefore pen and ink are very excellent things.

We had new brown bread for tea—when it came smoking on and we sat around the table, how I did wish a slice could be reserved for you! You shall have as many loaves as we have eaten slices if you will but come home. This suggests Thanksgiving, you will soon be here; then I can't help thinking of how, when we rejoice, so many hearts are breaking next Thanksgiving day. What will you say, Austin, if I tell you that Jennie Grout and merry Martha Kingman will spend the day above? They are not here— "While we delayed to let them forth, angels beyond stayed for them.". . .

Your affectionate
EMILY

AMHERST, *November* 17, 1851
Sunday Afternoon
DEAR AUSTIN,—We have just got home from meeting —it is very windy and cold—the hills from our kitchen window are just crusted with snow, which with their blue mantillas makes them seem so beautiful. You sat just here last Sunday, where I am sitting now; and our voices were nimbler than our pens can be, if they try never so hardly.

I should be quite sad to-day, thinking about last Sunday, didn't another Sabbath smile at me so pleasantly, promising me on its word to present you here again when "six days' work is done."

Father and mother sit in state in the sitting-room perusing such papers, only, as they are well assured, have nothing carnal in them; Vinnie is eating an apple which makes me think of gold, and accompanying it with her favorite *Observer*, which, if you recollect, deprives us many a time of her sisterly society. Pussy hasn't returned from the afternoon assembly, so you have us all just as we are at present. We were very glad indeed to hear from you so soon, glad that a cheerful fire met you at the door. I *do* well remember how chilly the west wind blew, and how everything shook and rattled before I went to sleep, and I often thought of you in the midnight car, and hoped you were not lonely. . . . We are thinking most of Thanksgiving than anything else just now—how full will be the circle, less then by none—how the things will smoke—how the board will groan with the thousand savory viands—how when the day is done, lo, the evening cometh, laden with merrie laugh and happy conversation, and then the sleep and the dream each of a knight or "Ladie"—how I love to see them, a beautiful company coming down the hill which men call the Future, with their hearts full of joy and their hands of gladness. Thanksgiving indeed to a family united once more together before they go away. . . . Don't mind the days—some of them are long ones, but who cares for length when breadth is in store for him? Or who minds the cross who knows he'll have a crown? I wish I could imbue you with all the strength and courage which can be given men—I wish I could assure you of the constant remembrance of those you leave at home—I wish

—but oh! how vainly—that I could bring you back again and never more to stray. You are tired now, dear Austin, with my incessant din, but I can't help saying any of these things.

The very warmest love from Vinnie and every one of us. I am never ready to go.

Reluctant

EMILY

December, 1851
Monday Morning

DEAR AUSTIN,— . . . I was so glad to get your letter. I had been making calls all Saturday afternoon, and came home very tired, and a little disconsolate, so your letter was more than welcome. . . . Oh Austin, you don't know how we all wished for you yesterday. We had such a splendid sermon from Professor Park—I never heard anything like it, and don't expect to again, till we stand at the great white throne, and "he reads from the Book, the Lamb's Book." The students and chapel people all came to our church, and it was very full, and still, so still the buzzing of a fly would have boomed like a cannon. And when it was all over, and that wonderful man sat down, people stared at each other, and looked as wan and wild as if they had seen a spirit, and wondered they had not died. How I wish you had heard him—I thought of it all the time. . . .

Affectionately,

EMILIE

AMHERST, *January*, 1852
Monday Morning

Did you think I was tardy, Austin? For two Sunday afternoons it has been so cold and cloudy that I didn't feel in my very happiest mood, and so I did not write until next Monday morning, determining in my heart never to write to you in any but cheerful spirits.

Even this morning, Austin, I am not in merry case, for it snows slowly and solemnly, and hardly an outdoor thing can be seen a-stirring—now and then a man goes by with a large cloak wrapped around him, and shivering at that; and now and then a stray kitten out on some urgent errand creeps through the flakes and crawls so fast as *may* crawl half frozen away. I am glad for the sake of your body that you are not here this morning, for it is a trying time for fingers and toes—for the heart's sake I would verily have you here. You know there are winter mornings when the cold without only adds to the warm within, and the more it snows and the harder it blows brighter the fires blaze, and chirps more merrily the "cricket on the hearth." It is hardly cheery enough for such a scene this morning, and yet me-thinks it would be if you were only here. The future full of sleigh-rides would chase the gloom from our minds which only deepens and darkens with every flake that falls.

Black Fanny would "toe the mark" if you should be here to-morrow; but as the prospects are, I presume Black Fanny's hoofs will not attempt to fly. Do you have any snow in Boston? Enough for a ride, I hope, for the sake of "Auld Lang Syne." Perhaps the "ladie" of curls would not object to a drive. . . . We miss you more and more, we do not become accustomed to separation from you. I almost wish sometimes we needn't miss you so much, since duty claims a year of you entirely to herself; and then again I think that it is pleasant to miss you if you must go away, and I would not have it otherwise, even if I could. In every pleasure and pain you come up to our minds so wishfully— we know you'd enjoy our joy, and if you were with us,

Austin, we could bear little trials more cheerfully. . . . When I know of anything funny I am just as apt to cry, far more so than to laugh, for I know who loves jokes best, and who is not here to enjoy them. We don't have many jokes, though, now, it is pretty much all sobriety; and we do not have much poetry, father having made up his mind that it's pretty much all real life. Father's real life and mine sometimes come into collision but as yet escape unhurt. . . . I am so glad you are well and in such happy spirits—both happy and well is a great comfort to us when you are far away.

EMILIE

February 6, 1852
Friday Morning

. . . Since we have written you the grand railroad decision is made, and there is great rejoicing throughout this town and the neighboring; that is, Sunderland, Montague, and Belchertown. Everybody is wide awake, everything is stirring, the streets are full of people walking cheeringly, and you should really be here to partake of the jubilee. The event was celebrated by D. Warner and cannon; and the silent satisfaction in the hearts of all is its crowning attestation.

Father is really sober from excessive satisfaction, and bears his honors with a most becoming air. Nobody believes it yet, it seems like a fairy tale, a most miraculous event in the lives of us all. The men begin working next week; only think of it, Austin; why, I verily believe we shall fall down and worship the first "son of Erin" that comes, and the first sod he turns will be preserved as an emblem of the struggle and victory of our heroic fathers. Such old fellows as Col. S. and his wife fold their arms complacently and

say, "Well, I declare, we have got it after all." Got it, *you*
good-for-nothings! and so we have, in spite of sneers and
pities and insults from all around; and we will keep it too,
in spite of earth and heaven! How I wish you were here—
it is really too bad, Austin, at such a time as now. I miss
your big hurrahs, and the famous stir you make upon all
such occasions; but it is a comfort to know that you are
here—that your whole soul is here, and though apparently
absent, yet present in the highest and the truest sense. . . .
Take good care of yourself, Austin, and think much of us
all, for we do so of you.

EMILIE

*Several subsequent letters, all piquant and breezy, but
dealing quite entirely with family matters, experiences with
callers, and other personal subjects, have been omitted.*

March 24, 1852
Wednesday Morn

You wouldn't think it was spring, Austin, if you were at
home this morning, for we had a great snowstorm yesterday, and things are all white this morning. It sounds funny
enough to hear birds singing and sleigh-bells at a time. But
it won't last long, so you needn't think 'twill be winter at
the time when you come home.

I waited a day or two, thinking I might hear from you,
but you will be looking for me, and wondering where I
am, so I sha'n't wait any longer. We're rejoiced that you're
coming home—the first thing we said to father when he
got out of the stage was to ask if you were coming. I was
sure you would all the while, for father said "of course you

would," he should "consent to no other arrangement," and as you say, Austin, "what father says he means." How very soon it will be now—why, when I really think of it, how near and how happy it is! My heart grows light so fast that I could mount a grasshopper and gallop around the world, and not fatigue him any! The sugar weather holds on, and I do believe it will stay until you come. . . . "Mrs. S." is very feeble; "can't bear allopathic treatment, can't have homœopathic, don't want hydropathic," oh, what a pickle she is in. Shouldn't think she would deign to live, it is so decidedly vulgar! They have not yet concluded where to move—Mrs. W. will perhaps obtain board in the celestial city, but I'm sure I can't imagine what will become of the rest. . . . Much love from us all.

EMILIE

May 10, 1852
Monday Morning, 5 o'c.
DEAR AUSTIN,— . . . Vinnie will tell you all the news, so I will take a little place to describe a thunder-shower which occurred yesterday afternoon,—the very first of the season. Father and Vinnie were at meeting, mother asleep in her room, and I at work by my window on a "Lyceum lecture." The air was really scorching, the sun red and hot, and you know just how the birds sing before a thunder-storm, a sort of hurried and agitated song—pretty soon it began to thunder, and the great "cream-colored heads" peeped out of their windows. Then came the wind and rain, and I hurried around the house to shut all the doors and windows. I wish you had seen it come, so cool and so refreshing—and everything glistening from it as with a golden dew—I thought of you all the time. This morning

is fair and delightful. You will awake in dust, and with it the ceaseless din of the untiring city. Wouldn't you change your dwelling for my palace in the dew? Good-by for now. I shall see you soon.

E.

Mr. Edward Dickinson was in Baltimore when the following letter was written, in attendance upon the Whig Convention which sought, unsuccessfully, the nomination of Daniel Webster for the presidency.

AMHERST, *June* 21, 1852
Sunday Morning

. . . Father has not got home, and we don't know when to expect him. We had a letter from him yesterday, but he didn't say when he should come. He writes that he "should think the whole world was there, and some from other worlds." He says he meets a great many old friends and acquaintances, and forms a great many new ones—he writes in very fine spirits, and says he enjoys himself very much. . . . I wish you could have gone with him, you would have enjoyed it so, but I did not much suppose that selfish old school would let you. . . . Last week the Senior levee came off at the President's. I believe Professor Haven is to give one soon—and there is to be a reception at Professor Tyler's next Tuesday evening which I shall attend. You see Amherst is growing lively, and by the time you come everything will be in a buzz. . . . We all send you our love.

EMILIE

AMHERST, *July* 23, 1852
Sunday Night

. . . You'd better not come home; I say the law will have you, a pupil of the law o'ertaken by the law, and brought to condign punishment,—scene for angels and men, or rather for archangels, who being a little higher would seem to have a 'vantage so far as view's concerned. "*Are* you pretty comfortable, though,"—and are you deaf and dumb and gone to the asylum where such afflicted persons learn to hold their tongues?

The next time you aren't going to write me, I'd thank you to let me know—this kind of *protracted* insult is what no man can bear. Fight with me like a man—let me have fair shot, and you are *caput mortuum et cap-a-pie*, and that ends the business! If you really think I so deserve this silence, tell me why—how—I'll be a thorough scamp or else I won't be any, just which you prefer.

T—— of S——'s class went to Boston yesterday; it was in my heart to send an apple by him for your private use, but father overheard some of my intentions, and said they were "rather small"—whether this remark was intended for the apple, or for my noble self I did not think to ask him; I rather think he intended to give us both a cut— however, he may not!

You are coming home on Wednesday, as perhaps you know, and I am very happy in prospect of your coming, and hope you want to see us as much as we do you. Mother makes nicer pies with reference to your coming, I arrange my thoughts in a convenient shape, Vinnie grows only perter and more pert day by day.

The horse is looking finely—better than in his life—by which you may think him dead unless I add *before*. The carriage stands in state all covered in the chaise-house—we have one foundling hen into whose young mind I seek to instil the fact "Massa is a-comin!"

The garden is amazing—we have beets and beans, have had splendid potatoes for three weeks now. Old Amos weeds and hoes and has an oversight of all thoughtless vegetables. The apples are fine and large in spite of my impression that father called them "small."

Yesterday there was a fire. At about three in the afternoon Mr. Kimberly's barn was discovered to be on fire; the wind was blowing a gale directly from the west, and having had no rain, the roofs [were] as dry as stubble. Mr. Palmer's house was charred—the little house of father's—and Mr. Kimberly's also. The engine was broken, and it seemed for a little while as if the whole street must go; the Kimberlys' barn was burnt down, and the house much charred and injured, though not at all destroyed—Mr. Palmer's barn took fire, and Deacon Leland's also, but were extinguished with only part burned roofs. We all feel very thankful at such a narrow escape. Father says there was never such imminent danger, and such miraculous escape. Father and Mr. Frink took charge of the fire—or rather of the *water*, since fire usually takes care of itself. The men all worked like heroes, and after the fire was out father gave commands to have them march to Howe's where an entertainment was provided for them. After the whole was over they gave "three cheers for Edward Dickinson," and three more for the insurance company. On the whole, it is very wonderful that we didn't all burn up, and we ought to hold our tongues and be very thankful. If there *must* be a fire, I'm sorry it couldn't wait until you had got home, because you seem to enjoy such things so very much.

There is nothing of moment now which I can find to tell

you, except a case of measles in Hartford. . . . Good-by, Sir. Fare you well. My benison to your school.

Amherst, *Spring*, 1853
Tuesday Noon

Dear Austin,— . . . How soon now you are coming, and how happy we are in thought of seeing you! I can't realize that you will come, it is so still and lonely it doesn't seem possible it can be otherwise; but we shall see, when the nails hang full of coats again, and the chairs hang full of hats, and I can count the slippers under the chair. Oh, Austin, how we miss them all, and more than them, somebody who used to hang them there, and get many a hint ungentle to carry them away. Those times seem far off now, a great way, as things we did when children. I wish we were children now— I wish we were always children, how to grow up I don't know. . . . Cousin J. has made us an Æolian harp which plays beautifully whenever there is a breeze.

Austin, you mustn't care if your letters do not get here just when you think they will—they are always new to us, and delightful always, and the more you send us the happier we shall be. We all send our love to you, and think much and say much of seeing you again—keep well till you come, and if knowing that we all love you makes you happier, then, Austin, you may sing the whole day long!

Affectionately,
Emilie

Amherst, *March* 18, 1853
Friday Morning

Dear Austin,—I presume you remember a story that Vinnie tells of a breach of promise case where the corre-

93

spondence between the parties consisted of a reply from the girl to one she had never received but was daily expecting. Well, *I* am writing an answer to the letter I haven't had, so you will see the force of the accompanying anecdote. I have been looking for you ever since despatching my last, but this is a fickle world, and it's a great source of complacency that 'twill all be burned up by and by. I should be pleased with a line when you've published your work to father, if it's perfectly convenient!

Your letters are very funny indeed—about the only jokes we have, now you are gone, and I hope you will send us one as often as you can. Father takes great delight in your remarks to him—puts on his spectacles and reads them o'er and o'er as if it was a blessing to have an only son. He reads all the letters you write, as soon as he gets them, at the post-office, no matter to whom addressed; then he makes me read them aloud at the supper table again, and when he gets home in the evening, he cracks a few walnuts, puts his spectacles on, and with your last in his hand, sits down to enjoy the evening. . . . I believe at this moment, Austin, that there's nobody living for whom father has such respect as for you. But my paper is getting low, and I must hasten to tell you that we are very happy to hear good news from you, that we hope you'll have pleasant times and learn a great deal while you're gone, and come back to us greater and happier for the life lived at Cambridge. We miss you more and more. I wish that we could see you, but letters come the next—write them often, and tell us everything.

Affectionately,

EMILIE

June 14, 1853

. . . We have been free from company by the "Amherst and Belchertown Railroad" since J. went home, though we live in constant fear of some other visitation. "Oh, would some power the giftie gie" folks to see themselves as we see them.—*Burns.*

I have read the poems, Austin, and am going to read them again. They please me very much, but I must read them again before I know just what I think of "Alexander Smith." They are not very coherent, but there's a good deal of exquisite frenzy, and some wonderful figures as ever I met in my life. We will talk about it again. The grove looks nicely, Austin, and we think must certainly grow. We love to go there—it is a charming place. Everything is singing now, and everything is beautiful that *can* be in its life. . . . The time for the New London trip has not been fixed upon. I sincerely wish it may wait until you get home from Cambridge if you would like to go.

The cars continue thriving—a good many passengers seem to arrive from somewhere, though nobody knows from where. Father expects his new buggy to arrive by the cars every day now, and that will help a little. I expect all our grandfathers and all their country cousins will come here to spend Commencement, and don't doubt the stock will rise several per cent that week. If we children could obtain board for the week in some "vast wilderness," I think we should have good times. Our house is crowded daily with the members of this world, the high and the low, the bond and the free, the "poor in this world's goods," and the "almighty dollar"; and what in the world they are after continues to be unknown. But I hope they will pass away as insects or vegetation, and let us reap together in golden harvest time. You and I and our sister Vinnie must have a pleasant time to be unmolested together when your school-days end. You must come home from school, not stopping to play by the way. . . . We all send our love to you, and miss you very much, and think of seeing you again very much. Write me again soon. I have said a good deal to-day.

EMILIE

The new railroad was opened for the first regular trip from Palmer to Amherst, May 9, 1853. Mr. Edward Dickinson wrote on that day, "We have no railroad jubilee till we see whether all moves right, then we shall glorify becomingly." Everything was apparently satisfactory, for the celebration occurred early in June, when more than three hundred New London people visited Amherst. In the following letter from Emily are indications of her growing distaste to mingle in a social mêlée, despite genuine interest in itself and its cause.

June 20, 1853
Monday Morning

MY DEAR AUSTIN,— . . . The New London day passed off grandly, so all the people said. It was pretty hot and dusty, but nobody cared for that. Father was, as usual, chief marshal of the day, and went marching around with New London at his heels like some old Roman general upon a triumph day. Mrs. H. got a capital dinner, and was very much praised. Carriages flew like sparks, hither and thither and yon, and they all said 'twas fine. I 'spose' it was. I sat in Professor Tyler's woods and saw the train move off, and then came home again for fear somebody would see me, or ask me how I did. Dr. Holland was here, and called to see us—was very pleasant indeed, inquired for you, and asked mother if Vinnie and I might come and see them in Springfield. . . . We all send you our love.

EMILIE

Postmarked July 2, 1853
Friday Afternoon

DEAR AUSTIN,— . . . Some of the letters you've sent us we have received, and thank you for affectionately. Some we have not received, but thank you for the memory, of which the emblem perished. Where all those letters go, yours and ours, somebody surely knows, but we do not. There's a new postmaster to-day, but we don't know who's to blame. You never wrote me a letter, Austin, which I liked half so well as the one father brought me. We think of your coming home with a great deal of happiness, and are glad you want to come.

Father said he never saw you looking in better health or seeming in finer spirits. He didn't say a word about the Hippodrome or the Museum, and he came home so stern that none of us dared to ask him, and besides grandmother was here, and you certainly don't think I'd allude to a Hippodrome in the presence of that lady! I'd as soon think of popping fire-crackers in the presence of Peter the Great. But you'll tell us when you get home—how soon—how soon! . . . I admire the "Poems" very much. We all send our love to you—shall write you again Sunday.

EMILIE

Summer, 1853
Sunday Afternoon

. . . It is cold here to-day, Austin, and the west wind blows—the windows are shut at home, and the fire burns

97

in the kitchen. How we should love to see you—how pleasant it would be to walk to the grove together. We will walk there when you get home. We all went down this morning, and the trees look beautifully—every one is growing, and when the west wind blows, the pines lift their light leaves and make sweet music. Pussy goes down there too, and seems to enjoy much in her own observations.

Mr. Dwight has not answered yet; he probably will this week. I do think he will come, Austin, and shall be so glad if he will. . . . We all wish you here always, but I hope 'twill seem only dearer for missing it so long. Father says you will come in three weeks—that won't be long now—keep well and happy, Austin, and remember us all you can, and much love from home and

EMILIE

Thursday Evening

. . . G. H. has just retired from an evening's visit here, and I gather my spent energies to write a word to you.

"Blessed are they that are persecuted for righteousness' sake, for they shall have their reward!" Dear Austin, I don't *feel* funny, and I hope you won't laugh at anything I say. I am thinking of you and Vinnie—what nice times you are having, sitting and talking together, while I am lonely here, and I *wanted* to sit and think of you, and fancy what you were saying, all the evening long, but—ordained otherwise. I hope you will have grand times, and don't forget the unit without you, at home.

I have had some things from you to which I perceive no meaning. They either were very vast, or they didn't mean anything, I don't know certainly which. What did you mean by a note you sent me day before yesterday?

Father asked me what you wrote, and I gave it to him to read. He looked very much confused, and finally put on his spectacles, which didn't seem to help him much—I don't think a telescope would have assisted him. I hope you will write to me—I love to hear from you, and now Vinnie is gone I shall feel very lonely. . . . Love for them all if there are those to love and think of me, and more and most for you, from

EMILY

Tuesday Evening

Well, Austin, dear Austin, you have got back again, codfish and pork and all—all but the slippers, so nicely wrapped to take, yet found when you were gone under the kitchen chair. I hope you won't want them. Perhaps you have some more there—I will send them by opportunity, should there be such a thing. Vinnie proposed franking them, but I fear they are rather large! What should you think of it? It isn't every day that we have a chance to sponge Congress, . . . but Cæsar is such "an honorable man" that we may all go to the poorhouse for all the American Congress will lift a finger to help us. . . .

The usual rush of callers, and this beleaguered family as yet in want of time. I do hope immortality will last a little while, but if the A——s should happen to get there first, we shall be driven *there*. . . .

EMILIE

March 17, 1854

. . . Since you went back to Cambridge the weather has been wonderful,—the thermometer every noon between 60 and 70 above zero, and the air full of birds.

To-day has not seemed like a day. It has been most unearthly,—so mild, so bright, so still, the windows open, and fires uncomfortable.

Since supper it lightens frequently. In the south you can see the lightning—in the north the northern lights. Now a furious wind blows just from the north and west, and winter comes back again. . . .

There is to be a party at Professor Haven's tomorrow night, for married people merely. Celibacy excludes me and my sister. Father and mother are invited. Mother will go. . . . Mother and Vinnie send love. They are both getting ready for Washington. Take care of yourself.

Emilie

Already Emily seems to have exhibited disinclination for journeys, as, in a letter to his son in Cambridge, dated at Washington, March 13, 1854, Mr. Edward Dickinson said, "I have written home to have Lavinia come with your mother and you, and Emily, too, if she will, but that I will not insist upon her coming." Emily, however, did go to Washington with her family, later in the spring, as a subsequent letter to Mrs. Holland will show.

Amherst, March 27, 1854
Sunday Evening

Well, Austin,—it's Sunday evening. Vinnie is sick with the ague—mother taking a tour of the second story as she is wont, Sabbath evening—the wind is blowing high, the weather very cold, and I am rather cast down in view of all these circumstances. . . . I went to meeting alone all day. I assure you I felt very solemn. I went to meeting five minutes before the bell rang, morning and afternoon, so not to have to go in after all the people had got there. I wish you had heard Mr. Dwight's sermons to-day. He has preached wonderfully, and I thought all the afternoon how I wished you were there. . . . I will tell you something funny. You know Vinnie sent father [at Washington] a box of maple sugar—she got the box at the store, and it said on the outside of it, "1 doz. genuine Quaker Soap." We didn't hear from the box, but so many days passed we began to feel anxious lest it had never reached him; and mother, writing soon, alluded in her letter to the "sugar sent by the girls," and the funniest letter from father came in answer to hers. It seems the box went straightway, but father not knowing the hand, merely took off the papers in which the box was wrapped, and the label "Quaker Soap" so far imposed upon him that he put the box in a drawer with his shaving materials, and supposed himself well stocked with an excellent Quaker Soap. . . . We all send our love to you, and want you should write us often. Good-night, from

EMILIE

. . . The Germanians gave a concert here the evening of exhibition day. Vinnie and I went with J. I never heard sounds before. They seemed like brazen robins, all wearing broadcloth wings, and I think they were, for they all flew away as soon as the concert was over.

Late Spring, 1854
Saturday Noon

DEAR AUSTIN,—I rather thought from your letter to me that my essays, together with the lectures at Cambridge, were too much for you, so I thought I would let you have a little vacation; but you must have got rested now, so I shall renew the series. Father was very severe to me; he thought I'd been trifling with you, so he gave me quite a trimming about "Uncle Tom" and "Charles Dickens" and these "modern literati" who, he says, are nothing, compared to past generations who flourished when he was a boy. Then he said there were "somebody's rev-e-ries," he didn't know whose they were, that he thought were very ridiculous—so I'm quite in disgrace at present, but I think of that "pinnacle" on which you always mount when anybody insults you, and that's quite a comfort to me. . . .

After a page or two of information about friends in the village, the letter continues:

This is all the news I can think of, but there is one old story, Austin, which you may like to hear—it is that we think about you the whole of the livelong day, and talk of you when we're together. And you can recollect when you are busy studying that those of us at home not so hard at work as you are, get much time to be with you. We all send our love to you.

Emilie

Amherst, *May,* 1854
Saturday Morn

Dear Austin,—A week ago we were all here—to-day we are not all here—yet the bee hums just as merrily, and all the busy things work on as if the same. They do not miss you, child, but there is a humming-bee whose song is not so merry, and there are busy ones who pause to drop a tear. Let us thank God, to-day, Austin, that we can love our friends, our brothers and our sisters, and weep when they are gone, and smile at their return. It is indeed a joy which we are blest to know.

To-day is very beautiful—just as bright, just as blue, just as green and as white and as crimson as the cherry-trees full in bloom, and the half-opening peach-blossoms, and the grass just waving, and sky and hill and cloud can make it, if they try. How I wish you were here, Austin; you thought last Saturday beautiful, yet to this golden day 'twas but one single gem to whole handfuls of jewels. You will ride to-day, I hope, or take a long walk somewhere, and recollect us all,—Vinnie and me and father and mother and home. Yes, Austin, every one of us, for we all think of you, and bring you to recollection many times each day —not bring you to recollection, for we never put you away, but keep recollecting on. . . .

You must think of us to-night while Mr. Dwight takes tea here, and we will think of you far away down in Cambridge.

Don't mind the can, Austin, if it is rather dry, don't mind the daily road though it is rather dusty, but remember the brooks and the hills, and remember while you're but one, we are but four at home!

EMILIE

T O *Mrs. Gordon L. Ford, Mr. Bowdoin, Mrs. Anthon, and Miss Lavinia Dickinson*

❧❧WITH A *number of early letters to herself, Mrs. Ford of Brooklyn sent me also a short sketch of her remembrance of Emily Dickinson's girlhood, which seems to show her in a somewhat different aspect from anything which other friends have given.*

Mrs. Ford was a daughter of the late Professor Fowler of Amherst College, and her recollections, making a pleasant picture of life in Amherst nearly fifty years ago, have all the charm of early friendship and intercourse in the days when plain living and high thinking were not an exceptional combination.

In speaking of several letters which she could not find, Mrs. Ford wrote, "The other things which I wish I could put my hand on were funny—sparkling with fun, and that is a new phase to the public; but she certainly began as a humorist." Although sent to me for publication in this volume of Letters, *Mrs. Ford had hoped to revise and per-*

haps shorten the sketch in the proof; and her sudden death, within a few days after writing it, lends a saddened interest to these memories of a vanished friendship.

"My remembrances of my friend Emily Dickinson are many and vivid, and delightful to me personally, yet they are all of trifles in themselves, and only interesting to the general public as they cast light on the growth and changes in her soul.

"Our parents were friends, and we knew each other from childhood, but she was several years younger, and how and when we drew together I cannot recall, but I think the friendship was based on certain sympathies and mutual admirations of beauty in nature and ideas. She loved the great aspects of nature, and yet was full of interest and affection for its smaller details. We often walked together over the lovely hills of Amherst, and I remember especially two excursions to Mount Norwottock, five miles away, where we found the climbing fern, and came home laden with pink and white trilliums, and later, yellow lady's-slippers. She knew the wood-lore of the region round about, and could name the haunts and the habits of every wild or garden growth within her reach. Her eyes were wide open to nature's sights, and her ears to nature's voices.

"My chief recollections of her are connected with these woodland walks, or out-door excursions with a merry party, perhaps to Sunderland for the 'sugaring off' of the maple sap, or to some wild brook in the deeper forest, where the successful fishermen would afterward cook the chowder. She was a free talker about what interested her, yet I cannot remember one personal opinion expressed of her mates, her home, or her habits.

"Later we met to discuss books. *The Atlantic Monthly* was a youngster then, and our joy over a new poem by Lowell, Longfellow, and Whittier, our puzzles over Emerson's 'If the red slayer think he slays,' our laughter at Oliver Wendell

Holmes, were full and satisfying. Lowell was especially dear to us, and once I saw a passionate fit of crying brought on, when a tutor of the College, who died while contesting the senatorship for Louisiana,[2] told us from his eight years of seniority, that 'Byron had a much better style,' and advised us 'to leave Lowell, Motherwell and Emerson alone.' Like other young creatures, we were ardent partisans.

"There was a fine circle of young people in Amherst, and we influenced each other strongly. We were in the adoring mood, and I am glad to say that many of those idols of our girlhood have proved themselves golden. The eight girls who composed this group had talent enough for twice their number, and in their respective spheres of mothers, authors or women, have been noteworthy and admirable. Three of them have passed from earth, but the others live in activity and usefulness.

"This group started a little paper in the Academy, now the village High School, which was kept up for two years. Emily Dickinson was one of the wits of the school, and a humorist of the 'comic column.' Fanny Montague often made the head title of the paper—*Forest Leaves*—in leaves copied from nature, and fantasies of her own penwork. She is now a wise member of art circles in Baltimore, a manager of the Museum of Art, and the appointed and intelligent critic of the Japanese exhibit at the Exposition in Chicago. Helen Fiske (the 'H. H.' of later days) did no special work on the paper for various reasons.

"This paper was all in script, and was passed around the school, where the contributions were easily recognized from the handwriting, which in Emily's case was very beautiful—small, clear, and finished. Later, though her writing retained its elegance, it became difficult to read. I wish very much I could find a copy of *Forest Leaves*, but we recklessly gave the numbers away, and the last one I ever saw turned up at the

---

[2] The Hon. Henry M. Spofford, Justice of the Supreme Court of Louisiana, a graduate of Amherst College in the Class of 1840, and brother of Mr. Ainsworth R. Spofford, the Librarian of Congress.

Maplewood Institute in Pittsfield, Massachusetts, where they
started a similar paper. Emily's contributions were irresistible,
but I cannot recall them. One bit was stolen by a roguish
editor for the College paper, where her touch was instantly
recognized; and there were two paragraphs in *The Springfield
Republican.*

"We had a Shakespeare Club—a rare thing in those days,—
and one of the tutors proposed to take all the copies of all
the members and mark out the questionable passages. This
plan was negatived at the first meeting, as far as 'the girls'
spoke, who said they did not want the strange things em-
phasized, nor their books spoiled with marks. Finally we told
the men to do as they liked—'we shall read everything.' I
remember the lofty air with which Emily took her departure,
saying, 'There's nothing wicked in Shakespeare, and if there
is I don't want to know it.' The men read for perhaps three
meetings from their expurgated editions, and then gave up
their plan, and the whole text was read out boldly.

"There were many little dances, with cake and lemonade
at the end, and one year there was a valentine party, where
the lines of various authors were arranged to make apparent
sense, but absolute nonsense, the play being to guess the names
and places of the misappropriated lines.

"Emily was part and parcel of all these gatherings, and there
were no signs, in her life and character, of the future recluse.
As a prophetic hint, she once asked me if it did not make
me shiver to hear a great many people talk—they took 'all the
clothes off their souls'—and we discussed this matter. She
mingled freely in all the companies and excursions of the
moment, and the evening frolics.

"Several of this group had beauty, all had intelligence and
character, and others had charm. Emily was not beautiful,
yet she had great beauties. Her eyes were lovely auburn, soft
and warm, her hair lay in rings of the same color all over her
head, and her skin and teeth were fine. At this time she had
a demure manner which brightened easily into fun where she

felt at home, but among strangers she was rather shy, silent, and even deprecating. She was exquisitely neat and careful in her dress, and always had flowers about her, another pleasant habit of modernity.

"I have so many times seen her in the morning at work in her garden where everything throve under her hand, and wandering there at eventide, that she is perpetually associated in my mind with flowers—a flower herself,—especially as for years it was her habit to send me the first buds of the arbutus which we had often hung over together in the woods, joying in its fresh fragrance as the very breath of coming spring.

"My busy married life separated me from these friends of my youth, and intercourse with them has not been frequent; but I rejoice that my early years were passed in scenes of beautiful nature, and with these mates of simple life, high cultivation and noble ideals. In Emily as in others, there was a rare combination of fervor and simplicity, with good practical living, great conscience and directness of purpose. She loved with all her might, there was never a touch of the worldling about her, and we all knew and trusted her love.

"Dr. Holland once said to me, 'Her poems are too ethereal for publication.' I replied, 'They are beautiful—so concentrated —but they remind me of air-plants that have no roots in earth.' 'That is true,' he said, 'a perfect description'; and I think these lyrical ejaculations, these breathed-out projectiles, sharp as lances, would at that time have fallen into idle ears. But gathered in a volume where many could be read at once as her philosophy of life, they explain each other, and so become intelligible and delightful to the public.

"The first poem I ever read was the robin chorister[3] which she gave my husband years ago. I think in spite of her seclusion, she was longing for poetic sympathy, and that some of her later habits of life originated in this suppressed and ungratified desire.

[3] "Some keep the Sabbath going to church," etc.

"I only wish the interest and delight her poems have aroused could have come early enough in her career to have kept her social and communicative, and at one with her friends. Still, these late tributes to her memory are most welcome to the circle that loved her, even though they are but laurels to lay on her grave.

E. E. F. F."

The first letter was written in 1848; the others at intervals until 1853. Though placed in order, they were not dated by Mrs. Ford.

1848

DEAR EMILY,—I said when the barber came I would save you a little lock, and fulfilling my promise, I send you one to-day. I shall never give you anything again that will be half so full of sunshine as this wee lock of hair, but I wish no hue more sombre might ever fall to you.

All your gifts should be rainbows if I owned half the shine, and but a bit of sea to furnish raindrops for one. Dear Emily, this is all—it will serve to make you remember me when locks are crisp and gray, and the quiet cap, and the spectacles, and "John Anderson my Jo" are all that is left of you.

I must have one of yours. Please spare me a little lock sometime when you have your scissors and there is one to spare.

Your very affectionate
EMILIE

The buds are small, dear Emily, but will you please accept one for your cousin and yourself? I quite forgot the rosebugs when I spoke of the buds, last evening, and I found a family of them taking an early breakfast on my most precious bud, with a smart little worm for land-lady, so the sweetest are gone, but accept my love with the smallest, and I'm

Your affectionate
EMILIE

Tuesday Morn

DEAR EMILY,—I come and see you a great many times every day, though I don't bring my body with me, so perhaps you don't know I'm there. But I love to come just as dearly, for nobody sees me then, and I sit and chat away, and look up in your face, and no matter who calls if "my Lord the King," he doesn't interrupt me. Let me say, dear Emily, both mean to come at a time, so you shall be very sure I am sitting by your side, and not have to trust the fancy. . . .

Affectionately,
E.

1849?
Thursday Morning

DEAR EMILY,—I fear you will be lonely this dark and stormy day, and I send this little messenger to say you must not be.

The day is long to me. I have wanted to come and see you. I have tried earnestly to come, but always have been detained by some ungenerous care, and now this falling snow sternly and silently lifts up its hand between.

How glad I am affection can always leave and go. How

glad that the drifts of snow pause at the outer door and go no farther, and it is as warm within as if no winter came. . . . Let us think of the pleasant summer whose gardens are far away, and whose robins are singing always. If it were not for blossoms . . . and for that brighter sunshine above, beyond, away, these days were dark indeed; but I try to keep recollecting that we are away from home, and have many brothers and sisters who are expecting us. Dear Emilie, don't weep, for you will both be so happy where "sorrow cannot come."

Vinnie left her Testament on a little stand in our room, and it made me think of her, so I thought I would open it, and the first words I read were in those sweetest verses, "Blessed are the poor—Blessed are they that mourn—Blessed are they that weep, for they shall be comforted." Dear Emily, I thought of you, and I hastened away to send this message to you.

EMILIE

Thursday Morn

DEAR EMILY,—I can't come in this morning, because I am so cold, but you will know I am here ringing the big front door-bell, and leaving a note for you.

Oh, I want to come in, I have a great mind now to follow little Jane into your warm sitting-room; are you there, dear Emily?

No, I resist temptation and run away from the door just as fast as my feet will carry me, lest if I once come in I shall grow so happy that I shall stay there always and never go home at all. You will have read this note by the time I reach the office, and you can't think how fast I run.

Affectionately,

EMILY

P. S. I have just shot past the corner, and now all the wayside houses, and the little gate flies open to see me coming home.

Saturday Morn

It has been a long week, dear Emily, for I have not seen your face, but I have contrived to think of you very much instead, which has half reconciled me to not seeing you for so long. I was coming several times, but the snow would start the first, and then the paths were damp, and then a friend would drop in to chat, and the short afternoon was gone before I was aware.

Did Mr. D—— give you a message from me? He promised to be faithful, but I don't suppose divines think earthly loves of much consequence. My flowers come in my stead to-day, dear Emily. I hope you will love to see them, and whatever word of love or welcome kindly you would extend to me, "do even so to them." They are small, but so full of meaning if they only mean the half of what I bid them.

Very affectionately,

EMILY

Thursday Morning

. . . When I am as old as you, and have had so many friends, perhaps they won't seem so precious, and then I sha'n't write any more little *billets-doux* like these, but you will forgive me now, because I can't find many so dear to me as you. Then I know I can't have you always; some day a "brave dragoon" will be stealing you away, and I will have farther to go to discover you at all, so I shall recollect all these sweet opportunities, and feel so sorry if I didn't improve them. . . .

About this time (December, 1849), the following little note was sent to Mr. Bowdoin, a law student in Mr. Dickinson's office, "on returning Jane Eyre." *The leaves mentioned were box leaves.*

December, 1849

MR. BOWDOIN,—If all these leaves were altars, and on every one a prayer that Currer Bell might be saved, and you were God—would you answer it?

Mr. Bowdoin, who was considered by the young girls at that time "a confirmed bachelor," also received the accompanying valentine from Emily.

Valentine Week, 1850

Awake, ye muses nine, sing me a strain divine,
Unwind the solemn twine, and tie my Valentine.

* * *

Oh the earth was *made* for lovers, for damsel, and hopeless
swain,
For sighing, and gentle whispering, and *unity* made of
twain.
All things do go a courting, in earth or sea, or air,
God hath made nothing single but *thee* in His world so fair!
The *bride* and then the *bridegroom*, the *two*, and then the
one,
Adam, and Eve, his consort, the moon and then the sun;
The life doth prove the precept, who obey shall happy be,
Who will not serve the sovereign, be hanged on fatal tree.
The high do seek the lowly, the great do seek the small,
None cannot find who seeketh, on this terrestrial ball;
The bee doth court the flower, the flower his suit receives.

And they make a merry wedding, whose guests are hundred
  leaves;
The wind doth woo the branches, the branches they are
  won,
And the father fond demandeth the maiden for his son.
The storm doth walk the seashore humming a mournful
  tune,
The wave with eye so pensive, looketh to see the moon,
Their spirits meet together, they make them solemn vows,
No more he singeth mournful, her sadness she doth lose.
The worm doth woo the mortal, death claims a living
  bride,
Night unto day is married, morn unto eventide;
Earth is a merry damsel, and heaven a knight so true,
And Earth is quite coquettish, and beseemeth in vain to
  sue.
Now to the application, to the reading of the roll,
To bringing thee to justice, and marshalling thy soul:
Thou art a *human* solo, a being cold, and lone,
Wilt have no kind companion, thou reapest what thou
  hast sown.
Hast never silent hours, and minutes all too long,
And a deal of sad reflection, and wailing instead of song?
There's *Sarah*, and *Eliza*, and *Emeline* so fair,
And *Harriet* and *Sabra*, and she with curling hair.
Thine eyes are sadly blinded, but yet thou mayest see
Six true and comely maidens sitting upon the tree;
Approach that tree with caution, then up it boldly climb,
And seize the one thou lovest, nor care for space, or time.
Then bear her to the greenwood, and build for her a
  bower,
And give her what she asketh, jewel, or bird, or flower—

And bring the fife, and trumpet, and beat upon the
     drum—
And bid the world Goodmorrow, and go to glory home!

*Valentines seemed ever near the thoughts of the young
people of this generation, and another clever one, written
by Emily in 1852, somehow found its way into* The
Republican, *probably through some friend. It was orig-
inally sent to Mr. William Howland.*

1852

Sic transit gloria mundi,
How doth the busy bee—
Dum vivimus vivamus,
I stay mine enemy.

Oh, *veni, vidi, vici,*
Oh, *caput, cap-a-pie,*
And oh, *memento mori*
When I am far from thee.

Hurrah for Peter Parley,
Hurrah for Daniel Boone,
Three cheers, sir, for the gentlemen
Who first observed the moon.

Peter put up the sunshine,
Pattie arrange the stars,
Tell Luna tea is waiting,
And call your brother Mars.

Put down the apple, Adam,
And come away with me;

So shall thou have a pippin
From off my father's tree.

I climb the hill of science
I "view the landscape o'er,"
Such transcendental prospect
I ne'er beheld before.

Unto the Legislature
My country bids me go.
I'll take my india-rubbers,
In case the wind should blow.

During my education,
It was announced to me
That gravitation, stumbling,
Fell from an apple-tree.

The earth upon its axis
Was once supposed to turn,
By way of a gymnastic
In honor to the sun.

It was the brave Columbus,
A-sailing on the tide,
Who notified the nations
Of where I would reside.

Mortality is fatal,
Gentility is fine,
Rascality heroic,
Insolvency sublime.

Our fathers being weary
Lay down on Bunker Hill,
And though full many a morning,
Yet they are sleeping still.

The trumpet, sir, shall wake them,
In dream I see them rise,
Each with a solemn musket
A-marching to the skies.

A coward will remain, sir,
Until the fight is done,
But an immortal hero
Will take his hat and run.

Good-by, sir, I am going—
My country calleth me.
Allow me, sir, at parting
To wipe my weeping e'e.

In token of our friendship
Accept this *Bonnie Doon,*
And when the hand that plucked it
Has passed beyond the moon,

The memory of my ashes
Will consolation be.
Then farewell, Tuscarora,
And farewell, sir, to thee.

T O *Mrs. Ford*

Sunday Afternoon, 1852

I have just come home from meeting, where I have been all day, and it makes me so happy to think of writing you that I forget the sermon and minister and all, and think of none but you. . . . Imiss you always, dear Emily, and I think now and then that I can't stay without you, and half make up my mind to make a little bundle of all my earthly things, bid my blossoms and home good-by, and set out on foot to find you. But we have so much matter of fact here that I don't dare to go, so I keep on sighing, and wishing you were here.

I know you would be happier amid this darling spring than in ever so kind a city, and you would get well much faster drinking our morning dew—and the world here is so beautiful, and things so sweet and fair, that your heart would be soothed and comforted.

I would tell you about the spring if I thought it might persuade you even now to return, but every bud and bird would only afflict you and make you sad where you are, so not one word of the robins, and not one word of the bloom, lest it make the city darker, and your own home more dear.

But nothing forgets you, Emily, not a blossom, not a bee; for in the merriest flower there is a pensive air, and in the bonniest bee a sorrow—they know that you are gone, they know how well you loved them, and in their little faces is sadness, and in their mild eyes, tears. But another spring, dear friend, you must and shall be here, and nobody can take you away, for I will hide you and keep you—and who would think of taking you if I hold you tight in my arms?

Your home looks very silent—I try to think of things funny, and turn the other way when I am passing near, for sure I am that looking would make my heart too heavy, and make my eyes so dim. How I do long once more to hear the household voices, and see you there at twilight sitting in the door—and I shall when the leaves fall, sha'n't I, and the crickets begin to sing?

You must not think sad thoughts, dear Emily. I fear you are doing so, from your sweet note to me, and it almost breaks my heart to have you so far away, where I cannot comfort you.

All will be well, I know, and I know all will be happy, and I so wish I was near to convince my dear friend so. I want very much to hear how Mr. Ford is now. I hope you will tell me, for it's a good many weeks since I have known anything of him. You and he may come this way any summer; and how I hope he may—and I shall pray for him, and for you, and for your home on earth, which will be next the one in heaven.

Your very affectionate

EMILIE

I thank you for writing me, one precious little "forget-me-not" to bloom along my way. But one little one is lonely —pray send it a blue-eyed mate, that it be not alone. Here is love from mother and father and Vinnie and me. . . .

1853

Wednesday Eve

DEAR EMILY,—Are you there, and shall you always stay there, and is it not dear Emily any more, but Mrs.

Ford of Connecticut, and must we stay alone, and will you not come back with the birds and the butterflies, when the days grow long and warm?

Dear Emily, we are lonely here. I know Col. S—— is left, and Mr. and Mrs. K——, but pussy has run away, and you do not come back again, and the world has grown so long! I knew you would go away, for I know the roses are gathered, but I guessed not yet, not till by expectation we had become resigned. Dear Emily, when it came, and hidden by your veil you stood before us all and made those promises, and when we kissed you, all, and went back to our homes, it seemed to me translation, not any earthly thing, and if a little after you'd ridden on the wind, it would not have surprised me.

And now five days have gone, Emily, and long and silent, and I begin to know that you will not come back again. There's a verse in the Bible, Emily, I don't know where it is, nor just how it goes can I remember, but it's a little like this—"I can go to her, but she cannot come back to me." I guess that isn't right, but my eyes are full of tears, and I'm sure I do not care if I make mistakes or not. Is it happy there, dear Emily, and is the fireside warm, and have you a little cricket to chirp upon the hearth?

How much we think of you—how dearly love you—how often hope for you that it may all be happy.

Sunday evening your father came in—he stayed a little while. I thought he looked solitary. I thought he had grown old. How lonely he must be—I'm sorry for him.

Mother and Vinnie send their love, and hope you are so happy. Austin has gone away. Father comes home to-morrow. I know father will miss you. He loved to meet you here.

"So fades a summer cloud away,
  So smiles the gale when storms are o'er,
So gently shuts the eye of day,
  So dies a wave along the shore."

Kiss me, dear Emily, and remember me if you will, with
much respect, to your husband. Will you write me sometime?

Affectionately,
EMILY

TO *Mrs. Anthon*

AMHERST, 1859

. . . Sweet at my door this March night another
candidate. Go home! We don't like Katies here! Stay! My
heart votes for you, and what am I, indeed, to dispute her
ballot!

What are your qualifications? Dare you dwell in the East
where we dwell? Are you afraid of the sun? When you hear
the new violet sucking her way among the sods, shall you
be resolute? All we are strangers, dear, the world is not
acquainted with us, because we are not acquainted with
her; and pilgrims. Do you hesitate? And soldiers, oft—some
of us victors, but those I do not see to-night, owing to the
smoke. We are hungry, and thirsty, sometimes, we are
barefoot and cold—will you still come?

Then, bright I record you—Kate, gathered in March!
It is a small bouquet, dear, but what it lacks in size it
gains in fadelessness. Many can boast a hollyhock, but few
can bear a rose! And should new flower smile at limited
associates, pray her remember were there many, they were

not worn upon the breast, but tilled in the pasture. So I rise wearing her—so I sleep holding,—sleep at last with her fast in my hand, and wake bearing my flower.

EMILIE

To the Same

There are two ripenings, one of sight,
Whose forces spheric wind,
Until the velvet product
Drops spicy to the ground.
A homelier maturing,
A process in the burr
That teeth of frosts alone disclose
On far October air.

EMILIE

To the Same, 1860

The prettiest of pleas, dear, but with a lynx like me quite unavailable. Finding is slow, facilities for losing so frequent, in a world like this, I hold with extreme caution. A prudence so astute may seem unnecessary, but plenty moves those most, dear, who have been in want, and Saviour tells us, Kate, the poor are always with us. Were you ever poor? I have been a beggar, and rich to-night, as by God's leave I believe I am, the "lazzaroni's" faces haunt, pursue me still!

You do not yet "dislimn," Kate. Distinctly sweet your face stands in its phantom niche—I touch your hand—my cheek your cheek—I stroke your vanished hair. Why did you enter, sister, since you must depart? Had not its heart been torn enough but you must send your shred?

Oh, our condor Kate! Come from your crags again! Oh, dew upon the bloom fall yet again a summer's night! Of

122

such have been the frauds which have vanquished faces, sown plant of flesh the church-yard plats, and occasioned angels.

There is a subject, dear, on which we never touch. Ignorance of its pageantries does not deter me. I too went out to meet the dust early in the morning. I too in daisy mounds possess hid treasure, therefore I guard you more. You did not tell me you had once been a "millionaire." Did my sister think that opulence could be mistaken? Some trinket will remain, some babbling plate or jewel.

I write you from the summer. The murmuring leaves fill up the chinks through which the winter red shone when Kate was here, and F—— was here, and frogs sincerer than our own splash in their Maker's pools. It's but a little past, dear, and yet how far from here it seems, fled with the snow! So through the snow go many loving feet parted by 'Alps.' How brief, from vineyards and the sun!

Parents and Vinnie request love to be given girl.

EMILIE

1861?

To the Same

KATIE,—Last year at this time I did not miss you, but positions shifted; until I hold your black in strong hallowed remembrance, and trust my colors are to you tints slightly beloved.

You cease, indeed, to talk, which is a custom prevalent among things parted and torn, but shall I class this, dear, among elect exceptions, and bear you just as usual unto the kind Lord?

We dignify our faith when we can cross the ocean with it, though most prefer ships.

123

How do you do this year? . . . How many years, I
wonder, will sow the moss upon them, before we bind
again, a little altered, it may be, elder a little it *will* be, and
yet the same, as suns which shine between our lives and
loss, and violets—not last year's, but having the mother's
eyes.

Do you find plenty of food at home? Famine is unpleasant.

It is too late for frogs—or what pleases me better, dear,
not quite early enough! The pools were full of you for a
brief period, but that brief period blew away, leaving me
with many stems, and but a few foliage! Gentlemen here
have a way of plucking the tops of the trees, and putting
the fields in their cellars annually, which in point of taste
is execrable, and would they please omit, I should have
fine vegetation and foliage all the year round, and never
a winter month. Insanity to the sane seems so unnecessary
—but I am only one, and they are "four and forty," which
little affair of numbers leaves me impotent. Aside from
this, dear Katie, inducements to visit Amherst are as they
were—I am pleasantly located in the deep sea, but love
will row you out, if her hands are strong, and don't wait
till I land, for I'm going ashore on the other side.

EMILIE

*Following are letters written to her sister, Miss Lavinia
Dickinson, while Emily was receiving treatment for her
eyes in Boston. She was there for this purpose twice,—
during the summer of 1864, and again in 1865, usually
writing of these years as "when I was sick so long," which
has given many persons the idea of an invalidism she never
had.*

1864

DEAR VINNIE,—Many write that they do not write because that they have too much to say, I that I have enough. Do you remember the whippoorwill that sang one night on the orchard fence, and then drove to the south, and we never heard of him afterward?

He will go home, and I shall go home, perhaps in the same train. It is a very sober thing to keep my summer in strange towns—what, I have not told, but I have found friends in the wilderness. You know Elijah did, and to see the "ravens" mending my stockings would break a heart long hard.

Fanny and Lou are solid gold, and Mrs. B—— and her daughter very kind, and the doctor enthusiastic about my getting well. I feel no gayness yet—I suppose I had been discouraged so long.

You remember the prisoner of Chillon did not know liberty when it came, and asked to go back to jail.

C—— and A—— came to see me and brought beautiful flowers. Do you know what made them remember me? Give them my love and gratitude.

They told me about the day at Pelham, you, dressed in daisies, and Mr. McD——. I couldn't see you, Vinnie. I am glad of all the roses you find, while your primrose is gone. How kind Mr. C—— grew. Was Mr. D—— dear?

Emily wants to be well—if any one alive wants to get well more, I would let him, first.

Give my love to father and mother and Austin. Tell Margaret I remember her, and hope Richard is well. . . . How I wish I could rest all those who are tired for me.

EMILY

125

To the Same, 1865

DEAR VINNIE,—The hood is far under way, and the girls think it a beauty. . . . I hope the chimneys are done, and the hemlocks set, and the two teeth filled in the front yard. How astonishing it will be to me! . . .

The pink lily you gave Lou has had five flowers since I came, and has more buds. The girls think it my influence. Lou wishes she knew father's view of Jeff Davis' capture—thinks no one but him can do it justice. She wishes to send a photograph of the arrest to Austin, including the skirt and spurs, but fears he will think her trifling with him. I advised her not to be rash.

How glad I should be to see you all, but it won't be long, Vinnie. You will be willing, won't you, for a little while? It has rained and been very hot, and mosquitoes, as in August. I hope the flowers are well. The tea-rose I gave Aunt L—— has a flower now. Is the lettuce ripe? Persons wear no bonnets here. Fanny has a blade of straw with handle of ribbon.

Affectionately,
EMILY

To the Same

. . . Father told me you were going. I wept for the little plants, but rejoiced for you. Had I loved them as well as I did, I could have begged you to stay with them, but they are foreigners now, and all, a foreigner. I have been sick so long I do not know the sun. I hope they may be alive, for home would be strange except them, now the world is dead.

A—— N—— lives here since Saturday, and two new people more, a person and his wife, so I do little but fly, yet always find a nest. I shall go home in two weeks. You will get me at Palmer?

Love for E—— and Mr. D——.

SISTER

To the Same

. . . The Doctor will let me go Monday of Thanksgiving week. He wants to see me Sunday, so I cannot before. . . . Love for the Middletown pearls. Shall write E—— after Tuesday, when I go to the Doctor. Thank her for sweet note.

The drums keep on for the still man—but Emily must stop.

Love of Fanny and Lou.

SISTER

Soon after the close of the war, a friend, Mrs. Vanderbilt of Long Island, met with a very serious bodily accident. Upon her recovery she received the following welcome to the realm of health:—

> To this world she returned,
> But with a tingle of that;
> A compound manner,
> As a sod
> Espoused a violet
> That chiefer to the skies
> Than to himself allied,
> Dwelt, hesitating,
> Half of dust,
> And half of day, the bride.

EMILY

On the occasion of another friend's departure from Amherst after a visit, Emily's good-by was embodied in the following lines, accompanied by an oleander blossom tied with black ribbon:

> We'll pass without a parting,
> So to spare
> Certificate of absence,
> Deeming where
> I left her I could find her
> If I tried.
> This way I keep from missing
> Those who died.

> EMILY

T O *Dr. J. G. Holland, and Mrs. Holland*

THE DATES *of these letters can be approximated only by the hand-writing—which varies from the early style, about 1853, to the latest—and by events mentioned, the time of whose occurrence is known. Mrs. Holland writes that there were many other letters, even more quaint and original, but unhappily not preserved.*

About 1853
Friday Evening

Thank you, dear Mrs. Holland—Vinnie and I will come, if you would like to have us. We should have written before, but mother has not been well, and we hardly knew whether we could leave her, but she is better now, and I write quite late this evening, that if you still desire it, Vinnie and I will come. Then, dear Mrs. Holland, if agreeable to you, we will take the Amherst train on Tuesday morning, for Springfield, and be with you at noon.

The cars leave here at nine o'clock, and I think reach

Springfield at twelve. I can think just how we dined with you a year ago from now, and it makes my heart beat faster to think perhaps we'll see you so little while from now.

To live a thousand years would not make me forget the day and night we spent there, and while I write the words, I don't believe I'm coming, so sweet it seems to me. I hope we shall not tire you; with all your other cares, we fear we should not come, but you *will* not let us trouble you, will you, dear Mrs. Holland?

Father and mother ask a very warm remembrance to yourself and Dr. Holland.

We were happy the grapes and figs seemed acceptable to you, and wished there were many more. I am very sorry to hear that "Kate" has such excellent lungs. With all your other cares, it must be quite a trial to you.

It is also a source of pleasure to me that Annie goes to sleep, on account of the "interregnum" it must afford to you.

Three days and we are there—happy—very happy! To-morrow I will sew, but I shall think of you, and Sunday sing and pray—yet I shall not forget you, and Monday's very near, and here's to me on Tuesday! Good-night, dear Mrs. Holland—I see I'm getting wild—you will forgive me all, and not *forget* me all, though? Vinnie is fast asleep, or her love would be here—though she is, it is. Once more, if it is fair, we will come on Tuesday, and you love to have us, but if not convenient, please surely tell us so.

Affectionately,

EMILIE

Tuesday Evening

DEAR DR. AND MRS. HOLLAND,—dear Minnie—it is cold to-night, but the thought of you so warm, that I sit by it as a fireside, and am never cold any more. I love to write to you—it gives my heart a holiday and sets the bells to ringing. If prayers had any answers to them, you were all here to-night, but I seek and I don't find, and knock and it is not opened. Wonder if God is just—presume He is, however, and 'twas only a blunder of Matthew's.

I think mine is the case, where when they ask an egg, they get a scorpion, for I keep wishing for you, keep shutting up my eyes and looking toward the sky, asking with all my might for you, and yet you do not come. I wrote to you last week, but thought you would laugh at me, and call me sentimental, so I kept my lofty letter for "Adolphus Hawkins, Esq."

If it wasn't for broad daylight, and cooking-stoves, and roosters, I'm afraid you would have occasion to smile at my letters often, but so sure as "this mortal" essays immortality, a crow from a neighboring farm-yard dissipates the illusion, and I am here again.

And what I mean is this—that I thought of you all last week, until the world grew rounder than it sometimes is, and I broke several dishes.

Monday, I solemnly resolved I would be *sensible,* so I wore thick shoes, and thought of Dr. Humphrey, and the Moral Law. One glimpse of *The Republican* makes me break things again—I read in it every night.

Who writes those funny accidents, where railroads meet each other unexpectedly, and gentlemen in factories get their heads cut off quite informally? The author, too, relates them in such a sprightly way, that they are quite attractive. Vinnie was disappointed to-night, that there were

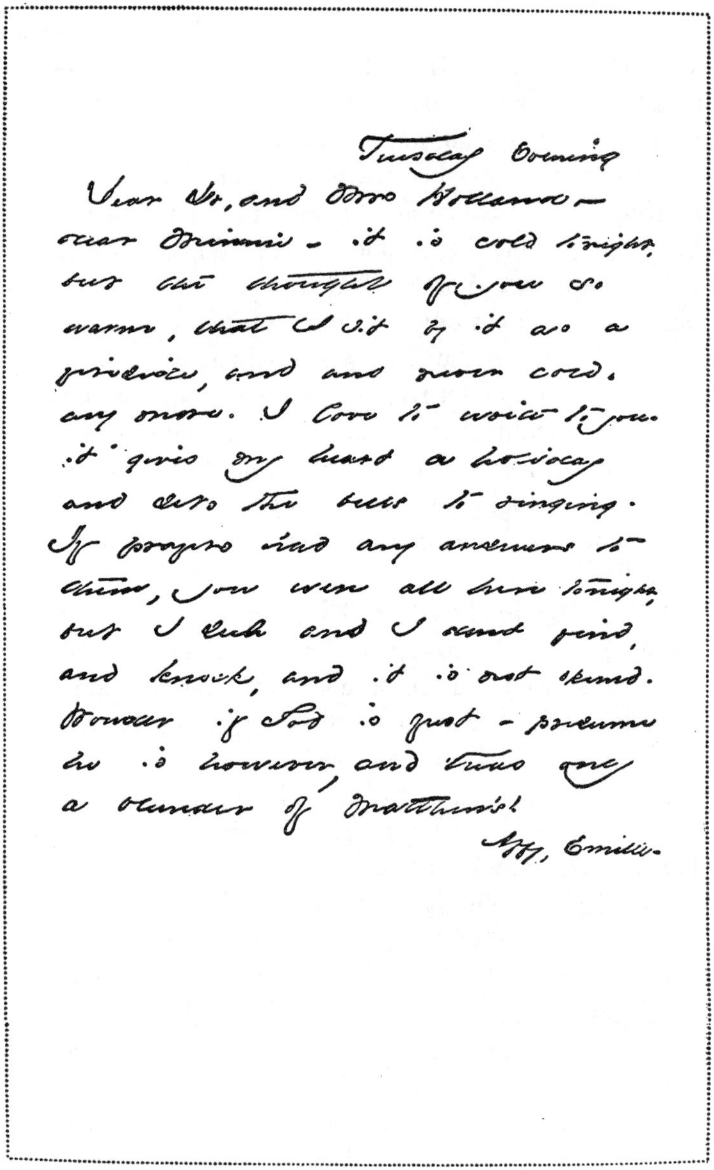

LETTER TO DR. AND MRS. HOLLAND, *facsimile*

not more accidents—I read the news aloud, while Vinnie was sewing. *The Republican* seems to us like a letter from you, and we break the seal and read it eagerly. . . .

Vinnie and I talked of you as we sewed, this afternoon. I said—"how far they seem from us," but Vinnie answered me "only a little way." . . . I'd love to be a bird or bee, that whether hum or sing, still might be near you.

Heaven is large—is it not? Life is short too, isn't it? Then when one is done, is there not another, and—and—then if God is willing, we are neighbors then. Vinnie and mother send their love. Mine too is here. My letter as a bee, goes laden. Please love us and remember us. Please write us very soon, and tell us how you are. . . .

Affectionately,
EMILIE

Late Autumn, 1853
Sabbath Afternoon

DEAR FRIENDS,—I thought I would write again. I write you many letters with pens which are not seen. Do you receive them?

I think of you all to-day, and dreamed of you last night. When father rapped on my door to wake me this morning, I was walking with you in the most wonderful garden, and helping you pick—roses, and though we gathered with all our might, the basket was never full. And so all day I pray that I may walk with you, and gather roses again, and as night draws on, it pleases me, and I count impatiently the hours 'tween me and the darkness, and the dream of you and the roses, and the basket never full.

God grant the basket fill not, till, with hands purer and whiter, we gather flowers of gold in baskets made of pearl; higher—higher! It seems long since we heard from you—

long, since how little Annie was, or any one of you—so long since Cattle Show, when Dr. Holland was with us. Oh, it always seems a long while from our seeing you, and even when at your house, the nights seemed much more long than they're wont to do, because separated from you. I want so much to know if the friends are all well in that dear cot in Springfield—and if well whether happy, and happy—*how* happy, and why, and what bestows the joy? And then those other questions, asked again and again, whose answers are so sweet, do they love—remember us— wish sometimes we were there? Ah, friends—dear friends —perhaps my queries tire you, but I so long to know.

The minister to-day, not our own minister, preached about death and judgment, and what would become of those, meaning Austin and me, who behaved improperly— and somehow the sermon scared me, and father and Vinnie looked very solemn as if the whole was true, and I would not for worlds have them know that it troubled me, but I longed to come to you, and tell you all about it, and learn how to be better. He preached such an awful sermon though, that I didn't much think I should ever see you again until the Judgment Day, and then you would not speak to me, according to his story. The subject of perdition seemed to please him, somehow. It seems very solemn to me. I'll tell you all about it, when I see you again.

I wonder what you are doing to-day—if you have been to meeting? To-day has been a fair day, very still and blue. To-night the crimson children are playing in the west, and to-morrow will be colder. How sweet if I could see you, and talk of all these things! Please write us very soon. The days with you last September seem a great way off, and to meet you again, delightful. I'm sure it won't be long before we sit together.

Then will I not repine, knowing that bird of mine, though flown—learneth beyond the sea, melody new for me, and will return.

> Affectionately,
> EMILY

This little poem was enclosed in the foregoing letter:—
> Truth is as old as God,
> His twin identity—
> And will endure as long as He,
> A co-eternity,
> And perish on the day
> That He is borne away
> From mansion of the universe,
> A lifeless Deity.

> *Enclosing some leaves,* 1854
> *January* 2d

May it come *to-day?*

Then New Year the sweetest, and long life the merriest, and the Heaven highest—by and by!

> EMILIE

> *Spring,* 1854
> PHILADELPHIA

DEAR MRS. HOLLAND AND MINNIE, AND DR. HOLLAND too—I have stolen away from company to write a note to you; and to say that I love you still.

I am not at home—I have been away just five weeks to-day, and shall not go quite yet back to Massachusetts. Vinnie is with me here, and we have wandered together into many new ways.

We were three weeks in Washington, while father was

there, and have been two in Philadelphia. We have had many pleasant times, and seen much that is fair, and heard much that is wonderful—many sweet ladies and noble gentlemen have taken us by the hand and smiled upon us pleasantly—and the sun shines brighter for our way thus far.

I will not tell you what I saw—the elegance, the grandeur; you will not care to know the value of the diamonds my Lord and Lady wore, but if you haven't been to the sweet Mount Vernon, then I *will* tell you how on one soft spring day we glided down the Potomac in a painted boat, and jumped upon the shore—how hand in hand we stole along up a tangled pathway till we reached the tomb of General George Washington, how we paused beside it, and no one spoke a word, then hand in hand, walked on again, not less wise or sad for that marble story; how we went within the door—raised the latch he lifted when he last went home—thank the Ones in Light that he's since passed in through a brighter wicket! Oh, I could spend a long day, if it did not weary you, telling of Mount Vernon —and I will sometime if we live and meet again, and God grant we shall!

I wonder if you have all forgotten us, we have stayed away so long. I hope you haven't—I tried to write so hard before I went from home, but the moments were so busy, and then they *flew* so. I was sure when days *did* come in which I was less busy, I should seek your forgiveness, and it did not occur to me that you might not forgive me. Am I too late to-day? Even if you are angry, I shall keep praying you, till from very weariness, you will take me in. It seems to me many a day since we were in Springfield, and Minnie and the *dumb-bells* seem as vague—as vague; and sometimes I wonder if I ever dreamed—then if I'm dreaming now, then if I *always* dreamed, and there is not a world, and not these darling friends, for whom I would not count my life too great a sacrifice. Thank God there is a world, and that the friends we love dwell forever and ever in a house above. I fear I grow incongruous, but to meet my friends does delight me so that I quite forget time and sense and so forth.

Now, my precious friends, if you won't forget me until I get home, and become more sensible, I will write again, and more properly. Why didn't I ask before, if you were well and happy?

Forgetful
EMILIE

November, 1854
Saturday Eve

I come in flakes, dear Dr. Holland, for verily it snows, and as descending swans, here a pinion and there a pinion, and anon a plume, come the bright inhabitants of the white home.

I know they fall in Springfield; perhaps you see them now—and therefore I look out again, to see if you are looking.

How pleasant it seemed to hear your voice—so said Vinnie and I, as we as individuals, and then collectively, read your brief note. Why didn't you speak to us before? We thought you had forgotten us—we concluded that one of the bright things had gone forever more. That is a sober feeling, and it mustn't come too often in such a world as this. A violet came up next day, and blossomed in our garden, and were it not for these same flakes, I would go in the dark and get it, so to send to you. Thank Him who is in Heaven, Katie Holland lives! Kiss her on every cheek for me—I really can't remember how many the bairn has—and give my warmest recollection to Mrs. Holland and Minnie, whom to love, this Saturday night, is no trifling thing. I'm very happy that you are happy—and that you cheat the angels of another one.

I would the many households clad in dark attire had succeeded so. You must all be happy and strong and well. I love to have the lamps shine on your evening table. I love to have the sun shine on your daily walks.

The "new house"! God bless it! You will leave the "maiden and married life of Mary Powell" behind.

Love and remember

EMILIE

While the family lived for many years in the old mansion built by Emily Dickinson's grandfather, the Hon. Samuel Fowler Dickinson, they had moved away from it about 1840; *and the following letter describes their return after fifteen years to their early home, where Emily was born, and where she died:—*

1855
Sabbath Day

Your voice is sweet, dear Mrs. Holland—I wish I heard it oftener.

One of the mortal musics Jupiter denies, and when indeed its gentle measures fall upon my ear, I stop the birds to listen. Perhaps you think I *have* no bird, and this is rhetoric—pray, Mr. Whately, what is *that* upon the cherry-tree? Church is done, and the winds blow, and Vinnie is in that pallid land the simple call "sleep." They will be wiser by and by, we shall all be wiser! While I sit in the snows, the summer day on which you came and the bees and the south wind, seem fabulous as *Heaven* seems to a sinful world—and I keep remembering it till it assumes a *spectral* air, and nods and winks at me, and then all of you turn to phantoms and vanish slow away. We cannot talk and laugh more, in the parlor where we met, but we learned to love for aye, there, so it is just as well.

We shall sit in a parlor "not made with hands" unless we are very careful!

I cannot tell you how we moved. I had rather not remember. I believe my "effects" were brought in a bandbox, and the "deathless me," on foot, not many moments after. I took at the time a memorandum of my several senses, and also of my hat and coat, and my best shoes—but it was lost in the *mêlée*, and I am out with lanterns, looking for myself.

Such wits as I reserved, are so badly shattered that repair is useless—and still I can't help laughing at my own catastrophe. I supposed we were going to make a "transit," as heavenly bodies did—but we came budget by budget, as our fellows do, till we fulfilled the pantomime contained in the word "moved." It is a kind of *gone-to-Kansas* feeling, and if I sat in a long wagon, with my family tied behind, I should suppose without doubt I was a party of emigrants!

They say that "home is where the heart is." I think it is where the *house* is, and the adjacent buildings.

But, my dear Mrs. Holland, I have another story, and lay my laughter all away, so that I can sigh. Mother has been an invalid since we came *home*, and Vinnie and I "regulated," and Vinnie and I "got settled," and still we keep our father's house, and mother lies upon the lounge, or sits in her easy-chair. I don't know what her sickness is, for I am but a simple child, and frightened at myself. I often wish I was a grass, or a toddling daisy, whom all these problems of the dust might not terrify—and should my own machinery get slightly out of gear, *please,* kind ladies and gentlemen, some one stop the wheel,—for I know that with belts and bands of gold, I shall whizz triumphant on the new stream! Love for you—love for Dr. Holland—thanks for his exquisite hymn—tears for your sister in sable, and kisses for Minnie and the bairns.

From your mad

EMILIE

Spring, 1856?

. . . February passed like a skate and I know March. Here is the "light" the stranger said "was not on sea or land." Myself could arrest it, but will not chagrin him.

. . . Cousin Peter told me the Doctor would address Commencement—trusting it insure you both for papa's *fête* I endowed Peter. We do not always know the source of the smile that flows to us. . . .

My flowers are near and foreign, and I have but to cross the floor to stand in the Spice Isles.

The wind blows gay to-day and the jays bark like blue terriers.

I tell you what I see—the landscape of the spirit requires a lung, but no tongue. I hold you few I love, till my heart is red as February and purple as March.

Hand for the Doctor.

EMILY

Late Summer, 1856
Sabbath Night

Don't tell, dear Mrs. Holland, but wicked as I am, I read my Bible sometimes, and in it as I read to-day, I found a verse like this, where friends should "go no more out"; and there were "no tears," and I wished as I sat down to-night that we were *there*—not *here*—and that wonderful world had commenced, which makes such promises, and rather than to write you, I were by your side, and the "hundred and forty and four thousand" were chatting pleasantly, yet not disturbing us. And I'm half tempted to take my seat in that Paradise of which the good man writes, and begin forever and ever *now*, so wondrous does it seem. My only sketch, profile, of Heaven is a large, blue sky, bluer and larger than the *biggest* I have seen in June, and in it are my friends—all of them—every one of them—those who are with me now, and those who were "parted" as we walked, and "snatched up to Heaven."

If roses had not faded, and frosts had never come, and one had not fallen here and there whom I could not waken, there were no need of other Heaven than the one below—and if God had been here this summer, and seen the things that *I* have seen—I guess that He would think His Paradise superfluous. Don't tell Him, for the world, though, for after all He's said about it, I should like to see what He *was* building for us, with no hammer, and no stone, and no journeyman either. Dear Mrs. Holland, I love, to-night—love you and Dr. Holland, and "time and sense"—and fading things, and things that do *not* fade.

I'm so glad you are not a blossom, for those in my garden fade, and then a "reaper whose name is Death" has come to get a few to help him make a bouquet for himself, so I'm glad you are not a rose—and I'm glad you are not a bee, for where they go when summer's done, only the thyme knows, and even were you a robin, when the west winds came, you would coolly wink at me, and away, some morning!

As "little Mrs. Holland," then, I think I love you most,

and trust that tiny lady will dwell below while we dwell, and when with many a wonder we seek the new Land, *her* wistful face, *with* ours, shall look the last upon the hills, and first upon—well, *Home!*

Pardon my sanity, Mrs. Holland, in a world *in*sane, and love me if you will, for I had rather *be* loved than to be called a king in earth, or a lord in Heaven.

Thank you for your sweet note—the clergy are very well. Will bring such fragments from them as shall seem me good. I kiss my paper here for you and Dr. Holland— would it were cheeks instead.

> Dearly,
> EMILIE

P. S. The bobolinks have gone.

1857?

DEAR SISTER,—After you went, a low wind warbled through the house like a spacious bird, making it high but lonely. When you had gone the love came. I supposed it would. The supper of the heart is when the guest has gone.

Shame is so intrinsic in a strong affection we must all experience Adam's reticence. I suppose the street that the lover travels is thenceforth divine, incapable of turnpike aims.

That you be with me annuls fear and I await Commencement with merry resignation. Smaller than David you clothe me with extreme Goliath.

Friday I tasted life. It was a vast morsel. A circus passed the house—still I feel the red in my mind though the drums are out.

The book you mention, I have not met. Thank you for tenderness.

The lawn is full of south and the odors tangle, and I hear to-day for the first the river in the tree.

You mentioned spring's delaying—I blamed her for the opposite. I would eat evanescence slowly.

Vinnie is deeply afflicted in the death of her dappled cat, though I convince her it is immortal which assists her some. Mother resumes lettuce, involving my transgression—suggestive of yourself, however, which endears disgrace.

"House" is being "cleaned." I prefer pestilence. That is more classic and less fell.

Yours was my first arbutus. It was a rosy boast.

I will send you the first witch hazel.

A woman died last week, young and in hope but a little while—at the end of our garden. I thought since of the power of Death, not upon affection, but its mortal signal. It is to us the Nile.

You refer to the unpermitted delight to be with those we love. I suppose that to be the license not granted of God.

> Count not that far that can be had,
> Though sunset lie between—
> Nor that adjacent, that beside,
> Is further than the sun.

Love for your embodiment of it.

EMILY

1859

God bless you, dear Mrs. Holland! I read it in the paper.

I'm so glad it's a little boy, since now the little sisters have some one to draw them on the sled—and if a grand old lady you should live to be, there's something sweet, they say, in a son's arm.

I pray for the tenants of that holy chamber, the wrestler,

and the wrestled for. I pray for distant father's heart, swollen, happy heart!

Saviour keep them all!

Emily

Autumn, 1859

Dear Hollands,—Belong to me! We have no fires yet, and the evenings grow cold. To-morrow, stoves are set. How many barefoot shiver I trust their Father knows who saw not fit to give them shoes.

Vinnie is sick to-night, which gives the world a russet tinge, usually so red. It is only a headache, but when the head aches next to you, it becomes important. When she is well, time leaps. When she is ill, he lags, or stops entirely.

Sisters are brittle things. God was penurious with me, which makes me shrewd with Him.

One is a dainty sum! One bird, one cage, one flight; one song in those far woods, as yet suspected by faith only!

This is September, and you were coming in September. Come! Our parting is too long. There has been frost enough. We must have summer now, and "whole legions" of daisies.

The gentian is a greedy flower, and overtakes us all. Indeed, this world is short, and I wish, until I tremble, to touch the ones I love before the hills are red—are gray—are white—are "born again"! If we knew how deep the crocus lay, we never should let her go. Still, crocuses stud many mounds whose gardeners till in anguish some tiny, vanished bulb.

We saw you that Saturday afternoon, but heedlessly forgot to ask where you were going, so did not know, and could not write. Vinnie saw Minnie flying by, one afternoon at Palmer. She supposed you were all there on your way from the sea, and untied her fancy! To say that her fancy wheedled her is superfluous.

We talk of you together, then diverge on life, then hide in you again, as a safe fold. Don't leave us long, dear friends! You know we're children still, and children fear the dark.

Are you well at home? Do you work now? Has it altered much since I was there? Are the children women, and the women thinking it will soon be afternoon? We will help each other bear our unique burdens.

Is Minnie with you now? Take her our love, if she is. Do her eyes grieve her now? Tell her she may have half ours.

Mother's favorite sister is sick, and mother will have to bid her good-night. It brings mists to us all;—the aunt whom Vinnie visits, with whom she spent, I fear, her last inland Christmas. Does God take care of those at sea? My aunt is such a timid woman!

Will you write to us? I bring you all their loves—*many*. They tire me.

EMILIE

1860

How is your little Byron? Hope he gains his foot without losing his genius. Have heard it ably argued that the poet's genius lay in his foot—as the bee's prong and his song are concomitant. Are you stronger than these? To assault so minute a creature seems to me malign, unworthy of Nature—but the frost is no respecter of persons.

I should be glad to be with you, or to open your letter. Blossoms belong to the bee, if needs be by *habeas corpus*.

EMILY

Probably about 1861 *came this brilliant, yet half pathetic, arraignment of the friends who had not written when Emily expected to hear. Who could resist such a plea?*

Friday

DEAR FRIENDS,—I write to you. I receive no letter.

I say "they dignify my trust." I do not disbelieve. I go again. *Cardinals* wouldn't do it. Cockneys wouldn't do it, but I can't *stop* to strut, in a world where bells toll. I hear through visitor in town, that "Mrs. Holland is not strong." The little peacock in me, tells me not to inquire again. Then I remember my tiny friend—how brief she is—how dear she is, and the peacock quite dies away. Now, you need not speak, for perhaps you are weary, and "Herod" requires all your thought, but if you are *well*—let Annie draw me a little picture of an erect flower; if you are *ill*, she can hang the flower a little on one side!

Then, I shall understand, and you need not stop to write me a letter. Perhaps you laugh at me! Perhaps the whole United States are laughing at me too! *I* can't stop for that! *My* business is to love. I found a bird, this morning, down —down—on a little bush at the foot of the garden, and wherefore sing, I said, since nobody *hears?*

One sob in the throat, one flutter of bosom—"*My* business is to *sing*"—and away she rose! How do I know but cherubim, once, themselves, as patient, listened, and applauded her unnoticed hymn?

EMILY

1864?

DEAR SISTER,—Father called to say that our steelyard was fraudulent, exceeding by an ounce the rates of honest men.

He had been selling oats. I cannot stop smiling, though it is hours since, that even our steelyard will not tell the truth.

Besides wiping the dishes for Margaret, I wash them now, while she becomes Mrs. Lawler, vicarious papa to four previous babes. Must she not be an adequate bride?

I winced at her loss, because I was in the habit of her, and even a new rolling-pin has an embarrassing element, but to all except anguish, the mind soon adjusts.

It is also November. The noons are more laconic and the sundowns sterner, and Gibraltar lights make the village foreign. November always seemed to me the Norway of the year. —— is still with the sister who put her child in an ice nest last Monday forenoon. The redoubtable God! I notice where Death has been introduced, he frequently calls, making it desirable to forestall his advances.

It is hard to be told by the papers that a friend is failing, not even know where the water lies. Incidentally, only, that he comes to land. Is there no voice for these? Where is Love to-day?

Tell the dear Doctor we mention him with a foreign accent, party already to transactions spacious and untold. Nor have we omitted to breathe shorter for our little sister. Sharper than dying is the death for the dying's sake.

News of these would comfort, when convenient or possible.

EMILY

DEAR SISTER,—It was incredibly sweet that Austin had seen you, and had stood in the dear house which had lost its friend. To see one who had seen you was a strange assurance. It helped dispel the fear that you departed too, for notwithstanding the loved notes and the lovely gift, there lurked a dread that you had gone or would seek to go. "Where the treasure is," there is the prospective.

Austin spoke very warmly and strongly of you, and we all felt firmer, and drew a vocal portrait of Kate at Vinnie's request, so vivid that we saw her. . . .

> Not all die early, dying young,
> Maturity of fate
> Is consummated equally
> In ages or a night.
> A hoary boy I've known to drop
> Whole-statured, by the side
> Of junior of fourscore—'t was act,
> Not period, that died.

EMILY

Will some one lay this little flower on Mrs. Holland's pillow?

EMILIE

In handwriting similar to the letters about 1862–68, *are several poems, enclosed to the Hollands, among them,—*

> Away from home are some and I,
> An emigrant to be
> In a metropolis of homes
> Is common possibility.
> The habit of a foreign sky
> We, difficult, acquire,
> As children who remain in face,
> The more their feet retire.

And—

> Though my destiny be fustian
> Hers be damask fine—
> Though she wear a silver apron,
> I, a less divine,
>
> Still, my little gypsy being,
> I would far prefer,
> Still my little sunburnt bosom,
> To her rosier.
>
> For when frosts their punctual fingers
> On her forehead lay,
> You and I and Doctor Holland
> Bloom eternally,
>
> Roses of a steadfast summer
> In a steadfast land,
> Where no autumn lifts her pencil,
> And no reapers stand.

In addition to these, many other poems were sent to the Hollands which have already been published; all of them, however, showing slight changes from copies which she retained.

Autumn, 1876
Saturday Eve

DEAR HOLLANDS,—Good-night! I can't stay any longer in a world of death. Austin is ill of fever. I buried my garden last week—our man, Dick, lost a little girl through the scarlet fever. I thought perhaps that *you* were dead, and not knowing the sexton's address, interrogate the daisies. Ah! dainty—dainty Death! Ah! democratic Death! Grasping the proudest zinnia from my purple garden,— then deep to his bosom calling the serf's child!

Say, is he everywhere? Where shall I hide my things? Who is alive? The woods are dead. Is Mrs. H. alive? Annie and Katie—are they below, or received to nowhere?

I shall not tell how short time is, for I was told by lips which sealed as soon as it was said, and the open revere the shut. You were not here in summer. *Summer?* My memory flutters—had I—was there a summer? You should have seen the fields go—gay little entomology! Swift little ornithology! Dancer, and floor, and cadence quite gathered away, and I, a phantom, to you a phantom, rehearse the story! An orator of feather unto an audience of fuzz,—and panto-mimic plaudits. "Quite as good as a play," indeed! Tell Mrs. Holland she is mine.

Ask her if *vice versa?* Mine is but just the thief's request —"Remember me to-day." Such are the bright chirographies of the "Lamb's Book." Good-night! My ships are in!—My window overlooks the wharf! One yacht, and a man-of-war; two brigs and a schooner! "Down with the topmast! Lay her a' hold, a' hold!"

EMILIE

A letter from Mrs. Holland to Emily and her sister jointly, in 1877, *called forth this unique protest.*

SISTER,—A mutual plum is not a plum. I was too respect-ful to take the pulp and do not like a stone.

Send no union letters. The soul must go by Death alone, so, it must by life, if it is a soul.

If a committee—no matter.

I saw the sunrise on the Alps since I saw you. Travel why to Nature, when she dwells with us? Those who lift their hats shall see her, as devout do God.

I trust you are merry and sound. The chances are all against the dear, when we are not with them, though paws of principalities cannot affront if we are by.

Dr. Vaill called here Monday on his way to your house to get the Doctor to preach for him. Shall search *The Republican* for a brief of the sermon. To-day is very homely and awkward as the homely are who have not mental beauty.

Then follows,—
        "The sky is low, the clouds are mean,"
printed in the Poems, *First Series.*

Spring, 1878

I thought that "Birnam Wood" had "come to Dunsinane." Where did you pick arbutus? In Broadway, I suppose. They say that God is everywhere, and yet we always think of Him as somewhat of a recluse. . . . It is hard not to hear again that vital "Sam is coming"—though if grief is a test of a priceless life, he is compensated. He was not ambitious for redemption—that was why it is his. "To him that hath, shall be given." Were it not for the eyes, we would know of you oftener. Have they no remorse for their selfishness? "This tabernacle" is a blissful trial, but the bliss predominates.

I suppose you will play in the water at Alexandria Bay, as the baby does at the tub in the drive. . . . Speak to us when your eyes can spare you, and "keep us, at home, or by the way," as the clergyman says, when he folds the church till another Sabbath.

Lovingly,
EMILY

August, 1879

LOVED AND LITTLE SISTER,—Vinnie brought in a sweet pea to-day, which had a pod on the "off" side. Startled by the omen, I hasten to you.

An unexpected impediment to my reply to your dear last, was a call from my Aunt Elizabeth—"the only male relative on the female side," and though many days since, its flavor of court-martial still sets my spirit tingling.

With what dismay I read of those columns of kindred in the Bible—the Jacobites and the Jebusites and the Hittites and the Jacqueminots!

I am sure you are better, for no rheumatism in its senses would stay after the thermometer struck ninety!

We are revelling in a gorgeous drought.

The grass is painted brown, and how nature would look in other than the standard colors, we can all infer. . . . I bade —— call on you, but Vinnie said you were "the other side the globe," yet Vinnie thinks Vermont is in Asia, so I don't intend to be disheartened by trifles.

Vinnie has a new pussy that catches a mouse an hour. We call her the "minute hand." . . .

Dr. Holland's death, in October of 1881, brought grief to many loving hearts, but to the quiet Amherst household peculiar pain, voiced in the notes to follow.

We read the words but know them not. We are too frightened with sorrow. If that dear, tired one must sleep, could we not see him first?

Heaven is but a little way to one who gave it, here. "Inasmuch," to him, how tenderly fulfilled!

Our hearts have flown to you before—our breaking voices follow. How can we wait to take you all in our sheltering arms?

Could there be new tenderness, it would be for you, but the heart is full—another throb would split it—nor would we dare to speak to those whom such a grief removes, but we have somewhere heard "A little child shall lead them."

EMILY

Thursday

After a while, dear, you will remember that there is a heaven—but you can't now. Jesus will excuse it. He will remember his shorn lamb.

The lost one was on such childlike terms with the Father in Heaven. He has passed from confiding to comprehending—perhaps but a step.

The *safety* of a beloved lost is the first anguish. With you, that is peace.

I shall never forget the Doctor's prayer, my first morning with you—so simple, so believing. *That* God must be a friend—*that* was a different God—and I almost felt warmer myself, in the midst of a tie so sunshiny.

I am yearning to know if he knew he was fleeing—if he

153

spoke to you. Dare I ask if he suffered? Some one will tell
me a very little, when they have the strength. . . . Cling
tight to the hearts that will not let you fall.

EMILY

Panting to help the dear ones and yet not knowing how,
lest any voice bereave them but that loved voice that will
not come, if I can rest them, here is down—or rescue, here
is power.

One who only said "I am sorry" helped me the most when
father ceased—it was too soon for language.

Fearing to tell mother, some one disclosed it unknown to
us. Weeping bitterly, we tried to console her. She only
replied "I loved him so."

Had he a tenderer eulogy?

EMILY

. . . I know you will live for our sake, dear, you would
not be willing to for your own. That is the duty which saves.
While we are trying for others, power of life comes back,
very faint at first, like the new bird, but by and by it has
wings.

How sweetly you have comforted me—the toil to comfort
you, I hoped never would come. A sorrow on your sunny
face is too dark a miracle—but how sweet that he rose in
the morning—accompanied by dawn. How lovely that he
spoke with you, that memorial time! How gentle that he left
the pang he had not time to feel! Bequest of darkness, yet of
light, since unborne by him. "Where thou goest, *we* will
go"—how mutual, how intimate! No solitude receives him,
but neighborhood and friend.

Relieved forever of the loss of those that must have fled, but for his sweet haste. Knowing he could not spare *them*, he hurried like a boy from that unhappened sorrow. Death has mislaid his sting—the grave forgot his victory. Because the flake fell not on him, we will accept the drift, and wade where he is lain.

Do you remember the clover leaf? The little hand that plucked it will keep tight hold of mine.

Please give her love to Annie, and Kate, who also gave a father.

EMILY

To Mrs. Holland, on the marriage of her daughter Annie, December 7, 1881.

SWEET SISTER,—We were much relieved to know that the dear event had occurred without overwhelming any loved one, and perhaps it is sweeter and safer so. I feared much for the parting, to you, to whom parting has come so thickly in the last few days. I knew all would be beautiful, and rejoice it was. Few daughters have the immortality of a father for a bridal gift. Could there be one more costly?

As we never have ceased to think of you, we will more tenderly, now. Confide our happiness to Annie, in her happiness. We hope the unknown balm may ease the balm withdrawn.

You and Katie, the little sisters, lose her, yet obtain her, for each new width of love largens all the rest. Mother and Vinnie think and speak. Vinnie hopes to write. Would that mother could, but her poor hand is idle. Shall I return to you your last and sweetest words—"But I love you all"?

EMILY

Christmas, 1881

Dare we wish the brave sister a sweet Christmas, who remembered us punctually in sorrow as in peace?

The broken heart is broadest. Had it come all the way in your little hand, it could not have reached us perfecter, though had it, we should have clutched the hand and forgot the rest.

Fearing the day had associations of anguish to you, I was just writing when your token came. Then, humbled with wonder at your self-forgetting, I delayed till now. Reminded again of gigantic Emily Brontë, of whom her Charlotte said "Full of ruth for others, on herself she had no mercy." The hearts that never lean, must fall. To moan is justified.

To thank you for remembering under the piercing circumstances were a profanation.

God bless the hearts that suppose they are beating and are not, and enfold in His infinite tenderness those that do not know they are beating and are.

Shall we wish a triumphant Christmas to the brother withdrawn? Certainly he possesses it.

> How much of Source escapes with thee—
> How chief thy sessions be—
> For thou hast borne a universe
> Entirely away.

With wondering love,
EMILY

"Whom seeing not, we" clasp.

EMILY

1883?

Concerning the little sister, not to assault, not to adjure, but to obtain those constancies which exalt friends, we followed her to St. Augustine, since which the trail was lost, or says George Stearns of his alligator, "there was no such aspect."

The beautiful blossoms waned at last, the charm of all who knew them, resisting the effort of earth or air to persuade them to root, as the great florist says "The flower that never will in other climate grow."

To thank you for its fragrance would be impossible, but then its other blissful traits are more than can be numbered. And the beloved Christmas, too, for which I never thanked you. I hope the little heart is well,—*big* would have been the width,—and the health solaced; any news of her as sweet as the first arbutus.

Emily and Vinnie give the love greater every hour.

v

TO *Mr. Samuel Bowles and Mrs. Bowles*

AS EMILY DICKINSON *approached middle life,
and even before her thirtieth year, it seemed to become
more and more impossible for her to mingle in general
society; and a growing feeling of shyness, as early as 1862
or 1863, caused her to abstain, sometimes, from seeing the
dearest friends who came to the house. In spite of her
sympathy with sadness, and her deep apprehension of the
tragic element in life, she was not only keenly humorous
and witty, as already said, but, while made serious by the
insistence of life's pathos, she was yet at heart as ecstatic
as a bird. This combination of qualities made her companionship, when she vouchsafed it, peculiarly breezy and
stimulating. Such a nature must inevitably know more pain
than pleasure.*

*Passionately devoted to her friends, her happiness in their
love and trust was at times almost too intense to bear; and
it will already have been seen how disproportionately great
pain was caused by even comparatively slight separations.*

With her, pathos lay very near raillery and badinage,—sadness very near delight.

Whether, in writing her poems, the joy of creating was sufficient, or whether a thought of future and wider recognition ever came, it is certain that during life her friends made her audience. She cared more for appreciation and approval from the few who were dear than for any applause from an impersonal public. She herself writes, "My friends are my estate."

All her letters show this rare loyalty of soul, those in the preceding chapter particularly, but none perhaps more strongly than those to Mr. and Mrs. Bowles. Beginning about 1858, the letters cover a period of twenty-six or twenty-seven years. Often a single short poem comprises the entire letter,—sometimes only four lines, and without title, date, or signature, but unmistakably pertinent to a special occasion or subject.

Late August, 1858?
AMHERST

DEAR MR. BOWLES,—I got the little pamphlet. I think you sent it to me, though unfamiliar with your hand—I may mistake.

Thank you, if I am right. Thank you, if not, since here I find bright pretext to ask you how you are to-night, and for the health of four more, elder and minor Mary, Sallie and Sam, tenderly to inquire.

I hope your cups are full.

I hope your vintage is untouched. In such a porcelain life one likes to be *sure* that all is well lest one stumble upon one's hopes in a pile of broken crockery.

My friends are my estate. Forgive me then the avarice

to hoard them! They tell me those were poor early have different views of gold. I don't know how that is.

God is not so wary as we, else He would give us no friends, lest we forget Him! The charms of the heaven in the bush are superseded, I fear, by the heaven in the hand, occasionally.

Summer stopped since you were here. Nobody noticed her—that is, no men and women. Doubtless, the fields are rent by petite anguish, and "mourners go about" the woods. But this is not for us. Business enough indeed, our stately resurrection! A special courtesy, I judge, from what the clergy say! To the "natural man" bumblebees would seem an improvement, and a spicing of birds, but far be it from me to impugn such majestic tastes!

Our pastor says we are a "worm." How is that reconciled? "Vain, sinful worm" is possibly of another species.

Do you think we shall "see God"? Think of Abraham strolling with Him in genial promenade!

The men are mowing the second hay. The cocks are smaller than the first, and spicier. I would distil a cup, and bear to all my friends, drinking to her no more astir, by beck, or burn, or moor!

Good-night, Mr. Bowles. This is what they say who come back in the morning; also the closing paragraph on repealed lips. Confidence in daybreak modifies dusk.

Blessings for Mrs. Bowles, and kisses for the bairns' lips. We want to see you, Mr. Bowles, but spare you the rehearsal of "familiar truths."

Good-night,
EMILY

Winter, 1858?

Monday Eve

DEAR MRS. BOWLES,—You send sweet messages. Remembrance is more sweet than robins in May orchards.

I love to trust that round bright fires, some, braver than I, take my pilgrim name. How are papa, mamma, and the little people? . . .

It storms in Amherst five days—it snows, and then it rains, and then soft fogs like veils hang on all the houses, and then the days turn topaz, like a lady's pin.

Thank you for bright bouquet, and afterwards verbena. I made a plant of a little bough of yellow heliotrope which the bouquet bore me, and call it Mary Bowles. It is many days since the summer day when you came with Mr. Bowles, and before another summer day it will be many days. My garden is a little knoll with faces under it, and only the pines sing tunes, now the birds are absent. I cannot walk to the distant friends on nights piercing as these, so I put both hands on the window-pane, and try to think how birds fly, and imitate, and fail, like Mr. "Rasselas." I could make a balloon of a dandelion, but the fields are gone, and only "Professor Lowe" remains to weep with me. If I built my house I should like to call you. I talk of all these things with Carlo, and his eyes grow meaning, and his shaggy feet keep a slower pace. Are you safe to-night? I hope you may be glad. I ask God on my knee to send you much prosperity, few winter days, and long suns. I have a childish hope to gather all I love together and sit down beside and smile. . . .

Will you come to Amherst? The streets are very cold now, but we will make you warm. But if you never came, perhaps you could write a letter, saying how much you would like to, if it were "God's will." I give good-night, and daily love to you and Mr. Bowles.

Emilie

1859
Amherst

I should like to thank dear Mrs. Bowles for the little book, except my cheek is red with shame because I write so often. Even the "lilies of the field" have their dignities.

Why did you bind it in green and gold? The *immortal* colors. I take it for an emblem. I never read before what Mr. Parker wrote.

I heard that he was "poison." Then I like poison very well. Austin stayed from service yesterday afternoon, and I . . . found him reading my Christmas gift. . . . I wish the "faith of the fathers" didn't wear brogans, and carry blue umbrellas. I give you all "New Year!" I think you kept gay Christmas, from the friend's account, and can only sigh with one not present at "John Gilpin," "and when he next doth ride a race," etc. You picked your berries from my holly. Grasping Mrs. Bowles!

To-day is very cold, yet have I much bouquet upon the window-pane of moss and fern. I call them saints' flowers, because they do not romp as other flowers do, but stand so still and white.

The snow is very tall, . . . which makes the trees so low that they tumble my hair, when I cross the bridge.

I think there will be no spring this year, the flowers are gone so far. Let us have spring in our heart, and never mind the orchises! . . . Please have my love, mother's, and Vinnie's. Carlo sends a brown kiss, and pussy a gray and white one, to each of the children.

Please, now I write so often, make lamplighter of me, then I shall not have lived in vain.

Dear Mrs. Bowles, dear Mr. Bowles, dear Sally—Sam and Mamie, now all shut your eyes, while I do benediction!

Lovingly,

EMILY

Written in 1861, *on the birth of a son*

DEAR MARY,—Can you leave your flower long enough just to look at mine?

Which is the prettiest? I shall tell you myself, some day. I used to come to comfort you, but now to tell you how glad I am, and how glad we all are. . . . You must not stay in New York any more—you must come back now, and bring the blanket to Massachusetts where we can all look. What a responsible shepherd! Four lambs in one flock! Shall you be glad to see us, or shall we seem old-fashioned, by the face in the crib?

Tell him I've got a pussy for him, with a spotted gown; and a dog with ringlets.

We have very cold days since you went away, and I think you hear the wind blow far as the Brevoort House, it comes from so far, and crawls so. Don't let it blow baby away. Will you call him Robert for me? He is the bravest man alive, but *his* boy has no mamma. That makes us all weep, don't it?

Good-night, Mary.

EMILY

One of the very few of Emily Dickinson's verses named by herself was sent Mrs. Bowles soon after the preceding letter.

BABY

Teach him, when he makes the names,
Such an one to say
On his babbling, berry lips
As should sound to me—
Were my ear as near his nest
As my thought, to-day—
As should sound—"forbid us not"—
Some like "Emily."

August, 1861

MARY,—I do not know of you, a long while. I remember
you—several times. I wish I knew if you kept me? The
doubt, like the mosquito, buzzes round my faith. We are
all human, Mary, until we are divine, and to some of
us, that is far off, and to some as near as the lady ringing
at the door; perhaps *that's* what alarms. I say I will go myself—I cross the river, and climb the fence—now I am at
the gate, Mary—now I am in the hall—now I am looking
your heart in the eye!

Did it wait for me—did it go with the company? Cruel
company, who have the stocks, and farms, and creeds
—and *it* has just its heart! I hope you are glad, Mary; no
pebble in the brook to-day—no film on noon.

I can think how you look; you can't think how I look;
I've got more freckles, since you saw me, playing with the
school-boys; then I pare the "Juneating" to make the pie,
and get my fingers "tanned."

Summer went very fast—she got as far as the woman
from the hill, who brings the blueberry, and that is a long
way. I shall have no winter this year, on account of the
soldiers. Since I cannot weave blankets or boots, I thought
it best to omit the season. Shall present a "memorial" to

God when the maples turn. Can I rely on your "name"?

How is your garden, Mary? Are the pinks true, and the sweet williams faithful? I've got a geranium like a sultana, and when the hummingbirds come down, geranium and I shut our eyes, and go far away.

Ask "Mamie" if I shall catch her a butterfly with a vest like a Turk? I will, if she will build him a house in her "morning-glory."

Vinnie would send her love, but she put on a white frock, and went to meet to-morrow—a few minutes ago; mother would send her love, but she is in the "eave spout," sweeping up a leaf that blew in last November; I brought my own, myself, to you and Mr. Bowles.

Please remember me, because I remember you—always.

Then follows the poem beginning "My river runs to thee," published in the First Series of the Poems.

Don't cry, dear Mary. Let us do that for you, because you are too tired now. We don't know how dark it is, but if you are at sea, perhaps when we say that we are there, you won't be as afraid.

The waves are very big, but every one that covers you, covers us, too.

Dear Mary, you can't see us, but we are close at your side. May we comfort you?

Lovingly,
EMILY

Autumn, 1861

FRIEND, SIR,—I did not see you. I am very sorry. Shall I keep the wine till you come again, or send it in by Dick? It is now behind the door in the library, also an unclaimed flower. I did not know you were going so soon. Oh! my tardy feet.

Will you not come again?

Friends are gems, infrequent. Potosi is a care, sir. I guard it reverently, for I could not afford to be poor now, after affluence. I hope the hearts in Springfield are not so heavy as they were. God bless the hearts in Springfield.

I am happy you have a horse. I hope you will get stalwart, and come and see us many years.

I have but two acquaintance, the "quick and the dead" —and would like more.

I write you frequently, and am much ashamed. My voice is not quite loud enough to cross so many fields, which will, if you please, apologize for my pencil.

Will you take my love to Mrs. Bowles, whom I remember every day?

Emilie

Vinnie hallos from the world of night-caps, "don't forget her love."

January, 1862

Dear Friend,—Are you willing? I am so far from land. To offer you the cup, it might some Sabbath come *my* turn. Of wine how solemn-full!

Did you get the doubloons—did you vote upon "Robert"? You said you would come in February. Only three weeks more to wait at the gate!

While you are sick, we—are homesick. Do you look out to-night? The moon rides like a girl through a topaz town. I don't think we shall ever be merry again—you are ill so long. When did the dark happen?

I skipped a page to-night, because I come so often, now,
I might have tired you.

That page is fullest, though.

Vinnie sends her love. I think father and mother care a
great deal for you, and hope you may be well. When you
tire with pain, to know that eyes would cloud, in Amherst
—might that comfort, *some?*

EMILY

We never forget Mary.

DEAR MR. BOWLES,—Thank you.

> Faith is a fine invention
> When gentlemen can see!
> But microscopes are prudent
> In an emergency![4]

You spoke of the "East." I have thought about it this
winter.

Don't you think you and I should be shrewder to take
the mountain road?

That bareheaded life, under the grass, worries one like
a wasp.

The rose is for Mary.

EMILY

> The zeros taught us phosphorus—
> We learned to like the fire
> By playing glaciers when a boy,
> And tinder guessed by power

---

[4] Second Series.

Of opposite to balance odd,
If white, a red must be![5]
Paralysis, our primer dumb
Unto vitality.

I couldn't let Austin's note go, without a word.

EMILY

Sunday Night

DEAR MARY,—Could you leave "Charlie" long enough? Have you time for *me*? I sent Mr. Bowles a little note, last Saturday morning, asking him to do an errand for me.

I forgot he was going to Washington, or I shouldn't have troubled him, so late. Now, Mary, I fear he did not get it, and *you* tried to do the errand for me—and it troubled you. Did it? Will you tell me? Just say with your pencil "It didn't tire me, Emily," and then I shall be sure, for with all your care, I would not have taxed you for the world.

You never refused me, Mary, you cherished me many times, but I thought it must seem so selfish to ask the favor of Mr. Bowles just as he went from home, only I forgot that. Tell me to-night just a word, Mary, with your own hand, so I shall know I harassed none—and I will be *so* glad.

Austin told us of Charlie—I send a rose for his small hands.

Put it in, when he goes to sleep, and then he will dream of Emily, and when you bring him to Amherst we shall be "old friends." Don't love him so well, you know, as to

---

[5] The poems enclosed in letters to friends are often slightly different from her own copies preserved in the manuscript volumes. This line, for instance, in another place reads 'Eclipses suns imply.'

forget us. We shall wish he wasn't *there,* if you do, I'm afraid, sha'n't we?

I'll remember you, if you like me to, while Mr. Bowles is gone, and that will stop the lonely, some, but I cannot agree to stop when he gets home from Washington.

Good-night, Mary. You won't forget my little note, to-morrow, in the mail. It will be the first one you ever wrote me in your life, and yet, was I the little friend a long time? *Was* I, Mary?

EMILY

March, 1862

Perhaps you thought I didn't care—because I stayed out, yesterday. I *did* care, Mr. Bowles. I pray for your sweet health to Allah every morning, but something troubled me, and I knew you needed light and air, so I didn't come. Nor have I conceit that you *noticed* me—but I couldn't bear that you, or Mary, so gentle to me, should think me forget-ful.

It's little at the most, we can do for ours, and we must do *that* flying, or our things are flown!

Dear friend, I wish you were well.

It grieves me till I cannot speak, that you are suffering. Won't you come back? Can't I bring you something? My little balm might be o'erlooked by wiser eyes, you know. Have you tried the breeze that swings the sign, or the hoof of the dandelion? *I* own 'em—wait for mine! This is all I have to say. Kinsmen need say nothing, but "Swiveller" may be sure of the

'MARCHIONESS'

Love for Mary.

DEAR FRIEND,— . . . Austin is disappointed—he expected to see you to-day. He is sure you won't go to sea without first speaking to him. I presume if Emily and Vinnie knew of his writing, they would entreat him to ask you not.

Austin is chilled by Frazer's murder.[6] He says his brain keeps saying over "Frazer is killed"—"Frazer is killed," just as father told it to him. Two or three words of lead, that dropped so deep they keep weighing. Tell Austin how to get over them!

He is very sorry you are not better. He cares for you when at the office, and afterwards, too, at home; and sometimes wakes at night, with a worry for you he didn't finish quite by day. He would not like it that I betrayed him, so you'll never tell. . . .

Mary sent beautiful flowers. Did she tell you?

Spring, 1862

DEAR FRIEND,—The hearts in Amherst ache to-night —you could not know how hard. They thought they could not wait, last night, until the engine sang a pleasant tune that time, because that you were coming. The flowers waited, in the vase, and love got peevish, watching. A railroad person rang, to bring an evening paper—Vinnie tipped pussy over, in haste to let you in, and I, for joy and dignity, held tight in my chair. My hope put out a petal.

You would come, to-day,—but . . . we don't believe it, now; "Mr. Bowles not coming!" Wouldn't you, to-morrow, and this but be a bad dream, gone by next morning?

Please do not take our *spring* away, since you blot summer out! We cannot count our tears for this, because they drop so fast. . . .

[6] A son of President Stearns of Amherst College, who was killed during the war, 13th March, 1862.

Dear friend, we meant to make *you* brave, but moaned before we thought. . . . If you'll be sure and get well, we'll try to bear it. If we could only care the less, it would be so much easier. Your letter troubled my throat. It gave that little scalding we could not know the reason for till we grew far up.

I must do my good-night in crayon I meant to in red. Love for Mary.

EMILY

After Mr. Bowles had sailed for Europe, Emily sent this quaintly consoling note to Springfield.

Early Summer, 1862

DEAR MARY,—When the best is gone, I know that other things are not of consequence. The heart wants what it wants, or else it does not care.

You wonder why I write so. Because I cannot help. I like to have you know some care—so when your life gets faint for its other life, you can lean on us. We won't break, Mary. We look very small, but the reed can carry weight.

Not to see what we love is very terrible, and talking doesn't ease it, and nothing does but just itself. The eyes and hair we chose are all there are—to us. Isn't it so, Mary?

I often wonder how the love of Christ is done when that below holds so.

I hope the little "Robert" coos away the pain. Perhaps your flowers help, some. . . .

The frogs sing sweet to-day—they have such pretty, lazy times—how nice to be a frog! . . .

Mother sends her love to you—she has a sprained foot,

and can go but little in the house, and not abroad at all.

Don't dishearten, Mary, we'll keep thinking of you. Kisses for all.

Emily

To Mr. Bowles, June, 1862

Dear Friend,—You go away—and where you go we cannot come—but then the months have names—and each one comes but once a year—and though it seems they never could, they sometimes do, go by.

We hope you are more well than when you lived in America, and that those foreign people are kind, and true, to you. We hope you recollect each life you left behind, even ours, the least.

We wish we knew how Amherst looked, in your memory. Smaller than it did, maybe, and yet things swell, by leaving, if big in themselves.

We hope you will not alter, but be the same we grieved for when the *China* sailed.

If you should like to hear the news, we did not die here—we did not change. We have the guests we did, except yourself—and the roses hang on the same stems as before you went. Vinnie trains the honeysuckle, and the robins steal the string for nests—quite, quite as they used to.

I have the errand from my heart—I might forget to tell it. Would you please to come home? The long life's years are scant, and fly away, the Bible says, like a told story—and sparing is a solemn thing, somehow, it seems to me —and I grope fast, with my fingers, for all out of my sight I own, to get it nearer.

I had one letter from Mary. I think she tries to be patient

—but you wouldn't want her to succeed, would you, Mr. Bowles?

It's fragrant news, to know they pine, when we are out of sight.

It is 'most Commencement. The little cousin from Boston has come, and the hearts in Pelham have an added thrill. We shall miss you, most, dear friend, who annually smiled with us, at the gravities. I question if even Dr. Vaill have his wonted applause.

Should anybody, where you go, talk of Mrs. Browning, you must hear for us, and if you touch her grave, put one hand on the head, for me—her unmentioned mourner.

Father and mother, and Vinnie and Carlo, send their love to you, and warm wish for your health—and I am taking lessons in prayer, so to coax God to keep you safe. Good-night, dear friend. You sleep so far, how can I know you hear?

EMILY

DEAR FRIEND,—I cannot see you. You will not less believe me. That you return to us alive is better than a summer, and more to hear your voice below than news of any bird.

EMILY

August, 1862

DEAR MR. BOWLES,—Vinnie is trading with a tin peddler —buying water-pots for me to sprinkle geraniums with when you get home next winter, and she has gone to the war.

Summer isn't so long as it was, when we stood looking at it before you went away; and when I finish August, we'll hop the autumn very soon, and then 'twill be yourself.

I don't know how many will be glad to see you,—because I never saw your whole friends, but I have heard that in large cities noted persons chose you—though how glad those I know will be, is easier told.

I tell you, Mr. Bowles, it is a suffering to have a sea —no care how blue—between your soul and you.

The hills you used to love when you were in Northampton, miss their old lover, could they speak; and the puzzled look deepens in Carlo's forehead as the days go by and you never come.

I've learned to read the steamer place in newspapers now. It's 'most like shaking hands with you, or more like your ringing at the door.

We reckon your coming by the fruit. When the grape gets by, and the pippin and the chestnut—when the days are a little short by the clock, and a little long by the want —when the sky has new red gowns, and a purple bonnet—then we say you will come. I am glad that kind of time goes by.

It is easier to look behind at a pain, than to see it coming.

A soldier called, a morning ago, and asked for a nosegay to take to battle. I suppose he thought we kept an aquarium.

How sweet it must be to one to come home, whose home is in so many houses, and every heart a "best room." I mean you, Mr. Bowles. . . . Have not the clovers names to the bees?

EMILY

> Before he comes
> We weigh the time,
> 'Tis heavy, and 'tis light.

When he departs
An emptiness
Is the superior freight.

EMILY

While asters
On the hill
Their everlasting fashions set,
And covenant gentians frill!

EMILY

Late Autumn, 1862

So glad we are, a stranger'd deem
'Twas sorry that we were;
For where the holiday should be
There publishes a tear;
Nor how ourselves be justified,
Since grief and joy are done
So similar, an optizan
Could not decide between.

Early Winter, 1862

DEAR FRIEND,—Had we the art like you, to endow so many, by just recovering our health, 'twould give us tender pride, nor could we keep the news, but carry it to you, who seem to us to own it most.

So few that live have life, it seems of quick importance not one of those escape by death. And since you gave us fear, congratulate us for ourselves—you give us safer peace.

How extraordinary that life's large population contain so few of power to us—and those a vivid species who leave no mode, like Tyrian dye.

175

Remembering these minorities, permit our gratitude for you. We ask that you be cautious, for many sakes, excelling ours. To recapitulate the stars were useless as supreme. Yourself is yours, dear friend, but ceded, is it not, to here and there a minor life? Do not defraud these, for gold may be bought, and purple may be bought, but the sale of the spirit never did occur.

Do not yet work. No public so exorbitant of any as its friend, and we can wait your health. Besides, there is an idleness more tonic than toil.

> The loss of sickness—was it loss?
> Or that ethereal gain
> You earned by measuring the grave,
> Then measuring the sun.

Be sure, dear friend, for want you have estates of lives.

Emily

> *With Flowers*
> If she had been the mistletoe,
> And I had been the rose,
> How gay upon your table
> My velvet life to close!
> Since I am of the Druid,
> And she is of the dew,
> I'll deck tradition's buttonhole,
> And send the rose to you.

E.

Dear Mr. Bowles,—I can't thank you any more. You are thoughtful so many times you grieve me always; *now* the old words are numb, and there aren't any new ones.

Brooks are useless in freshet time. When you come to

Amherst—please God it were to-day—I will tell you about
the picture—if I *can*, I will.

> *Speech* is a prank of Parliament,
> *Tears* a trick of the nerve,—
> But the heart with the heaviest freight on
> Doesn't always swerve.

EMILY

> Perhaps you think me stooping!
> I'm not ashamed of that!
> Christ stooped until he touched the grave!
> Do those at sacrament
> Commemorate dishonor—
> Or love, annealed of love,
> Until it bend as low as death
> Re-royalized above?

> The juggler's hat her country is,
> The mountain gorse the bee's.

> I stole them from a bee,
> Because—thee!
> Sweet plea—
> He pardoned me!

EMILY

*Besides the verses given here, many others were sent to
Mr. and Mrs. Bowles, as to the Hollands, which, having
already been published in one or the other volume of the
Poems, will not be reprinted.*

Summer, 1863

DEAR FRIENDS,—I am sorry you came, because you went away.

Hereafter, I will pick no rose, lest it fade or prick me.

I would like to have you dwell here.

Though it is almost nine o'clock, the skies are gay and yellow, and there's a purple craft or so, in which a friend could sail. To-night looks like "Jerusalem"! . . . I hope we may all behave so as to reach Jerusalem.

How are your hearts to-day? Ours are pretty well. I hope your tour was bright, and gladdened Mrs. Bowles. Perhaps the retrospect will call you back some morning.

You shall find us all at the gate if you come in a hundred years, just as we stood that day. If it become of "jasper" previously, you will not object, so that we lean there still, looking after you.

I rode with Austin this morning. He showed me mountains that touched the sky, and brooks that sang like bobolinks. Was he not very kind? I will give them to you, for they are mine, and "all things are mine," excepting "Cephas and Apollos," for whom I have no taste. Vinnie's love brims mine.

Take

EMILIE

DEAR MRS. BOWLES,—Since I have no sweet flower to send you, I enclose my heart. A little one, sunburnt, half broken sometimes, yet close as the spaniel to its friends. Your flowers come from heaven, to which, if I should ever go, I will pluck you palms.

My words are far away when I attempt to thank you, so take the silver tear instead, from my full eye.

You have often remembered me.

I have little dominion. Are there not wiser than I, who, with curious treasure, could requite your gift?

Angels fill the hand that loaded

EMILY'S

Nature and God, I neither knew,
Yet both, so well knew me
They startled, like executors
Of an identity.
Yet neither told, that I could learn;
My secret as secure
As Herschel's private interest,
Or Mercury's affair.

1863

DEAR FRIEND,—You remember the little "meeting" we held for you last spring? We met again, Saturday.

'Twas May when we "adjourned," but then adjourns are all. The meetings were alike, Mr. Bowles.

The topic did not tire us, so we chose no new. We voted to remember you so long as both should live, including immortality; to count you as ourselves, except sometimes more tenderly, as now, when you are ill, and we, the haler of the two—and so I bring the bond we sign so many times, for you to read when chaos comes, or treason, or decay, still witnessing for morning. . . . We hope our joy to see you gave of its own degree to you. We pray for your new health, the prayer that goes not down when they shut the church. We offer you our cups—stintless, as to the bee, —the lily, her new liquors.

Would you like summer? Taste of ours.
Spices? Buy here!

Ill! We have berries, for the parching!
Weary! Furloughs of down!
Perplexed! Estates of violet trouble ne'er looked on!
Captive! We bring reprieve of roses!
Fainting! Flasks of air!
Even for Death, a fairy medicine.
But, which is it, sir?

EMILY

I'll send the feather from my hat!
Who knows but at the sight of *that*
My sovereign will relent?
As trinket, worn by faded child,
Confronting eyes long comforted
Blisters the adamant!

EMILY

Her breast is fit for pearls,
But I was not a diver.
Her brow is fit for thrones,
But I had not a crest.
Her heart is fit for rest—
I, a sparrow, build there
Sweet of twigs and twine,
My perennial nest.

1864?

DEAR FRIEND,—How hard to thank you—but the large
heart requites itself. Please to need me. I wanted to ask
you to receive Mr. Browning from me, but you denied my
Brontë—so I did not dare.

Is it too late now? I should like so much to remind you
how kind you had been to me.

You could choose—as you did before—if it would not

be obnoxious—except where you "measured by your heart,"
you should measure this time by mine. I wonder which
would be biggest!

Austin told, Saturday morning, that you were not so
well. 'Twas sundown, all day, Saturday—and Sunday such
a long bridge no news of you could cross!

Teach us to miss you less because the fear to miss you
more haunts us all the time. We didn't care so much, once.
I wish it was then, now, but you kept tightening, so it can't
be stirred to-day. You didn't mean to be worse, did you?
Wasn't it a mistake?

Won't you decide soon to be the strong man we first
knew? 'Twould lighten things so much—and yet that man
was not so dear—I guess you'd better not.

We pray for you, every night. A homely shrine our knee,
but Madonna looks at the heart first.

Dear friend—don't discourage!

Affectionately,
EMILY

> No wilderness can be
> Where *this* attendeth thee—
> No desert noon,
> No fear of frost to come
> Haunt the perennial bloom,
> But certain June!

EMILY

*The following lines, sent with flowers, have almost as
quaint and "seventeenth century" a flavor as the now famous quatrain beginning,—*

"A death-blow is a life-blow to some."

If recollecting were forgetting
Then I remember not.
And if forgetting, recollecting,
How near I had forgot!
And if to miss were merry,
And if to mourn were gay,
How very blithe the fingers
That gathered this, to-day!

EMILIE

Other verses, sent at different times, were written in the same general hand,—that of the early middle period, from about 1863 *to* 1870; *among them:—*

"They have not chosen me," he said,
"But I have chosen them."
Brave, broken-hearted statement
Uttered in Bethlehem!

I could not have told it,
But since Jesus dared,
Sovereign! know a daisy
Thy dishonor shared.

EMILY

Saturday

Mother never asked a favor of Mr. Bowles before—that he accept from her the little barrel of apples.

"Sweet apples," she exhorts me, with an occasional Baldwin for Mary and the squirrels.

EMILY

Saturday

Mother never asked
a favor of Mr Bowles
before - that he
accept from her
the little Barrel
of Apples.

"Sweet Apples". She
exhorts me - with an
occasional Baldwin -
in Theirs, and the
Squirrels - Emily

LETTER TO MR. SAMUEL BOWLES, *facsimile*

Just once—oh! least request!
Could adamant refuse
So small a grace,
So scanty put,
Such agonizing terms?

Would not a God of flint
Be conscious of a sigh,
As down his heaven dropt remote,
"Just once, sweet Deity?"

A spray of white pine was enclosed with this note:—

A feather from the whippoorwill
That everlasting sings!
Whose galleries are sunrise,
Whose opera the springs,
Whose emerald nest the ages spin
Of mellow, murmuring thread,
Whose beryl egg, what school boys-hunt
In "recess" overhead!

EMILY

We part with the river at the flood through a timid custom, though with the same waters we have often played.

EMILY

1865?

DEAR FRIEND,—Vinnie accidentally mentions that you hesitated between the *Theophilus* and the *Junius.*

Would you confer so sweet a favor as to accept that too, when you come again?

I went to the room as soon as you left, to confirm your presence, recalling the Psalmist's sonnet to God beginning

> I have no life but this—
> To lead it here,
> Nor any death but lest
> Dispelled from there.
> Nor tie to earths to come,
> Nor action new,
> Except through this extent—
> The love of you.

It is strange that the most intangible thing is the most adhesive.

Your "rascal."

I washed the adjective.

1868?

I should think you would have few letters, for your own are so noble that they make men afraid. And sweet as your approbation is, it is had in fear, lest your depth convict us.

You compel us each to remember that when water ceases to rise, it has commenced falling. That is the law of flood.

The last day that I saw you was the newest and oldest of my life.

Resurrection can come but once, first, to the same house. Thank you for leading us by it.

Come always, dear friend, but refrain from going. You spoke of not liking to be forgotten. Could you, though you would?

Treason never knew you.

EMILY

1869?

DEAR FRIEND,—You have the most triumphant face out of Paradise, probably because you are there constantly, instead of ultimately.

Ourselves we do inter with sweet derision the channel of the dust; who once achieves, invalidates the balm of that religion, that doubts as fervently as it believes.

EMILY

Wednesday

Dear Mr. Bowles's note, of itself a blossom, came only to-night.

I am glad it lingered, for each was all the heart could hold.

EMILY

Of your exquisite act there can be no acknowledgment but the ignominy that grace gives.

EMILY

Could mortal lip divine
The undeveloped freight
Of a delivered syllable,
'Twould crumble with the weight!

1873

DEAR FRIEND,—It was so delicious to see you—a peach before the time—it makes all seasons possible, and zones a caprice.

We, who arraign the *Arabian Nights* for their understatement, escape the stale sagacity of supposing them sham.

We miss your vivid face, and the besetting accents you bring from your Numidian haunts.

Your coming welds anew that strange trinket of life which each of us wear and none of us own; and the phosphorescence of yours startles us for its permanence.

Please rest the life so many own—for gems abscond.

In your own beautiful words—for the voice is the palace of all of us,—

"Near, but remote."

EMILY

1874

DEAR FRIEND,—The paper wanders so I cannot write my name on it, so I give you father's portrait instead.

> As summer into autumn slips
> And yet we sooner say
> "The summer" than "the autumn," lest
> We turn the sun away,
>
> And almost count it an affront
> The presence to concede
> Of one however lovely, not
> The one that we have loved,—
>
> So we evade the charge of years,
> One, one attempting shy
> The circumvention of the shaft
> Of life's declivity.

EMILY

If we die, will you come for us, as you do for father? "Not born," yourself "to die," you must reverse us all.

Last to adhere
When summers swerve away—
Elegy of
Integrity

To remember our own Mr. Bowles is all we can do.
With grief it is done, so warmly and long, it can never
be new.

EMILY

*In January of 1878, Mr. Bowles died, leaving a sense
of irreparable loss, not only to his friends, but to his great
constituency through* The Republican, *into whose success
he had woven the very tissue of his own magnetic personality.*

January, 1878

I hasten to you, Mary, because no moment must be lost
when a heart is breaking, for though it broke so long, each
time is newer than the last, if it broke truly. To be willing
that I should speak to you was so generous, dear.

Sorrow almost resents love, it is so inflamed.

I am glad if the broken words helped you. I had not
hoped so much, I felt so faint in uttering them, thinking
of your great pain. Love makes us "heavenly" without
our trying in the least. 'Tis easier than a Saviour—it does
not stay on high and call us to its distance; its low "Come
unto me" begins in every place. It makes but one mistake,
it tells us it is "rest"—perhaps its toil is rest, but what we
have not known we shall know again, that divine "again"
for which we are all breathless.

I am glad you "work." Work is a bleak redeemer, but it

does redeem; it tires the flesh so that can't tease the spirit.

Dear "Mr. Sam" is very near, these midwinter days. When purples come on Pelham, in the afternoon, we say "Mr. Bowles's colors." I spoke to him once of his Gem chapter, and the beautiful eyes rose till they were out of reach of mine, in some hallowed fathom.

Not that he goes—we love him more who led us while he stayed. Beyond earth's trafficking frontier, for what he moved, he made.

Mother is timid and feeble, but we keep her with us. She thanks you for remembering her, and never forgets you. . . . Your sweet "and left me all alone," consecrates your lips.

EMILY

Spring, 1878

Had you never spoken to any, dear, they would not up-braid you, but think of you more softly, as one who had suffered too much to speak. To forget you would be im-possible, had we never seen you; for you were his for whom we moan while consciousness remains. As he was himself Eden, he is with Eden, for we cannot become what we were not.

I felt it sweet that you needed me—though but a simple shelter I will always last. I hope your boys and girls assist his dreadful absence, for sorrow does not stand so still on their flying hearts.

How fondly we hope they look like him—that his beau-tiful face may be abroad.

Was not his countenance on earth graphic as a spirit's? The time will be long till you see him, dear, but it will be short, for have we not each our heart to dress—heavenly as his?

He is without doubt with my father. Thank you for thinking of him, and the sweet, last respect you so faithfully paid him.

Mother is growing better, though she cannot stand, and has not the power to raise her head for a glass of water. She thanks you for being sorry, and speaks of you with love. . . . Your timid "for his sake," recalls that sheltering passage, "for his sake who loved us, and gave himself to die for us."

EMILY

1879

How lovely to remember! How tenderly they told of you! Sweet toil for smitten hands to console the smitten!

Labors as endeared may engross our lost. Buds of other days quivered in remembrance. Hearts of other days lent their solemn charm.

Life of flowers lain in flowers—what a home of dew! And the bough of ivy; was it as you said? Shall I plant it softly?

There were little feet, white as alabaster.

Dare I chill them with the soil?

Nature is our eldest mother, she will do no harm.

Let the phantom love that enrolls the sparrow shield you softer than a child.

April, 1880

DEAR MARY,—The last April that father lived, lived I mean below, there were several snow-storms, and the birds were so frightened and cold, they sat by the kitchen door. Father went to the barn in his slippers and came back with a breakfast of grain for each, and hid himself while he scattered it, lest it embarrass them. Ignorant of the name or fate of their benefactor, their descendants are singing this afternoon.

As I glanced at your lovely gift, his April returned. I am powerless toward your tenderness.

Thanks of other days seem abject and dim, yet antiquest altars are the fragrantest. The past has been very near this week, but not so near as the future—both of them pleading, the latter priceless.

David's grieved decision haunted me when a little girl. I hope he has found Absalom.

Immortality as a guest is sacred, but when it becomes as with you and with us, a member of the family, the tie is more vivid. . . .

If affection can reinforce, you, dear, shall not fall.

EMILY

Probably the famous "Yellow Day," September 6, 1881
Tuesday

DEAR MARY,—I give you only a word this mysterious morning in which we must light the lamps to see each other's faces, thanking you for the trust too confiding for speech.

You spoke of enclosing the face of your child. As it was not there, forgive me if I tell you, lest even the copy of sweetness abscond; and may I trust you received the flower the mail promised to take you, my foot being incompetent?

The timid mistake about being "forgotten," shall I caress or reprove? Mr. Samuel's "sparrow" does not "fall" without the fervent "notice."

"Would you see us, would Vinnie?" Oh, my doubting Mary! Were you and your brave son in my father's house, it would require more prowess than mine to resist seeing you.

Shall I still hope for the picture? And please address to my full name, as the little note was detained and opened, the name being so frequent in town, though not an Emily but myself.

Vinnie says "give her my love, and tell her I would delight to see her"; and mother combines.

There should be no tear on your cheek, dear, had my hand the access to brush it away.

EMILY

1881

DEAR MARY,—To have been the mother of the beautiful face, is of itself fame, and the look of Arabia in the eyes is like Mr. Samuel. "Mr. Samuel" is his memorial name. "Speak, that we may see thee," and Gabriel no more ideal than his swift eclipse. Thank you for the beauty, which I reluctantly return, and feel like committing a "startling fraud" in that sweet direction. If her heart is as magical as her face, she will wreck many a spirit, but the sea is ordained.

Austin looked at her long and earnestly.

"Yes, it is Sam's child." His Cashmere confederate. It is best, dear, you have so much to do. Action is redemption.

"And again a little while and ye shall not see me," Jesus confesses is temporary.

Thank you indeed.

EMILY

vi

TO *the Misses* ———

𝒔𝒆̃ AMONG THE *most natural and spontaneous of Emily Dickinson's letters are these to her cousins. They are, perhaps, more than usually full of her real self, or one unmistakable phase of that elusive individuality. Many, indeed, are so completely personal that they are of necessity omitted, and the final letter has been reserved for the closing chapter.*

January, 1859

Since it snows this morning, dear L———, too fast for interruption, put your brown curls in a basket, and come and sit with me.

I am sewing for Vinnie, and Vinnie is flying through the flakes to buy herself a little hood. It's quite a fairy morning, and I often lay down my needle, and "build a castle in the air" which seriously impedes the sewing project. What if I pause a little longer, and write a note to you!

Who will be the wiser? I have known little of you, since the October morning when our families went out driving, and you and I in the dining-room decided to be distinguished. It's a great thing to be "great," L——, and you and I might tug for a life, and never accomplish it, but no one can stop our looking on, and you know some cannot sing, but the orchard is full of birds, and we all can listen. What if we learn, ourselves, some day! Who indeed knows? —— said you had many little cares; I hope they do not fatigue you. I would not like to think of L—— as weary, now and then. Sometimes *I* get tired, and I would rather none I love would understand the word. . . .

Do you still attend Fanny Kemble? "Aaron Burr" and father think her an "animal," but I fear zoölogy has few such instances. I have heard many notedly *bad* readers, and a fine one would be almost a fairy surprise. When will you come again, L——? For you remember, dear, you are one of the ones from whom I do not run away! I keep an ottoman in my heart exclusively for you. My love for your father and F——.

Emily

March, 1859

The little "apple of my eye," is not dearer than L——; she knows I remember her,—why waste an instant in defence of an absurdity? My birds fly far off, nobody knows where they go to, but you see I know they are coming back, and other people don't, that makes the difference.

I've had a curious winter, very swift, sometimes sober, for I haven't felt well, much, and March amazes me! I didn't think of it, that's all! Your "hay" don't look so dim as it did at one time. I hayed a little for the horse two Sundays ago, and mother thought it was summer, and set one plant outdoors which she brought from the deluge, but it snowed since, and we have fine sleighing, now, on *one* side of the road, and wheeling on the other, a kind of variegated turnpike quite picturesque to see!

You are to have Vinnie, it seems, and I to tear my hair, or engage in any other vocation that seems fitted to me. Well, the earth is round, so if Vinnie rolls your side sometimes, 'tisn't strange; I wish I were there too, but the geraniums felt so I couldn't think of leaving them, and one minute carnation pink cried, till I shut her up—see box!

Now, my love, robins, for both of you, and when you and Vinnie sing at sunrise on the apple boughs, just cast your eye to my twig.

POOR PLOVER

Early Summer, 1859

DEAR L——,—You did not acknowledge my vegetable; perhaps you are not familiar with it. I was reared in the garden, you know. It was to be eaten with mustard! Bush eighty feet high, just under chamber window—much used at this season when other vegetables are gone. You should snuff the hay if you were here to-day, infantile as yet, homely, as cubs are prone to be, but giving brawny promise of hay-cocks by and by. "Methinks I see you," as schoolgirls say, perched upon a cock with the "latest work," and confused visions of bumblebees tugging at your hat. Not so far off, cousin, as it used to be, that vision and the hat. It makes me feel so hurried, I run and brush my hair so to be all ready.

I enjoy much with a precious fly, during sister's absence, not one of your blue monsters, but a timid creature, that hops from pane to pane of her white house, so very cheerfully, and hums and thrums, a sort of speck piano. Tell Vinnie I'll kill him the day she comes, for I sha'n't need him any more, and she don't mind flies!

Tell F—— and papa to come with the sweetwilliams.

Tell Vinnie I counted three peony noses, red as Sammie Matthews's, just out of the ground, and get her to make the accompanying face. "By-Bye."

EMILY

Miss Lavinia Dickinson was visiting her cousins when their mother died, and Emily's letter to her sister at that time seems more appropriate here than in any other connection:—

April, 1860

VINNIE,—I can't believe it, when your letters come, saying what Aunt L—— said "just before she died." Blessed Aunt L—— now; all the world goes out, and I see nothing but her room, and angels bearing her into those great countries in the blue sky of which we don't know anything.

Then I sob and cry till I can hardly see my way 'round the house again; and then sit still and wonder if she sees us now, if she sees *me,* who said that she "loved Emily." Oh! Vinnie, it is dark and strange to think of summer afterward! How she loved the summer! The birds keep singing just the same. Oh! The thoughtless birds!

Poor little L——! Poor F——! You must comfort them!

If you were with me, Vinnie, we could talk about her together.

And I thought she would live! I wanted her to live so, I thought she could not die! To think how still she lay

while I was making the little loaf, and fastening her flowers! Did you get my letter in time to tell her how happy I
would be to do what she requested? Mr. Brady is coming
to-morrow to bring arbutus for her. Dear little aunt! Will
she look down?

You must tell me all you can think about her. Did she
carry my little bouquet? So many broken-hearted people
have got to hear the birds sing, and see all the little flowers
grow, just the same as if the sun hadn't stopped shining
forever! . . . How I wish I could comfort you! How I wish
you could comfort me, who weep at what I did not see
and never can believe. I will try and share you a little
longer, but it is so long, Vinnie.

We didn't think, that morning when I wept that you left
me, and you, for other things, that we should weep more
bitterly before we saw each other.

Well, she is safer now than "we know or even think."
Tired little aunt, sleeping ne'er so peaceful! Tuneful little
aunt, singing, as we trust, hymns than which the robins
have no sweeter ones.

Good-night, broken hearts, L——, and F——, and
Uncle L——. Vinnie, remember

SISTER

Autumn, 1860

Bravo, L——, the cape is a beauty, and what shall I
render unto F——, for all her benefits? I will take my
books and go into a corner and give thanks! Do you think
I am going "upon the boards" that I wish so smart attire?
Such are my designs, though. I beg you not to disclose
them! May I not secure L—— for drama, and F—— for
comedy? You are a brace of darlings, and it would give
me joy to see you both, in any capacity. . . . Will treasure

all till I see you. Never fear that I shall forget! In event of my decease, I will still exclaim "Dr. Thompson," and he will reply "Miss Montague." My little L—— pined for the hay in her last communication. Not to be saucy, dear, we sha'n't have any more before the first of March, Dick having hid it all in a barn in a most malicious manner; but he has not brought the sunset in, so there is still an inducement to my little girls. We have a sky or two, well worth consideration, and trees so fashionable they make us all *passée.*

I often remember you both, last week. I thought that flown mamma could not, as was her wont, shield from crowd, and strangers, and was glad Eliza was there. I knew she would guard my children, as she has often guarded me, from publicity, and help to fill the deep place never to be full. Dear cousins, I know you both better than I did, and love you both better, and always I have a chair for you in the smallest parlor in the world, to wit, my heart.

This world is just a little place, just the red in the sky, before the sun rises, so let us keep fast hold of hands, that when the birds begin, none of us be missing.

"Burnham" must think F—— a scholastic female. I wouldn't be in her place! If she feels delicate about it, she can tell him the books are for a friend in the East Indies.

Won't F—— give my respect to the "Bell and Everett party" if she passes that organization on her way to school? I hear they wish to make me Lieutenant-Governor's daughter. Were they cats I would pull their tails, but as they are only patriots, I must forego the bliss. . . .

Love to papa.

EMILY

Winter, 1860–61

DEAR FRIENDS,—L——'s note to Miss W—— only stopped to dine. It went out with a beautiful name on its face in the evening mail. "Is there nothing else," as the clerk says? So pleased to enact a trifle for my little sister. It is little sisters you are, as dear F—— says in the hallowed note. Could mamma read it, it would blur her light even in Paradise.

It was pretty to lend us the letters from the new friends. It gets us acquainted. We will preserve them carefully. . . . I regret I am not a scholar in the Friday class. I believe the love of God may be taught not to seem like bears. Happy the reprobates under that loving influence.

I have one new bird and several trees of old ones. A snow slide from the roof, dispelled mother's "sweetbrier." You will of course feel for her, as you were named for him! There are as yet no streets, though the sun is riper, and these small bells have rung so long I think it "tea-time" always.

Spring, 1861

. . . Send a sundown for L——, please, and a crocus for F——. Shadow had no stem, so they could not pick him.

. . . —— fed greedily upon *Harper's Magazines* while here. Suppose he is restricted to Martin Luther's works at home. It is a criminal thing to be a boy in a godly village, but maybe he will be forgiven.

. . . The seeing pain one can't relieve makes a demon of one. If angels have the heart beneath their silver jackets, I think such things could make them weep, but Heaven is so cold! It will never look kind to me that God, who causes all, denies such little wishes. It could not hurt His glory, unless it were a lonesome kind. I 'most conclude it is.

. . . Thank you for the daisy. With nature in my ruche I shall not miss the spring. What would become of us, dear, but for love to reprieve our blunders?

. . . I'm afraid that home is 'most done, but do not say I fear so. Perhaps God will be better. They're happy, you know. That makes it doubtful. Heaven hunts round for those that find itself below, and then it snatches.

. . . Think Emily lost her wits—but she found 'em, likely. Don't part with wits long in this neighborhood.

. . . Your letters are all real, just the tangled road children walked before you, some of them to the end, and others but a little way, even as far as the fork in the road. That Mrs. Browning fainted, we need not read *Aurora Leigh* to know, when she lived with her English aunt; and George Sand "must make no noise in her grandmother's bedroom." Poor children! Women, now, queens, now! And one in the Eden of God. I guess they both forget that now, so who knows but we, little stars from the same night, stop twinkling at last? Take heart, little sister, twilight is but the short bridge, and the moon stands at the end. If we can only get to her! Yet, if she sees us fainting, she will put out her yellow hands. . . .

December, 1861

DEAR PEACOCK,—I received your feather with profound emotion. It has already surmounted a work, and crossed the Delaware. Doubtless you are moulting *à la* canary bird —hope you will not suffer from the reduction of plumage these December days. The latitude is quite stiff for a few nights, and gentlemen and ladies who go barefoot in our large cities must find the climate uncomfortable. A land of frosts and zeros is not precisely the land for me; hope you find it congenial. I believe it is several hundred years since I met you and F——, yet I am pleased to say, you do not become dim; I think you rather brighten as the hours fly. I should love to see you dearly, girls; perhaps I may, before south winds, but I feel rather confused to-day, and the future looks "higglety-pigglety."

You seem to take a smiling view of my finery. If you knew how solemn it was to me, you might be induced to curtail your jests. My sphere is doubtless calicoes, nevertheless I thought it meet to sport a little wool. The mirth it has occasioned will deter me from further exhibitions! Won't you tell "the public" that at present I wear a brown dress with a cape if possible browner, and carry a parasol of the same! We have at present one cat, and twenty-four hens, who do nothing so vulgar as lay an egg, which checks the ice-cream tendency.

I miss the grasshoppers much, but suppose it is all for the best. I should become too much attached to a trotting world.

My garden is all covered up by snow; picked gilliflower Tuesday, now gilliflowers are asleep. The hills take off their purple frocks, and dress in long white nightgowns.

There is something fine and something sad in the year's toilet. . . .

We often talk of you and your father these new winter days. Write, dear, when you feel like it.

Lovingly,

EMILY

December 29, 1861

. . . Your letter didn't surprise me, L——; I brushed away the sleet from eyes familiar with it—looked again to be sure I read it right—and then took up my work hemming strings for mother's gown. I think I hemmed them faster for knowing you weren't coming, my fingers had nothing else to do. . . . Odd, that I, who say "no" so much, cannot bear it from others. Odd, that I, who run from so many, cannot brook that one turn from me. Come when you will, L——, the hearts are never shut here. I don't remember "May." Is that the one that stands next April? And is that the month for the river-pink?

Mrs. Adams had news of the death of her boy to-day, from a wound at Annapolis. Telegram signed by Frazer Stearns. You remember him. Another one died in October —from fever caught in the camp. Mrs. Adams herself has not risen from bed since then. "Happy new year" step softly over such doors as these! "Dead! Both her boys! One of them shot by the sea in the East, and one of them shot in the West by the sea.". . . Christ be merciful! Frazer Stearns is just leaving Annapolis. His father has gone to see him to-day. I hope that ruddy face won't be brought home frozen. Poor little widow's boy, riding to-night in the mad wind, back to the village burying-ground where he never dreamed of sleeping! Ah! the dreamless sleep!

Did you get the letter I sent a week from Monday? You did not say, and it makes me anxious, and I sent a scrap for Saturday last, that too? L——, I wanted you very much, and I put you by with sharper tears than I give to many. Won't you tell me about the chills—what the doctor says? I must not lose you, sweet. Tell me if I could send a tuft to keep the cousin warm, a blanket of a thistle, say, or something!

Much love and Christmas, and sweet year, for you and F—— and papa.

EMILIE

Dear little F——'s note received, and shall write her soon.

Meanwhile, we wrap her in our heart to keep her tight and warm.

. . . Uncle told us you were too busy. Fold your little hands—the heart is the only workman we cannot excuse.

. . . Gratitude is not the mention of a tenderness, but its mute appreciation, deeper than we reach—all our LORD demands, who sizes better knows than we. Willing unto death, if only we perceive He die.

February, 1862

DEAR F——, —I fear you are getting as driven as Vinnie. We consider her standard for superhuman effort erroneously applied. Dear L—— remembers the basket Vinnie "never got to." But we must blame with lenience. Poor Vinnie has been very sick, and so have we all, and I feared one day our little brothers would see us no more, but God was not so hard. Now health looks so beautiful, the tritest "How do you do" is living with meaning. No doubt you "heard a bird," but which route did he take? Hasn't reached here yet. Are you sure it wasn't a "down brakes"? Best of ears will blunder! Unless he come by the first of April, I sha'n't countenance him. We have had fatal weather—thermometer two below zero all day, without a word of apology. Summer was always dear, but such a kiss as she'll get from me if I ever see her again, will make her cry, I know. . . .

April, 1862

DEAR CHILDREN,—You have done more for me—'tis least that I can do, to tell you of brave Frazer—"killed at Newbern," darlings. His big heart shot away by a "Minie ball."

I had read of those—I didn't think that Frazer would carry one to Eden with him. Just as he fell, in his soldier's cap, with his sword at his side, Frazer rode through Amherst. Classmates to the right of him, and classmates to the left of him, to guard his narrow face! He fell by the side of Professor Clark, his superior officer—lived ten minutes in a soldier's arms, asked twice for water—murmured just, "My God!" and passed! Sanderson, his classmate, made a box of boards in the night, put the brave boy in, covered with a blanket, rowed six miles to reach the boat,—so poor Frazer came. They tell that Colonel Clark cried like a little child when he missed his pet, and could hardly resume his post. They loved each other very much. Nobody here could look on Frazer—not even his father. The doctors would not allow it.

The bed on which he came was enclosed in a large casket shut entirely, and covered from head to foot with the sweetest flowers. He went to sleep from the village church. Crowds came to tell him good-night, choirs sang to him, pastors told how brave he was—early-soldier heart. And the family bowed their heads, as the reeds the wind shakes.

So our part in Frazer is done, but you must come next summer, and we will mind ourselves of this young crusader —too brave that he could fear to die. We will play his tunes—maybe he can hear them; we will try to comfort his broken-hearted Ella, who, as the clergyman said, "gave

him peculiar confidence.". . . Austin is stunned completely.
Let us love better, children, it's most that's left to do.

Love from

EMILY

. . . Sorrow seems more general than it did, and not the
estate of a few persons, since the war began; and if the
anguish of others helped one with one's own, now would
be many medicines.

'Tis dangerous to value, for only the precious can alarm.
I noticed that Robert Browning had made another poem,
and was astonished—till I remembered that I, myself, in
my smaller way, sang off charnel steps. Every day life feels
mightier, and what we have the power to be, more stu-
pendous.

May, 1862

When you can leave your little children, L——, you
must tell us all you know about dear Myra's going, so
sudden, and shocking to us all, we are only bewildered
and cannot believe the telegrams. I want so much to see
you, and ask you what it means, and why this young life's
sacrifice should come so soon, and not far off. I wake in the
morning saying "Myra, no more Myra in this world," and
the thought of that young face in the dark, makes the
whole so sorrowful, I cover my face with the blanket, so
the robins' singing cannot get through—I had rather not
hear it. Was Myra willing to leave us all? I want so much
to know if it was very hard, husband and babies and big
life and sweet home by the sea. I should think she would
rather have stayed. . . . She came to see us first in May.

I remember her frock, and how prettily she fixed her hair, and she and Vinnie took long walks, and got home to tea at sundown; and now remembering is all there is, and no more Myra. I wish 'twas plainer, L——, the anguish in this world. I wish one could be sure the suffering had a loving side. The thought to look down some day, and see the crooked steps we came, from a safer place, must be a precious thing. . . .

L——, you are a dear child to go to Uncle J——, and all will thank you, who love him. We will remember you every day, and the little children, and make a picture to ourself, of the small mamma. . . . Father and Vinnie would have gone immediately to Lynn, but got the telegram too late. Tell Uncle they wanted to. But what can Emily say? Their Father in Heaven remember them and her.

My little girls have alarmed me so that notwithstanding the comfort of Austin's assurance that "they will come," I am still hopeless and scared, and regard Commencement as some vast anthropic bear, ordained to eat me up. What made 'em scare 'em so? Didn't they know Cousin Aspen couldn't stand alone? I remember a tree in McLean Street, when you and we were a little girl, whose leaves went topsy-turvy as often as a wind, and showed an ashen side —that's fright, that's Emily. L—— and F—— were that wind, and the poor leaf, who? Won't they stop a' blowing? . . . Commencement would be a dreary spot without my double flower, that sows itself, and just comes up, when Emily seeks it most. Austin gives excellent account, I trust not overdrawn. "Health and aspect admirable, and lodgings very fine." Says the rooms were marble, even to the flies. Do they dwell in Carrara? Did they find the garden in the gown? Should have sent a farm, but feared for our button-hole. Hope to hear favorable news on receipt of this. Please give date of coming, so we might prepare our heart.

EMILY

July, 1862?

. . . Just a word for my children, before the mails shut. L—— left a tumbler of sweet-peas on the green room bureau. I am going to leave them there till they make pods and sow themselves in the upper drawer, and then I guess they'll blossom about Thanksgiving time. There was a thundershower here Saturday at car-time, and Emily was glad her little ones had gone before the hail and rain, lest it frighten them. . . . We wish the visit had just begun instead of ending now; next time we'll leave "the mountains" out, and tell good Dr. Gregg to recommend the orchards. I defrauded L—— of 1 spool of thread; we will "settle," however—and F——'s ruff is set high in my book of remembrance. They must be good children and recollect, as they agreed, and grow so strong in health that Emily won't know them when they show again. . . . Such a purple morning—even to the morning-glory that climbs the cherry-tree. The cats desire love to F——.

EMILY

About May 30, 1863

I said I should come "in a day." Emily never fails except for a cause; that you know, dear L——.

The nights turned hot, when Vinnie had gone, and I must keep no window raised for fear of prowling "booger," and I must shut my door for fear front door slide open on me at the "dead of night," and I must keep "gas" burning to light the danger up, so I could distinguish it—these gave me a snarl in the brain which don't unravel yet, and that old nail in my breast pricked me; these, dear, were my cause. Truth is so best of all I wanted you to know. Vinnie will tell of her visit. . . .

About Commencement, children, I can have no doubt, if you should fail me then, my little life would fail of itself. Could you only lie in your little bed and smile at me, that would be support. Tell the doctor I am inexorable, besides I shall heal you quicker than he. You need the balsam. And who is to cut the cake, ask F——, and chirp to those trustees? Tell me, dears, by the coming mail, that you will not fail me. . . .

Jennie Hitchcock's mother was buried yesterday, so there is one orphan more, and her father is very sick besides. My father and mother went to the service, and mother said while the minister prayed, a hen with her chickens came up, and tried to fly into the window. I suppose the dead lady used to feed them, and they wanted to bid her good-by.

> Life is death we're lengthy at,
> Death the hinge to life.

Love from all,

EMILY

Autumn, 1863
Wednesday

DEAR CHILDREN,—Nothing has happened but loneliness, perhaps too daily to relate. Carlo is consistent, has asked for nothing to eat or drink, since you went away. Mother thinks him a model dog, and conjectures what he might have been, had not Vinnie "demoralized" him. Margaret objects to furnace heat on account of bone decrepitudes, so I dwell in my bonnet and suffer comfortably. . . .

Miss Kingman called last evening to inspect your garden; I gave her a lanthorn, and she went out, and thanks you very much. No one has called so far, but one old lady to look at a house. I directed her to the cemetery to spare expense of moving.

I got down before father this morning, and spent a few moments profitably with the South Sea rose. Father detecting me, advised wiser employment, and read at devotions the chapter of the gentleman with one talent. I think he thought my conscience would adjust the gender.

Margaret washed to-day, and accused Vinnie of calicoes. I put her shoe and bonnet in to have them nice when she got home. I found a milliner's case in Miss N——'s wardrobe, and have opened business. I have removed a geranium leaf, and supplied a lily in Vinnie's parlor vase. The sweet-peas are unchanged. Cattle-show is to-morrow. The coops and committees are passing now. . . . They are picking the Baldwin apples. Be good children, and mind the vicar. Tell me precisely how Wakefield looks, since I go not myself.

EMILY

Autumn, 1863
. . . I should be wild with joy to see my little lovers. The writing them is not so sweet as their two faces that seem so small way off, and yet have been two weeks from me— two wishful, wandering weeks. Now, I begin to doubt if they ever came.

I bid the stiff "good-night" and the square "good-morning" to the lingering guest, I finish mamma's sack, all but the overcasting—that fatal sack, you recollect. I pick up tufts of mignonette, and sweet alyssum for winter, dim as winter seems these red, and gold, and ribbon days.

I am sure I feel as Noah did, docile, but somewhat sceptic, under the satinet.

No frost at our house yet. Thermometer frost, I mean. Mother had a new tooth Saturday. You know Dr. S—— had promised her one for a long time. "Teething" didn't agree with her, and she kept her bed, Sunday, with a face that would take a premium at any cattle-show in the land. Came to town next morning with slightly reduced features, but no eye on the left side. Doubtless we are "fearfully and wonderfully made," and occasionally grotesquely.

L—— goes to Sunderland, Wednesday, for a minute or two; leaves here at half-past six—what a fitting hour—and will breakfast the night before; such a smart atmosphere! The trees stand right up straight when they hear her boots, and will bear crockery wares instead of fruit, I fear. She hasn't starched the geraniums yet, but will have ample time, unless she leaves before April. Emily is very mean, and her children in dark mustn't remember what she says about damsel.

Grateful for little notes, and shall ask for longer when my birds locate. Would it were here. Three sisters are prettier than one. . . . Tabby is a continual shrine, and her jaunty ribbons put me in mind of fingers far out at sea. F——'s admonition made me laugh and cry too. In the hugest haste, and the engine waiting.

EMILY

After the death of the Misses——'s father, Jan. 1864

What shall I tell these darlings except that my father and mother are half their father and mother, and my home half theirs, whenever, and for as long as, they will. And sometimes a dearer thought than that creeps into my mind, but it is not for to-night. Wasn't dear papa so tired always after mamma went, and wasn't it almost sweet to think of the two together these new winter nights? The grief is our side, darlings, and the glad is theirs. Vinnie and I sit down to-night, while mother tells what makes us cry, though we know it is well and easy with uncle and papa, and only our part hurts. Mother tells how gently he looked on all who looked at him—how he held his bouquet sweet, as he were a guest in a friend's parlor and must still do honor. The meek, mild gentleman who thought no harm, but peace toward all.

Vinnie intended to go, but the day was cold, and she wanted to keep Uncle L—— as she talked with him, always, instead of this new way. She thought too, for the crowd, she could not see you, children, and she would be another one to give others care. Mother said Mr. V——, yes, dears, even Mr. V——, at whom we sometimes smile, talked about "Lorin" and "Laviny" and his friendship towards them, to your father's guests. We won't smile at him any more now, will we? Perhaps he'll live to tell some gentleness of us, who made merry of him.

But never mind that now. When you have strength, tell us how it is, and what we may do for you, of comfort, or of service. Be sure you crowd all others out, precious little cousins. Good-night. Let Emily sing for you because she cannot pray:—

It is not dying hurts us so,—
'Tis living hurts us more;
But dying is a different way,
A kind, behind the door,—
The southern custom of the bird
That soon as frosts are due
Adopts a better latitude.

We are the birds that stay,
The shiverers round farmers' doors,
For whose reluctant crumb
We stipulate, till pitying snows
Persuade our feathers home.

EMILY

1864

So many ask for the children that I must make a separate letter to tell them what they say, and leave my kisses till next time.

Eliza wrote last week, faint note in pencil—dressed in blankets, and propped up, having been so sick—and yet too weak to talk much, even with her slate. She said this of you, I give it in her own word, "Make them know I love them," and added, should have written immediately herself, except for weakness.

Mr. Dwight asks for you in the phrase "Of your sweet cousins." He does not yet know papa is asleep—only very weary.

The milliner at the head of the street wipes her eye for F—— and L——, and a tear rumples her ribbons. Mr. and Mrs. Sweetser care—Mrs. Sweetser most tenderly.

. . . Even Dick's wife, simple dame, with a kitchen full, and the grave besides, of little ragged ones, wants to know "more about" you, and follows mother to the door, who has called with bundle.

Dick says, in his wise way, he "shall always be interested in them young ladies." One little young lady of his own, you know, is in Paradise. That makes him tenderer-minded.

Be sure you don't doubt about the sparrow.

Poor—— and ——, in their genteel, antique way, express their sympathy, mixing admiring anecdotes of your father and mother's youth, when they, God help them, were not so sere. Besides these others, children, shall we tell them who else cherishes, every day the same, the bright one and the black one too? Could it be Emily?

Would it interest the children to know that crocuses come up, in the garden off the dining-room, and a fuchsia, that pussy partook, mistaking it for strawberries? And that we have primroses, like the little pattern sent in last winter's note, and heliotrope by the aprons full—the mountain colored one—and a jasmine bud, you know the little odor like Lubin—and gilliflowers, magenta, and few mignonette, and sweet alyssum bountiful, and carnation bud?

Will it please them to know that the ice-house is filled, to make their tumblers cool next summer, and once in a while a cream?

And that father has built a new road round the pile of trees between our house and Mr. S——'s, where they can take the soldier's shirt to make, or a sweet poem, and no man find them but the fly, and he such a little man?

Love, dears, from us all, and won't you tell us how you are?

We seem to hear so little.

EMILY

January, 1865

. . . I am glad my little girl is at peace. Peace is a deep place. Some, too faint to push, are assisted by angels.

I have more to say to you all than March has to the maples, but then I cannot write in bed. I read a few words since I came home—John Talbot's parting with his son, and Margaret's with Suffolk. I read them in the garret, and the rafters wept.

Remember me to your company, their Bedouin guest.

Every day in the desert, Ishmael counts his tents. New heart makes new health, dear.

Happiness is haleness. I dreamed last night I heard bees fight for pond-lily stamens, and waked with a fly in my room.

Shall you be strong enough to lift me by the first of April? I won't be half as heavy as I was before. I will be good and chase my spools.

I shall think of my little Eve going away from Eden. Bring me a jacinth for every finger, and an onyx shoe.

EMILY

1865

DEAR SISTER,—Brother has visited, and the night is falling, so I must close with a little hymn.

I had hoped to express more. Love more I never can, sweet D—— or yourself.

> This was in the white of the year,
> That was in the green.
> Drifts were as difficult then to think,
> As daisies now to be seen.
> Looking back is best that is left,
> Or if it be before,
> Retrospection is prospect's half,
> Sometimes almost more.

EMILY

February, 1865

All that my eyes will let me shall be said for L——, dear little solid gold girl. I am glad to the foot of my heart that you will go to M——. It will make you warm. Touches "from home," tell Gungl, are better than "sounds."[7]

---

[7] Referring to an old piece of piano-forte music.

You persuade me to speak of my eyes, which I shunned doing, because I wanted you to rest. I could not bear a single sigh should tarnish your vacation, but, lest through me one bird delay a change of latitude, I will tell you, dear.

The eyes are as with you, sometimes easy, sometimes sad. I think they are not worse, nor do I think them better than when I came home.

The snow-light offends them, and the house is bright; notwithstanding, they hope some. For the first few weeks I did nothing but comfort my plants, till now their small green cheeks are covered with smiles. I chop the chicken centres when we have roast fowl, frequent now, for the hens contend and the Cain is slain. . . . Then I make the yellow to the pies, and bang the spice for cake, and knit the soles to the stockings I knit the bodies to last June. They say I am a "help." Partly because it is true, I suppose, and the rest applause. Mother and Margaret are so kind, father as gentle as he knows how, and Vinnie good to me, but "cannot see why I don't get well." This makes me think I am long sick, and this takes the ache to my eyes. I shall try to stay with them a few weeks more before going to Boston, though what it would be to see you and have the doctor's care—that cannot be told. You will not wait for me. Go to M—— now. I wish I were there, myself, to start your little feet "lest they seem to come short of it." I have so much to tell I can tell nothing, except a sand of love. When I dare I shall ask if I may go, but that will not be now.

Give my love to my lamp and spoon, and the small lantana. Kindest remembrance for all the house, and write next from M——. Go, little girl, to M——. Life is so fast it will run away, notwithstanding our sweetest *whoa*.

Already they love you. Be but the maid you are to me, and they will love you more.

Carry your heart and your curls, and nothing more but your fingers. Mr. D—— will ask for these every candle-light. How I miss ten robins that never flew from the rose-wood nest!

Dear L——, —This is my letter—an ill and peevish thing, but when my eyes get well I'll send you thoughts like daisies, and sentences could hold the bees. . . .

1866

. . . Oh, L——, why were the children sent too faint to stand alone? . . . Every hour is anxious now, and heaven protect the lamb who shared her fleece with a timider, even Emily.

1868

Dear Children,—The little notes shall go as fast as steam can take them.

Our hearts already went. Would we could mail our faces for your dear encouragement.

Remember

> The longest day that God appoints
> Will finish with the sun.
> Anguish can travel to its stake,
> And then it must return.

I am in bed to-day—a curious place for me, and cannot write as well as if I was firmer, but love as well, and long more. Tell us all the load. Amherst's little basket is never so full but it holds more. That's a basket's cause. Not a flake assaults my birds but it freezes me. Comfort, little creatures—whatever befall us, this world is but this world.

Think of that great courageous place we have never seen!
Write at once, please, I am so full of grief and surprise
and physical weakness. I cannot speak until I know.

> Lovingly,
> EMILY

Of this letter her cousin writes, "All this trouble has become only a myth now; it must have been some illness, or other forgotten calamity."

Autumn, 1869

Vinnie was "gone" indeed and is due to-day, and before
the tumult that even the best bring we will take hold of
hands. It was sweet and antique as birds to hear L——'s
voice, worth the lying awake from five o'clock summer
mornings to hear. I rejoice that my wren can rise and touch
the sky again. We all have moments with the dust, but
the dew is given. Do you wish you heard "A—— talk"?
Then I would you did, for then you would be here always,
a sweet premium. Would you like to "step in the kitchen"?
Then you shall by faith, which is the first sight. Mr. C——
is not in the tree, because the rooks won't let him, but I
ate a pear as pink as a plum that he made last spring,
when he was ogling you. Mother has on the petticoat
you so gallantly gathered while he sighed and grafted.

Tabby is eating a stone dinner from a stone plate, . . .
Tim is washing Dick's feet, and talking to him now and
then in an intimate way. Poor fellow, how he warmed
when I gave him your message! The red reached clear to
his beard, he was so gratified; and Maggie stood as still
for hers as a puss for patting. The hearts of these poor
people lie so unconcealed you bare them with a smile.

Thank you for recollecting my weakness. I am not so well as to forget I was ever ill, but better and working. I suppose we must all "ail till evening."

Read Mr. Lowell's *Winter*. One does not often meet anything so perfect.

In many little corners how much of L—— I have.

Maggie "dragged" the garden for this bud for you. You have heard of the "last rose of summer." This is that rose's son.

Into the little port you cannot sail unwelcome at any hour of day or night. Love for F——, and stay close to

EMILY

Spring, 1870

DEAR CHILDREN,—I think the bluebirds do their work exactly like me. They dart around just so, with little dodging feet, and look so agitated. I really feel for them, they seem to be so tired.

The mud is very deep—up to the wagons' stomachs— arbutus making pink clothes, and everything alive.

Even the hens are touched with the things of Bourbon, and make republicans like me feel strangely out of scene.

Mother went rambling, and came in with a burdock on her shawl, so we know that the snow has perished from the earth. Noah would have liked mother.

I am glad you are with Eliza. It is next to shade to know that those we love are cool on a parched day.

Bring my love to —— and Mr.——. You will not need a hod. C—— writes often, full of joy and liberty. I guess it is a case of peace. . . .

Pussy has a daughter in the shavings barrel.

Father steps like Cromwell when he gets the kindlings.

Mrs. —— gets bigger, and rolls down the lane to church

like a reverend marble. Did you know little Mrs. Holland was in Berlin for her eyes? . . .

Did you know about Mrs. J——? She fledged her antique wings. 'Tis said that "nothing in her life became her like the leaving it."

"Great streets of silence led away," etc.

EMILY

May

This little sheet of paper has lain for several years in my Shakespeare, and though it is blotted and antiquated is endeared by its resting-place.

I always think of you peculiarly in May, as it is the peculiar anniversary of your loving kindness to me, though you have always been dear cousins, and blessed me all you could.

I cooked the peaches as you told me, and they swelled to beautiful fleshy halves and tasted quite magic. The beans we fricasseed and they made a savory cream in cooking that "Aunt Emily" liked to sip. She was always fonder of julep food than of more substantial. Your remembrance of her is very sweetly touching.

Maggie is ironing, and a cotton and linen and ruffle heat makes the pussy's cheeks red. It is lonely without the birds to-day, for it rains badly, and the little poets have no umbrellas. . . .

. . . Fly from Emily's window for L——. Botanical name unknown.

Enclosing a pressed insect

September, 1870

LITTLE SISTERS,—I wish you were with me, not precisely here, but in those sweet mansions the mind likes to suppose. Do they exist or nay? We believe they may, but do they, how know we? "The light that never was on sea or land" might just as soon be had for the knocking.

F——'s rustic note was as sweet as fern; L——'s token also tenderly estimated. Maggie and I are fighting which shall give L—— the "plant," though it is quite a pleasant war. . . . A—— went this morning, after a happy egg and toast provided by Maggie, whom he promised to leave his sole heir.

The "pussum" is found. "Two dollars reward" would return John Franklin. . . .

Love for Aunt O——. Tell her I think to instruct flowers will be her labor in heaven. . . .

Nearly October, sisters! No one can keep a sumach and keep a secret too. That was my "pipe" F—— found in the woods.

Affectionately,

MODOC

1870

UNTIRING LITTLE SISTERS,—What will I ever do for you, yet have done the most, for love is that one perfect labor nought can supersede. I suppose the pain is still there, for pain that is worthy does not go so soon. The small can crush the great, however, only temporarily. In a few days we examine, muster our forces, and cast it away. Put it out of your hearts, children. Faith is too fair to taint it so. There are those in the morgue that bewitch us with sweetness, but that which is dead must go with the ground. There is a verse in the Bible that says there are those who shall not see death. I suppose them to be the faithful. Love will not expire. There was never the instant when it was lifeless in the world, though the quicker deceit dies, the better for the truth, who is indeed our dear friend.

I am sure you will gain, even from this wormwood. The martyrs may not choose their food.

> God made no act without a cause,
> Nor heart without an aim,
> Our inference is premature,
> Our premises to blame.

. . . Sweetest of Christmas to you both, and a better year.

EMILY

DEAR CHILDREN,—When I think of your little faces I feel as the band does before it makes its first shout. . . .

EMILY

1870

. . . Mother drives with Tim to carry pears to settlers. Sugar pears with hips like hams, and the flesh of bonbons. Vinnie fastens flowers from the frosts. . . .

Lifetime is for two, never for committee.

I saw your Mrs. H——. She looks a little tart, but Vinnie says makes excellent pies after one gets acquainted.

Spring, 1871

The will is always near, dear, though the feet vary. The terror of the winter has made a little creature of me, who thought myself so bold.

Father was very sick. I presumed he would die, and the sight of his lonesome face all day was harder than personal trouble. He is growing better, though physically reluctantly. I hope I am mistaken, but I think his physical life don't want to live any longer. You know he never played, and the straightest engine has its leaning hour. Vinnie was not here. Now we will turn the corner. All this while I was with you all, much of every hour, wishing we were near enough to assist each other. Would you have felt more at home, to know we were both in extremity? That would be my only regret that I had not told you.

As regards the "pine" and the "jay," it is a long tryst, but I think they are able. I have spoken with them.

Of the "thorn," dear, give it to me, for I am strongest. Never carry what I can carry, for though I think I bend, something straightens me. Go to the "wine-press," dear, and come back and say has the number altered. I descry but one. What I would, I cannot say in so small a place.

Interview is acres, while the broadest letter feels a bandaged place. . . .

Tell F—— we hold her tight. Tell L—— love is oldest and takes care of us, though just now in a piercing place.

                                                                EMILY

Written to Milwaukee, just after the Chicago fire, 1871

We have the little note and are in part relieved, but have been too alarmed and grieved to hush immediately. The heart keeps sobbing in its sleep. It is the speck that makes the cloud that wrecks the vessel, children, yet no one fears a speck. I hope what is not lost is saved. Were any angel present, I feel it could not be allowed. So grateful that our little girls are not on fire too. Amherst would have quenched them. Thank you for comforting innocent blamed creatures. We are trying, too. The mayor of Milwaukee cuts and you and L—— sew, don't you? The *New York Times* said so. Sorrow is the "funds" never quite spent, always a little left to be loaned kindly. We have a new cow. I wish I could give Wisconsin a little pail of milk. Dick's Maggie is wilting. Awkward little flower, but transplanting makes it fair. How are the long days that made the fresh afraid?

BROTHER EMILY

March, 1872

Thank you, own little girls, for the sweet remembrance —sweet specifically. Be sure it was pondered with loving thoughts not unmixed with palates.

But love, like literature, is "its exceeding great reward." . . . I am glad you heard "Little Em'ly." I would go far to hear her, except I have lost the run of the roads. . . . Infinite March is here, and I "hered" a bluebird. Of course I am standing on my head!

> Go slow, my soul, to feed thyself
> Upon his rare approach.
> Go rapid, lest competing death
> Prevail upon the coach.
> Go timid, should his testing eye
> Determine thee amiss,
> Go boldly, for thou paidst the price,
> Redemption for a kiss.

Tabby is singing *Old Hundred,* which, by the way, is her maiden name. Would they address and mail the note to their friend J—— W——?

Tidings of a book.

EMILY

1872

I like to thank you, dear, for the annual candy. Though you make no answer, I have no letter from the dead, yet daily love them more. No part of mind is permanent. This startles the happy, but it assists the sad.

This is a mighty morning. I trust that L—— is with it, on hill or pond or wheel. Too few the mornings be, too scant the nights. No lodging can be had for the delights that come to earth to stay, but no apartment find and ride away. F—— was brave and dear, and helped as much by counsel as by actual team. Whether we missed L—— we will let her guess; riddles are healthful food.

Eliza was not with us, but it was owing to the trains. We know she meant to come.

Oh! Cruel Paradise! We have a chime of bells given for brave Frazer. You'll stop and hear them, won't you?

"We conquered, but Bozzaris fell." That sentence always chokes me.   EMILY

The new College church was given in 1870 by Mr. William French Stearns, brother of the Frazer so mourned; and its chime of bells was a memorial[8] to the Amherst students who were killed in the war. A cannon, now in Williston Hall, Amherst College, was given by General Burnside at the request of Colonel Clark, in loving memory of Frazer Stearns, the first of all the Amherst students who enlisted, nearly two hundred and fifty in number.

[8] Following is the inscription on the fundamental bell:—

THESE BELLS ARE PLACED HERE BY GEORGE HOWE OF BOSTON AND ARE TO BE MADE TO CHIME ON ALL SUITABLE OCCASIONS IN COMMEMORATION OF THE BRAVE PATRIOTS CONNECTED WITH AMHERST COLLEGE WHO LOST THEIR LIVES IN THE WAR AGAINST THE GREAT REBELLION OF 1861

An ill heart, like a body, has its more comfortable days, and then its days of pain, its long relapse, when rallying requires more effort than to dissolve life, and death looks choiceless.

Of Miss P—— I know but this, dear. She wrote me in October, requesting me to aid the world by my chirrup more. Perhaps she stated it as my duty, I don't distinctly remember, and always burn such letters, so I cannot obtain it now. I replied declining. She did not write to me again—she might have been offended, or perhaps is extricating humanity from some hopeless ditch. . . .

Emily was often besieged by different persons, literary and otherwise, to benefit the world by her "chirrup," but she steadily refused to publish during her lifetime. In all these years she was constantly writing verses; and while, as already apparent, she frequently enclosed poems in letters to friends, the fact that scores in addition were being written every year was her own secret. Her literary methods were also her own,—she must frequently have tossed off, many times daily, the stray thoughts which came to her. The box of "scraps" found by her sister after her death proves this conclusively, as some of Emily's rarest flashes were caught upon the margins of newspapers, backs of envelopes, or whatever bit of paper was nearest at hand, in the midst of other occupations. In the more carefully copied poems are many alterations, but it is a curious fact that not one change has reference to improvement in rhyme or rhythm. Every suggestion for a different word or phrase was in the evident hope that by some one of them the thought might be made clearer, and not in a single instance merely to smooth the form.

Whether Emily Dickinson had any idea that her work

would ever be published cannot be known. Except when a friend occasionally "turned love to larceny" as some one has aptly said, nothing was printed before her death. One of the poems, indeed, begins,—

> Publication is the auction
> Of the mind of man.

But the Prelude to the Poems, First Series, almost seems to indicate the thought of a possible future public, when she herself should be beyond the reach of the praise or criticism which her writing might call forth.

Early Summer, 1872

DEAR CHILDREN,—We received the news of your loving kindness through Uncle J—— last evening, and Vinnie is negotiating with neighbor Gray, who goes to a wedding in Boston next week, for the procuring of the nest. Vinnie's views of expressage do not abate with time. The crocuses are with us and several other colored friends. Cousin H—— broke her hip, and is in a polite bed, surrounded by mint juleps. I think she will hate to leave it as badly as *Marian Erle* did. Vinnie says there is a tree in Mr. Sweetser's woods that shivers. I am afraid it is cold. I am going to make it a little coat. I must make several, because it is tall as the barn, and put them on as the circus men stand on each other's shoulders. . . . There is to be a "show" next week, and little Maggie's bed is to be moved to the door so she can see the tents. Folding her own like the Arabs gives her no apprehension. While I write, dear children, the colors Eliza loved quiver on the pastures, and day goes gay to the northwest, innocent as she.

EMILY

. . . Thank you for the passage. How long to live the truth is! A word is dead when it is said, some say. I say it just begins to live that day.

July 27, 1872

Little Irish Maggie went to sleep this morning at six o'clock, just the time grandpa rises, and will rest in the grass at Northampton to-morrow. She has had a hard sickness, but her awkward little life is saved and gallant now. Our Maggie is helping her mother put her in the cradle. . . .

Month after this—after that is October, isn't it? That isn't much long. Joy to enfold our little girls in so close a future. That was a lovely letter of F——'s. It put the cat to playing and the kettle to purring, and two or three birds in plush teams reined nearer to the window. . . . You will miss the nasturtiums, but you will meet the chestnuts. You also will miss the south wind, but I will save the west. . . .

Of course we shall have a telegram that you have left for Nebraska. . . .

EMILY

. . . J—— is coming to put away her black hair on the children's pillow. I hoped she'd come while you were here, to help me with the starch, but Satan's ways are not as our ways. I'm straightening all the property, and making things erect and smart, and to-morrow, at twilight, her little heel boots will thump into Amherst. It being summer season she will omit the sleigh-bell gown, and that's a palliative. Vinnie is all disgust, and I shall have to smirk for two to make the manners even.

1872, or 1873

Thank you, dear, for the love. I am progressing timidly. Experiment has a stimulus which withers its fear.

> This is the place they hoped before,
> Where I am hoping now.
> The seed of disappointment grew
> Within a capsule gay,
> Too distant to arrest the feet
> That walk this plank of balm—
> Before them lies escapeless sea—
> The way is closed they came.

Since you so gently ask, I have had but one serious adventure—getting a nail in my foot, but Maggie pulled it out. It only kept me awake one night, and the birds insisted on sitting up, so it became an occasion instead of a misfortune. There was a circus, too, and I watched it away at half-past three that morning. They said "hoy, hoy" to their horses.

Glad you heard Rubinstein. Grieved L—— could not hear him. He makes me think of polar nights Captain Hall could tell! Going from ice to ice! What an exchange of awe!

I am troubled for L——'s eye. Poor little girl! Can I help her? She has so many times saved me. Do take her to Arlington Street.[9] Xerxes must go now and see to her worlds. You shall "taste," dear.

Lovingly.

Winter, 1873

. . . I know I love my friends—I feel it far in here where neither blue nor black eye goes, and fingers cannot reach. I know 'tis love for them that sets the blister in my throat,

---

[9] To the physician who had already done so much for Emily's eyes.

many a time a day, when winds go sweeter than their wont, or a different cloud puts my brain from home.

> I cannot see my soul, but know 'tis there,
> Nor ever saw his house nor furniture,
> Who has invited me with him to dwell;
> But a confiding guest consult as well,
> What raiment honor him the most,
> That I be adequately dressed,
> For he insures to none
> Lest men specifical adorn
> Procuring him perpetual drest
> By dating it a sudden feast.

Love for the glad if you know them, for the sad if they know you.

March, 1873

. . . I open my window, and it fills the chamber with white dirt. I think God must be dusting; and the wind blows so I expect to read in *The Republican* "Cautionary signals for Amherst," or "No ships ventured out from Phœnix Row." . . . Life is so rotatory that the wilderness falls to each, sometime. It is safe to remember that. . . .

Autumn, 1873

. . . I think of your little parlor as the poets once thought of Windermere,—peace, sunshine, and books.

> There is no frigate like a book
> To take us lands away,
> Nor any coursers like a page
> Of prancing poetry.
> This traverse may the poorest take,
> Without oppress of toll;
> How frugal is the chariot
> That bears the human soul!

What words could more vividly express the uplift, the expansion, the wider horizon which books bring! To Emily Dickinson, they were always solace and delight,—"frigates" and "coursers" indeed, to her quiet life, taking her over the world and into the infinite spaces, bringing Cathay and Brazil, Cashmere and Teneriffe, into an intimacy as near and familiar as the summer bees and butterflies of her own home noon. Without the help of books even, her nimble fancy leaped intervening leagues as if it commanded the magic carpet of Prince Houssain; but her love for books and indebtedness to them are many times expressed in the poems, both published and unpublished.

Autumn, 1873

DEAR BERKELEYS,—I should feel it my duty to lay my "net" on the national altar, would it appease finance, but as Jay Cooke can't wear it, I suppose it won't. I believe he opened the scare. M—— says D—— pulled her hair, and D—— says M—— pulled her hair, but the issue at court will be, which pulled the preliminary hair. I am not yet "thrown out of employment," nor ever receiving "wages" find them materially "reduced," though when bread may be a "tradition" Mr. C—— alone knows. I am deeply indebted to F——, also to her sweet sister *Mrs. Ladislaw*; add the funds to the funds, please. Keep the cap till I send— I could not insult my country by incurring expressage now. . . . Buff sings like a nankeen bumble-bee, and a bird's nest on the syringa is just in line with the conservatory fence, so I have fitted a geranium to it and the effect is deceitful.

I see by the paper that father spends the winter with you. Will you be glad to see him? . . . Tell L—— when I was a baby father used to take me to mill for my health. I was then in consumption! While he obtained the "grist," the horse looked round at me, as if to say " 'eye hath not seen nor ear heard the things that' I would do to you if I weren't tied!" That is the way I feel toward her. . . .

Maggie will write soon, says it was Mount Holyoke, and not sweet-brier she gave you! Thanks for the little "news." Did get F——'s note and thank it. Have thousands of things to say as also ten thousands, but must abate now.

Lovingly,

EMILY

1874

DEAR CHILDREN,—Father is ill at home. I think it is the "Legislature" reacting on an otherwise obliging constitution. Maggie is ill at Tom's—a combination of cold and superstition of fever—of which her enemy is ill—and longing for the promised land, of which there is no surplus. "Apollyon" and the "Devil" fade in martial lustre beside Lavinia and myself. "As thy day is so shall thy" stem "be." We can all of us sympathize with the man who wanted the roan horse to ride to execution, because he said 'twas a nimble hue, and 'twould be over sooner. . . .

Dear L——, shall I enclose the slips, or delay till father? Vinnie advises the latter. I usually prefer formers, latters seeming to me like Dickens's hero's dead mamma, "too some weeks off" to risk. Do you remember the "sometimes" of childhood, which invariably never occurred? . . .

Be pleased you have no cat to detain from justice. Ours have taken meats, and the wife of the "general court" is trying to lay them out, but as she has but two wheels and they have four, I would accept their chances. Kitties eat kindlings now. Vinnie thinks they are "cribbers." I wish I could make you as long a call as De Quincey made North, but that morning cannot be advanced.

EMILY

1874

. . . I was sick, little sister, and write you the first that I am able.

The loveliest sermon I ever heard was the disappointment of Jesus in Judas. It was told like a mortal story of intimate young men. I suppose no surprise we can ever have will be so sick as that. The last "I never knew you" may resemble it. I would your hearts could have rested from the first severity before you received this other one, but "not as I will." I suppose the wild flowers encourage themselves in the dim woods, and the bird that is bruised limps to his house in silence, but we have human natures, and these are different. It is lovely that Mrs. W—— did not disappoint you; not that I thought it possible, but you were so much grieved. . . . A finite life, little sister, is that peculiar garment that were it optional with us we might decline to wear. Tender words to L——, not most, I trust, in need of them.

Lovingly,
EMILY

. . . How short it takes to go, dear, but afterward to come so many weary years—and yet 'tis done as cool as a general trifle. Affection is like bread, unnoticed till we starve, and then we dream of it, and sing of it, and paint it, when every urchin in the street has more than he can eat. We turn not older with years, but newer every day.

Of all these things we tried to talk, but the time refused

us. Longing, it may be, is the gift no other gift supplies.
Do you remember what you said the night you came to
me? I secure that sentence. If I should see your face no
more it will be your portrait, and if I should, more vivid
than your mortal face. We must be careful what we say.
No bird resumes its egg.

> A word left careless on a page
> May consecrate an eye,
> When folded in perpetual seam
> The wrinkled author lie.

> EMILY

. . . A tone from the old bells, perhaps, might wake the
children.

> We send the wave to find the wave,
> An errand so divine
> The messenger enamored too,
> Forgetting to return,
> We make the sage decision still
> Soever made in vain,
> The only time to dam the sea
> Is when the sea is gone.

> EMILY, with love

Spring, 1874

SISTERS,—I hear robins a great way off, and wagons a
great way off, and rivers a great way off, and all appear to
be hurrying somewhere undisclosed to me. Remoteness is
the founder of sweetness; could we see all we hope, or
hear the whole we fear told tranquil, like another tale,
there would be madness near. Each of us gives or takes
heaven in corporeal person, for each of us has the skill

of life. I am pleased by your sweet acquaintance. It is not recorded of any rose that it failed of its bee, though obtained in specific instances through scarlet experience. The career of flowers differs from ours only in inaudibleness. I feel more reverence as I grow for these mute creatures whose suspense or transport may surpass my own. Pussy remembered the judgment, and remained with Vinnie. Maggie preferred her home to "Miggles" and "Oakhurst," so with a few spring touches, nature remains unchanged.

> The most triumphant bird
> I ever knew or met,
> Embarked upon a twig to-day,—
> And till dominion set
> I perish to behold
> So competent a sight—
> And sang for nothing scrutable
> But impudent delight.
> Retired and resumed
> His transitive estate;
> To what delicious accident
> Does finest glory fit!

EMILY

. . . There is that which is called an "awakening" in the church, and I know of no choicer ecstasy than to see Mrs.—— roll out in crape every morning, I suppose to intimidate antichrist; at least it would have that effect on me. It reminds me of Don Quixote demanding the surrender of the wind-mill, and of Sir Stephen Toplift, and of Sir Alexander Cockburn.

Spring is a happiness so beautiful, so unique, so unexpected, that I don't know what to do with my heart. I dare not take it, I dare not leave it—what do you advise?

Life is a spell so exquisite that everything conspires to break it.

"What do I think of *Middlemarch?*" What do I think of glory—except that in a few instances this "mortal has already put on immortality."

George Eliot is one. The mysteries of human nature surpass the "mysteries of redemption," for the infinite we only suppose, while we see the finite. . . . I launch Vinnie on Wednesday; it will require the combined efforts of Maggie, Providence and myself, for whatever advances Vinnie makes in nature and art, she has not reduced departure to a science. . . .

Your loving
EMILY

When, in June of 1874, *Emily's father died suddenly in Boston,—taken ill, indeed, while making a speech in the Legislature, and dying within a few hours,—the effect upon her was as if the foundations of her world had given way. She gathered herself together in a measure, and after a few days wrote to her cousins:—*

You might not remember me, dears. I cannot recall myself. I thought I was strongly built, but this stronger has undermined me.

We were eating our supper the fifteenth of June, and Austin came in. He had a despatch in his hand, and I saw by his face we were all lost, though I didn't know how. He said that father was very sick, and he and Vinnie must go. The train had already gone. While horses were dressing, news came he was dead.

Father does not live with us now—he lives in a new

house. Though it was built in an hour it is better than this. He hasn't any garden because he moved after gardens were made, so we take him the best flowers, and if we only knew he knew, perhaps we could stop crying. . . . The grass begins after Pat has stopped it.

I cannot write any more, dears. Though it is many nights, my mind never comes home. Thank you each for the love, though I could not notice it. Almost the last tune that he heard was, "Rest from thy loved employ."

EMILY

April, 1875

I have only a buttercup to offer for the centennial, as an "embattled farmer" has but little time.

Begging you not to smile at my limited meadows, I am modestly

Yours

Summer, 1875

DEAR CHILDREN,—I decide to give you one more package of lemon drops, as they only come once a year. It is fair that the bonbons should change hands, you have so often fed me. This is the very weather that I lived with you those amazing years that I had a father. W. D.——'s wife came in last week for a day and a night, saying her heart drove her. I am glad that you loved Miss W—— on knowing her nearer. Charlotte Brontë said "Life is so constructed that the event does not, cannot, match the expectation."

The birds that father rescued are trifling in his trees. How flippant are the saved! They were even frolicking at his grave, when Vinnie went there yesterday. Nature must be too young to feel, or many years too old.

Now children, when you are cutting the loaf, a crumb, peradventure, a crust, of love for the sparrows' table. . . .

August, 1876

DEAR COUSINS,—Mr. S—— had spoken with pleasure of you, before you spoke of him. Good times are always mutual; that is what makes good times. I am glad it cheered you.

We have had no rain for six weeks except one thunder shower, and that so terrible that we locked the doors, and the clock stopped—which made it like Judgment day. The heat is very great, and the grass so still that the flies speck it. I fear L—— will despair. The notices of the "fall trade" in the hurrying dailies, have a whiff of coolness.

Vinnie has a new pussy the color of Branwell Brontë's hair. She thinks it a little "lower than the angels," and I concur with her. You remember my ideal cat has always a huge rat in its mouth, just going out of sight—though going out of sight in itself has a peculiar charm. It is true that the unknown is the largest need of the intellect, though for it, no one thinks to thank God. . . . Mother is worn with the heat, but otherwise not altering. I dream about father every night, always a different dream, and forget what I am doing daytimes, wondering where he is. Without anybody, I keep thinking. What kind can that be?

Dr. Stearns died homelike, asked Eliza for a saucer of strawberries, which she brought him, but he had no hands. "In such an hour as ye think not" means something when you try it.

Lovingly,
EMILY

November

. . . Oh that beloved witch-hazel which would not reach me till part of the stems were a gentle brown, though one loved stalk as hearty as if just placed in the mail by the woods. It looked like tinsel fringe combined with staider fringes, witch and witching too, to my joyful mind.

I never had seen it but once before, and it haunted me like childhood's Indian pipe, or ecstatic puff-balls, or that mysterious apple that sometimes comes on river-pinks; and is there not a dim suggestion of a dandelion, if her hair were ravelled and she grew on a twig instead of a tube,— though this is timidly submitted. For taking Nature's hand to lead her to me, I am softly grateful—was she willing to come? Though her reluctances are sweeter than other ones' avowals.

> Trusty as the stars
> Who quit their shining working
> Prompt as when I lit them
> In Genesis' new house,
> Durable as dawn
> Whose antiquated blossom
> Makes a world's suspense
> Perish and rejoice.

Love for the cousin sisters, and the lovely alien. . . .

Lovingly,

EMILY

About July 4, 1879

DEAR COUSINS,—Did you know there had been a fire here, and that but for a whim of the wind Austin and Vinnie and Emily would have all been homeless? But perhaps you saw *The Republican.*

We were waked by the ticking of the bells,—the bells tick in Amherst for a fire, to tell the firemen.

I sprang to the window, and each side of the curtain saw that awful sun. The moon was shining high at the time, and the birds singing like trumpets.

Vinnie came soft as a moccasin, "Don't be afraid, Emily, it is only the fourth of July."

I did not tell that I saw it, for I thought if she felt it best to deceive, it must be that it was.

She took hold of my hand and led me into mother's room. Mother had not waked, and Maggie was sitting by her. Vinnie left us a moment, and I whispered to Maggie, and asked her what it was.

"Only Stebbins's barn, Emily"; but I knew that the right and left of the village was on the arm of Stebbins's barn. I could hear buildings falling, and oil exploding, and people walking and talking gayly, and cannon soft as velvet from parishes that did not know that we were burning up.

And so much lighter than day was it, that I saw a caterpillar measure a leaf far down in the orchard; and Vinnie kept saying bravely, "It's only the fourth of July."

It seemed like a theatre, or a night in London, or perhaps like chaos. The innocent dew falling "as if it thought no evil," . . . and sweet frogs prattling in the pools as if there were no earth.

At seven people came to tell us that the fire was stopped, stopped by throwing sound houses in as one fills a well.

Mother never waked, and we were all grateful; we knew she would never buy needle and thread at Mr. Cutler's store, and if it were Pompeii nobody could tell her.

The post-office is in the old meeting-house where L——

and I went early to avoid the crowd, and —— fell asleep with the bumble-bees and the Lord God of Elijah.

Vinnie's "only the fourth of July" I shall always remember. I think she will tell us so when we die, to keep us from being afraid.

Footlights cannot improve the grave, only immortality.

Forgive me the personality; but I knew, I thought, our peril was yours.

Love for you each.

EMILY

1880

. . . Did the "stars differ" from each other in anything but "glory," there would be often envy. The competitions of the sky corrodeless ply.

. . . We asked Vinnie to say in the rear of one of her mental products that we had neuralgia, but evidently her theme or her time did not admit of trifles. . . . I forget no part of that sweet, smarting visit, not even the nettle that stung my rose.

When Macbeth asked the physician what could be done for his wife, he made the mighty answer, "That sort must heal itself"; but, sister, that was guilt, and love, you know, is God, who certainly "gave the love to reward the love," even were there no Browning.

. . . The slips of the last rose of summer repose in kindred soil with waning bees for mates. How softly summer shuts, without the creaking of a door, abroad for evermore.

. . . Vinnie has also added a pilgrim kitten to her flock, which besides being jet black, is, I think, a lineal descendant of the "beautiful hearse horse" recommended to Austin.

December, 1880

. . . The look of the words [stating the death of George Eliot] as they lay in the print I shall never forget. Not their face in the casket could have had the eternity to me. Now, *my* George Eliot. The gift of belief which her greatness denied her, I trust she receives in the childhood of the kingdom of heaven. As childhood is earth's confiding time, perhaps having no childhood, she lost her way to the early trust, and no later came. Amazing human heart, a syllable can make to quake like jostled tree, what infinite for thee? . . .

February, 1881

. . . God is rather stern with his "little ones." "A cup of cold water in my name" is a shivering legacy February mornings.

. . . Maggie's brother is killed in the mine, and Maggie wants to die, but Death goes far around to those that want to see him. If the little cousins would give her a note—she does not know I ask it—I think it would help her begin, that bleeding beginning that every mourner knows.

Spring, 1881

The divine deposit came safely in the little bank. We have heard of the "deeds of the spirit," but are his acts gamboge and pink? A morning call from Gabriel is always a surprise. Were we more fresh from Eden we were expecting him—but Genesis is a "far journey." Thank you for the loveliness.

We have had two hurricanes within as many hours, one of which came near enough to untie my apron—but this moment the sun shines, Maggie's hens are warbling, and a man of anonymous wits is making a garden in the lane to set out slips of bluebird. The moon grows from the seed. . . . Vinnie's pusssy slept in grass Wednesday—a Sicilian symptom—the sails are set for summer, East India wharf. Sage and saucy ones talk of an equinoctial, and are trying the chimneys, but I am "short of hearing," as the deaf say. Blessed are they that play, for theirs is the kingdom of heaven. Love like a rose from each one, and Maggie's a Burgundy one she ardently asks.

EMILY

1881

My DEAR LITTLE COUSINS,—I bring you a robin who is eating a remnant oat on the sill of the barn. The horse was not as hungry as usual, leaving an ample meal for his dulcet friend. . . .

Maggie was charmed with her donkeys, and has long been talking of writing, but has not quite culminated. They stand on the dining-room side-board, by the side of an orange, and a *Springfield Republican*. It will please you to know that the clover in the bill of the brown one is fresh as at first, notwithstanding the time, though the only "pastures" I know gifted with that duration, are far off as the psalms.

Mr. C—— called with a twilight of you. It reminded me of a supper I took, with the pictures on Dresden china. Vinnie asked him "what he had for supper," and he said he "could easier describe the nectar of the gods." . . . We read in a tremendous Book about "an enemy," and armed a confidential fort to scatter him away. The time has passed, and years have come, and yet not any "Satan." I think he must be making war upon some other nation.

EMILY

242

1881

The dear ones will excuse—they knew there was a cause. Emily was sick, and Vinnie's middle name restrained her loving pen.

These are my first words since I left my pillow—that will make them faithful, although so long withheld. We had another fire—it was in Phœnix Row, Monday a week ago, at two in the night. The horses were harnessed to move the office—Austin's office, I mean. After a night of terror, we went to sleep for a few moments, and I could not rise. The others bore it better. The brook from Pelham saved the town. The wind was blowing so, it carried the burning shingles as far as Tom's piazza. We are weak and grateful. The fire-bells are oftener now, almost, than the church-bells. Thoreau would wonder which did the most harm.

The little gifts came sweetly. The bulbs are in the sod—the seeds in homes of paper till the sun calls them. It is snowing now. . . . "Fine sleighing we have this summer," says Austin with a scoff. The box of dainty ones—I don't know what they were, buttons of spice for coats of honey—pleased the weary mother. Thank you each for all.

The beautiful words for which L—— asked were that genius is the ignition of affection—not intellect, as is supposed,—the exaltation of devotion, and in proportion to our capacity for that, is our experience of genius. Precisely as they were uttered I cannot give them, they were in a letter that I do not find, but the suggestion was this.

It is startling to think that the lips, which are keepers of thoughts so magical, yet at any moment are subject to the seclusion of death.

. . . I must leave you, dear, to come perhaps again,—

We never know we go—when we are going
We jest and shut the door—
Fate following behind us bolts it
And we accost no more.

I give you my parting love.

EMILY

Autumn, 1881
Saturday

DEAR ONES,—If I linger, this will not reach you before Sunday; if I do not, I must write you much less than I would love. "Do unto others as ye would that they should do unto you." I would rather they would do unto me *so*.

After infinite wanderings the little note has reached us. It was mailed the twelfth—we received it the twenty-third. The address "Misses Dickinson" misled the rustic eyes— the postmaster knows Vinnie, also by faith who Emily is, because his little girl was hurt, and Emily sent her juleps —but he failed of the intellectual grasp to combine the names. So after sending it to all the *Mrs.* Dickinsons he could discover, he consigned it to us, with the request that we would speedily return it if not ours, that he might renew his research. Almost any one under the circumstances would have doubted if it were theirs, or indeed if they were themself—but to us it was clear. Next time, dears, direct Vinnie, or Emily, and perhaps Mr. ——'s astuteness may be adequate. I enclose the battered remains for your Sabbath perusal, and tell you we think of you tenderly, which I trust you often believe.

Maggie is making a flying visit to cattle-show, on her very robust wings—for Maggie is getting corpulent. Vinnie is picking a few seeds—for if a pod "die, shall he not live again"; and with the shutting mail I go to read to mother

about the President. When we think of the lone effort to
live, and its bleak reward, the mind turns to the myth
"for His mercy endureth forever," with confiding revulsion.
Still, when Professor Fisk died on Mount Zion, Dr. Humphrey prayed "to whom shall we turn but thee?" "I have
finished," said Paul, "the faith." We rejoice that he did not
say discarded it.

The little postman has come—Thomas's "second oldest,"
and I close with reluctant and hurrying love.

EMILY

1881

What is it that instructs a hand lightly created, to
impel shapes to eyes at a distance, which for them have the
whole area of life or of death? Yet not a pencil in the street
but has this awful power, though nobody arrests it. An
earnest letter is or should be life-warrant or death-warrant,
for what is each instant but a gun, harmless because
"unloaded," but that touched "goes off"?

Men are picking up the apples to-day, and the pretty
boarders are leaving the trees, birds and ants and bees. I
have heard a chipper say "dee" six times in disapprobation.
How should we like to have our privileges wheeled away
in a barrel? . . .

The Essex visit was lovely. Mr. L—— remained a week.
Mrs. —— re-decided to come with her son Elizabeth. Aunt
L—— shouldered arms. I think they lie in my memory,
a muffin and a bomb. Now they are all gone, and the
crickets are pleased. Their bombazine reproof still falls
upon the twilight, and checks the softer uproars of the
departing day.

Earnest love to F——. This is but a fragment, but
wholes are not below.

EMILY

DEAR L——, —Thank you, with love, for the kindness; it would be very sweet to claim if we needed it, but we are quite strong, and mother well as usual, and Vinnie spectacular as Disraeli and sincere as Gladstone, —was only sighing in fun. When she sighs in earnest, Emily's throne will tremble, and she will need both L—— and F——; but Vinnie "still prevails." When one or all of us are lain on *"Marian Erle's* dim pallet," so cool that she deplored to live because that she must leave it, L—— and the ferns, and F—— and her fan shall supplement the angels, if they have not already joined them.

Lovingly,
EMILY

October, 1881

Did the little sisters know that Dr. Holland had died— the dark man with the doll-wife, whom they used to see at "Uncle Edward's" before "Uncle Edward" went too?

Do they know any of the circumstances?

Did they know that the weary life in the second story had mourned to hear from them, and whether they were "comfortable"? "Comfortable" seems to comprise the whole to those whose days are weak. "Happiness" is for birds and other foreign nations, in their faint esteem.

Mother heard F—— telling Vinnie about her graham bread. She would like to taste it. Will F—— please write Emily how, and not too inconvenient? Every particular, for Emily is dull, and she will pay in gratitude, which, though not canned like quinces, is fragrantest of all we know.

Tell us just how and where they are, and if October sunshine is thoughtful of their heads.

EMILY

. . . Thank you, dear, for the quickness which is the blossom of request, and for the definiteness—for a new rule is a chance. The bread resulted charmingly, and such pretty little proportions, quaint as a druggist's formula—"I do remember an apothecary." Mother and Vinnie think it the nicest they have ever known, and Maggie so extols it.

Mr. Lathrop's poem was piteously sweet.[10]

To know of your homes is comforting. I trust they are both peace. Home is the riddle of the wise—the booty of the dove. God bless the sunshine in L——'s room, and could he find a sweeter task than to "temper the wind" to her curls? . . .

Tell us when you are happy, but be sure and tell us when you are sad, for Emily's heart is the edifice where the "wicked cease from troubling."

January, 1882

I have only a moment, exiles, but you shall have the largest half. Mother's dear little wants so engross the time, —to read to her, to fan her, to tell her health will come to-morrow, to explain to her *why* the grasshopper is a burden, because he is not so new a grasshopper as he was, —this is so ensuing, I hardly have said "Good-morning, mother," when I hear myself saying "Mother, good-night."

November, 1882

DEAR COUSINS,—I hoped to write you before, but mother's dying almost stunned my spirit.

[10] This reference is to the pathetic verses to his little boy, by Mr. George Parsons Lathrop, beginning,—"Do *you remember, my sweet absent son.*"

I have answered a few inquiries of love, but written little intuitively. She was scarcely the aunt you knew. The great mission of pain had been ratified—cultivated to tenderness by persistent sorrow, so that a larger mother died than had she died before. There was no earthly parting. She slipped from our fingers like a flake gathered by the wind, and is now part of the drift called "the infinite."

We don't know where she is, though so many tell us.

I believe we shall in some manner be cherished by our Maker—that the One who gave us this remarkable earth has the power still farther to surprise that which He has caused. Beyond that all is silence. . . .

Mother was very beautiful when she had died. Seraphs are solemn artists. The illumination that comes but once paused upon her features, and it seemed like hiding a picture to lay her in the grave; but the grass that received my father will suffice his guest, the one he asked at the altar to visit him all his life.

I cannot tell how Eternity seems. It sweeps around me like a sea. . . . Thank you for remembering me. Remembrance—mighty word.

"Thou gavest it to me from the foundation of the world."

Lovingly,

EMILY

Spring, 1883

Thank you, dears, for the sympathy. I hardly dare to know that I have lost another friend, but anguish finds it out.

> Each that we lose takes part of us;
> A crescent still abides,
> Which like the moon, some turbid night,
> Is summoned by the tides.

. . . I work to drive the awe away, yet awe impels the work.

I almost picked the crocuses, you told them so sincerely. Spring's first conviction is a wealth beyond its whole experience.

The sweetest way I think of you is when the day is done, and L—— sets the "sunset tree" for the little sisters. Dear F—— has had many stormy mornings; . . . I hope they have not chilled her feet, nor dampened her heart. I am glad the little visit rested you. Rest and water are most we want.

I know each moment of Miss W—— is a gleam of boundlessness. "Miles and miles away," said Browning, "there's a girl"; but "the colored end of evening smiles" on but few so rare.

Thank you once more for being sorry. Till the first friend dies, we think ecstasy impersonal, but then discover that he was the cup from which we drank it, itself as yet unknown. Sweetest love for each, and a kiss besides for Miss W——'s cheek, should you again meet her.

EMILY

July, 1884

DEAR COUSINS,—I hope you heard Mr. Sanborn's lecture. My *Republican* was borrowed before I waked, to read till my own dawn, which is rather tardy, for I have been quite sick, and could claim the immortal reprimand, "Mr. Lamb, you come down very late in the morning." Eight Saturday noons ago, I was making a loaf of cake with Maggie, when I saw a great darkness coming and knew no more until late at night. I woke to find Austin and Vinnie and a strange physician bending over me, and supposed I was dying, or had died, all was so kind and hallowed. I had fainted and lain unconscious for the first time in my life. Then I grew very sick and gave the others much alarm, but am now staying. The doctor calls it "revenge of the nerves"; but who but Death had wronged them? F——'s dear note has lain unanswered for this long season, though its "Good-night, my dear," warmed me to the core. I have all to say, but little strength to say it; so we must talk by degrees. I do want to know about L——, what pleases her most, book or tune or friend.

I am glad the housekeeping is kinder; it is a prickly art. Maggie is with us still, warm and wild and mighty, and we have a gracious boy at the barn. We remember you always, and one or the other often comes down with a "we dreamed of F—— and L—— last night"; then that day we think we shall hear from you, for dreams are couriers.

The little boy we laid away never fluctuates, and his dim society is companion still. But it is growing damp and I must go in. Memory's fog is rising.

> The going from a world we know
>   To one a wonder still
> Is like the child's adversity
>   Whose vista is a hill,
> Behind the hill is sorcery
>   And everything unknown,
> But will the secret compensate
>   For climbing it alone?

Vinnie's love and Maggie's, and mine is presupposed.
                                                      EMILY

January 14, 1885
Had we less to say to those we love, perhaps we should say it oftener, but the attempt comes, then the inundation, then it is all over, as is said of the dead.

Vinnie dreamed about F—— last night, and designing for days to write dear L——, —dear, both of you, —indeed, with the astounding nearness which a dream brings, I must speak this morning. I do hope you are well, and that the last enchanting days have refreshed your spirits, and I hope the poor little girl is better, and the sorrow at least adjourned.

L—— asked "what books" we were wooing now—watching like a vulture for Walter Cross's life of his wife. A friend sent me *Called Back.* It is a haunting story, and as loved Mr. Bowles used to say, "greatly impressive to me." Do you remember the little picture with his deep face in the centre, and Governor Bross on one side, and Colfax on the other? The third of the group died yesterday, so somewhere they are again together.

Moving to Cambridge seems to me like moving to Westminster Abbey, as hallowed and as unbelieved, or moving to Ephesus with Paul for a next-door neighbor.

Holmes's *Life of Emerson* is sweetly commended, but you, I know, have tasted that. . . . But the whistle calls me—I have not begun—so with a moan, and a kiss, and a promise of more, and love from Vinnie and Maggie, and the half-blown carnation, and the western sky, I stop.

That we are permanent temporarily, it is warm to know, though we know no more.

EMILY

vii

T O *Mr. Thomas Wentworth Higginson*

IN HIS *article upon Emily Dickinson* in The Atlantic Monthly *for* October, 1891, Colonel Higginson *has
already given many of her letters to himself. The rest are
here added.*

*The first one, enclosing four of her now widely known
poems for his criticism, was without signature, but accompanied by a card bearing her name. Her wish for an im-
partial and extrinsic judgment from a stranger may, perhaps, illustrate Mrs. Ford's suggestion that "she was longing for poetic sympathy." At a time when she was but
newly trying her own wings, she must have felt something
warmly and essentially human in Colonel Higginson's writing to be thus led to ask his help rather than another's,—
an intuition most happily justified.*

*He received the first of her unique letters at the begin-
ning of "war time." Unfortunately his answers cannot now
be found:*

April 16, 1862

MR. HIGGINSON,—Are you too deeply occupied to say if my verse is alive?

The mind is so near itself it cannot see distinctly, and I have none to ask.

Should you think it breathed, and had you the leisure to tell me, I should feel quick gratitude.

If I make the mistake, that you dared to tell me would give me sincerer honor toward you.

I enclosed my name, asking you, if you please, sir, to tell me what is true?

That you will not betray me it is needless to ask, since honor is its own pawn.

April 26, 1862

MR. HIGGINSON,—Your kindness claimed earlier gratitude, but I was ill, and write to-day from my pillow.

Thank you for the surgery; it was not so painful as I supposed. I bring you others, as you ask, though they might not differ. While my thought is undressed, I can make the distinction; but when I put them in the gown, they look alike and numb.

You asked how old I was? I made no verse, but one or two, until this winter, sir.

I had a terror since September, I could tell to none; and so I sing, as the boy does of the burying ground, because I am afraid.

You inquire my books. For poets, I have Keats, and Mr. and Mrs. Browning. For prose, Mr. Ruskin, Sir Thomas Browne, and the *Revelations*. I went to school, but in your manner of the phrase had no education. When a little girl, I had a friend who taught me Immortality; but venturing too near, himself, he never returned. Soon after my tutor died, and for several years my lexicon was my only companion. Then I found one more, but he was not contented I be his scholar, so he left the land.

You ask of my companions. Hills, sir, and the sundown, and a dog large as myself, that my father bought me. They are better than beings because they know, but do not tell; and the noise in the pool at noon excels my piano.

I have a brother and sister; my mother does not care for thought, and father, too busy with his briefs to notice what we do. He buys me many books, but begs me not to read them, because he fears they joggle the mind. They are religious, except me, and address an eclipse, every morning, whom they call their "Father."

But I fear my story fatigues you. I would like to learn. Could you tell me how to grow, or is it unconveyed, like melody or witchcraft?

You speak of Mr. Whitman. I never read his book, but was told that it was disgraceful.

I read Miss Prescott's *Circumstance*, but it followed me in the dark, so I avoided her.

Two editors of journals came to my father's house this winter, and asked me for my mind, and when I asked them "why" they said I was penurious, and they would use it for the world.

I could not weigh myself, myself. My size felt small to me. I read your chapters in *The Atlantic*, and experienced honor for you. I was sure you would not reject a confiding question.

Is this, sir, what you asked me to tell you?

Your friend,
E. DICKINSON

June 8, 1862

DEAR FRIEND,—Your letter gave no drunkenness, because I tasted rum before. Domingo comes but once; yet I have had few pleasures so deep as your opinion, and if I tried to thank you, my tears would block my tongue.

My dying tutor told me that he would like to live till I had been a poet, but Death was much of mob as I could master, then. And when, far afterward, a sudden light on orchards, or a new fashion in the wind troubled my attention, I felt a palsy, here, the verses just relieve.

Your second letter surprised me, and for a moment, swung. I had not supposed it. Your first gave no dishonor, because the true are not ashamed. I thanked you for your justice, but could not drop the bells whose jingling cooled my tramp. Perhaps the balm seemed better, because you bled me first. I smile when you suggest that I delay "to publish," that being foreign to my thought as firmament to fin.

If fame belonged to me, I could not escape her; if she did not, the longest day would pass me on the chase, and the approbation of my dog would forsake me then. My barefoot rank is better.

You think my gait "spasmodic." I am in danger, sir. You think me "uncontrolled." I have no tribunal.

Would you have time to be the "friend" you should think I need? I have a little shape: it would not crowd your desk, nor make much racket as the mouse that dents your galleries.

If I might bring you what I do—not so frequent to trouble you—and ask you if I told it clear, 'twould be control to me. The sailor cannot see the north, but knows the needle can. The "hand you stretch me in the dark" I put mine in, and turn away. I have no Saxon now:—

As if I asked a common alms,
And in my wondering hand
A stranger pressed a kingdom,
And I, bewildered, stand;
As if I asked the Orient
Had it for me a morn,
And it should lift its purple dikes
And shatter me with dawn!

But, will you be my preceptor, Mr. Higginson?

After these startling letters it was but natural that Mr. Higginson should have asked to see a photograph of his "enigmatical correspondent." But there was none. She had an unconquerable aversion to seeing herself reproduced in any sort of "mould." The frontispiece to the first volume of these Letters *is taken from an oil painting of Emily, when she was but eight years old, in a group with her brother and sister. The only other known representation of her face is a daguerrotype made a few years later; but it is entirely unsatisfactory, both in expression and individuality. Instead of her photograph, she sent this verbal portrait. Her coy avoidance of Mr. Higginson's request was as characteristically piquant as her answer to his question of her age:—*

July, 1862

Could you believe me without? I had no portrait, now, but am small, like the wren; and my hair is bold, like the chestnut burr; and my eyes, like the sherry in the glass that the guest leaves. Would this do just as well?

It often alarms father. He says death might occur, and he has moulds of all the rest, but has no mould of me; but I noticed the quick wore off those things in a few days, and forestall the dishonor. You will think no caprice of me.

You said "dark." I know the butterfly, and the lizard, and the orchis. Are not those *your* countrymen?

I am happy to be your scholar, and will deserve the kindness I cannot repay.

If you truly consent, I recite now. Will you tell me my fault, frankly, as to yourself, for I had rather wince than die. Men do not call the surgeon to commend the bone, but to set it, sir, and fracture within is more critical. And for this, preceptor, I shall bring you obedience, the blossom from my garden, and every gratitude I know.

Perhaps you smile at me. I could not stop for that. My business is circumference. An ignorance, not of customs, but if caught with the dawn, or the sunset see me, myself the only kangaroo among the beauty, sir, if you please, it afflicts me, and I thought that instruction would take it away.

Because you have much business, beside the growth of me, you will appoint, yourself, how often I shall come without your inconvenience.

And if at any time you regret you received me, or I prove a different fabric to that you supposed, you must banish me.

When I state myself, as the representative of the verse, it does not mean me, but a supposed person.

You are true about the "perfection." To-day makes yesterday mean.

You spoke of *Pippa Passes*. I never heard anybody speak of *Pippa Passes* before. You see my posture is benighted.

To thank you baffles me. Are you perfectly powerful? Had I a pleasure you had not, I could delight to bring it.

YOUR SCHOLAR

Colonel Higginson wrote, "It would seem that at first I tried a little—a very little—to lead her in the direction of rules and traditions; but I fear it was only perfunctory, and that she interested me more in her—so to speak—unregenerate condition. Still, she recognizes the endeavor. In this case, as will be seen, I called her attention to the fact that while she took pains to correct the spelling of a word, she was utterly careless of greater irregularities. It will be seen by her answer that with her usual naïve adroitness she turns my point":—

DEAR FRIEND,—Are these more orderly? I thank you for the truth.

I had no monarch in my life, and cannot rule myself; and when I try to organize, my little force explodes and leaves me bare and charred.

I think you called me "wayward." Will you help me improve?

I suppose the pride that stops the breath, in the core of woods, is not of ourself.

You say I confess the little mistake, and omit the large. Because I can see orthography; but the ignorance out of sight is my preceptor's charge.

Of "shunning men and women,"—they talk of hallowed things, aloud, and embarrass my dog. He and I don't object to them, if they'll exist their side. I think Carl would please you. He is dumb, and brave. I think you would like the chestnut-tree I met in my walk. It hit my notice suddenly, and I thought the skies were in blossom.

Then there's a noiseless noise in the orchard that I let persons hear.

You told me in one letter you could not come to see me "now," and I made no answer; not because I had none, but did not think myself the price that you should come so far.

I do not ask so large a pleasure, lest you might deny me.

You say, "Beyond your knowledge." You would not jest with me, because I believe you; but, preceptor, you cannot mean it?

All men say "What" to me, but I thought it a fashion.

When much in the woods, as a little girl, I was told that the snake would bite me, that I might pick a poisonous flower, or goblins kidnap me; but I went along and met no one but angels, who were far shyer of me than I could be of them, so I haven't that confidence in fraud which many exercise.

I shall observe your precept, though I don't understand it, always.

I marked a line in one verse, because I met it after I made it, and never consciously touch a paint mixed by another person. I do not let go it, because, it is mine.

Have you the portrait of Mrs. Browning? Persons sent me three. If you had none, will you have mine?

YOUR SCHOLAR

After entering the volunteer army of the Civil War, Colonel Higginson received the following letter while in camp in South Carolina, early in 1863:—

AMHERST

DEAR FRIEND,—I did not deem that planetary forces annulled, but suffered an exchange of territory, or world.

I should have liked to see you before you became improbable. War feels to me an oblique place. Should there be other summers, would you perhaps come?

I found you were gone, by accident, as I find systems are, or seasons of the year, and obtain no cause, but suppose it a treason of progress that dissolves as it goes. Carlo still remained, and I told him.

> Best gains must have the losses' test,
> To constitute them gains.

My shaggy ally assented.

Perhaps death gave me awe for friends, striking sharp and early, for I held them since in a brittle love, of more alarm than peace. I trust you may pass the limit of war; and though not reared to prayer, when service is had in church for our arms, I include yourself. . . . I was thinking to-day, as I noticed, that the "supernatural" was only the natural disclosed.

> Not "Revelation" 'tis that waits,
> But our unfurnished eyes.

But I fear I detain you. Should you, before this reaches you, experience Immortality, who will inform me of the exchange? Could you, with honor, avoid death, I entreat you, sir. It would bereave

Your Gnome

I trust the *Procession of Flowers* was not a premonition.

Of this curious letter Colonel Higginson wrote: "Mr. Howells reminds me that Swedenborg somewhere has an image akin to her 'oblique place,' where he symbolizes evil as simply an oblique angle."

In the summer of 1863 *Colonel Higginson was wounded;*

*in September of the same year began Emily's trouble with
her eyes, frequently referred to. In the April following she
went to Boston,—her mention of Hawthorne's death (May,
1864) of itself placing the date:—*

Summer, 1864

DEAR FRIEND,—Are you in danger? I did not know that
you were hurt. Will you tell me more? Mr. Hawthorne
died.

I was ill since September, and since April in Boston for
a physician's care. He does not let me go, yet I work in
my prison, and make guests for myself.

Carlo did not come, because that he would die in jail;
and the mountains I could not hold now, so I brought
but the gods.

I wish to see you more than before I failed. Will you
tell me your health? I am surprised and anxious since
receiving your note.

> The only news I know
> Is bulletins all day
> From Immortality.

Can you render my pencil? The physician has taken
away my pen. I enclose the address from a letter, lest my
fingers fail.

Knowledge of your recovery would excel my own.

E. DICKINSON

1865
AMHERST

DEAR FRIEND,—You were so generous to me, that if
possible I offended you, I could not too deeply apologize.

To doubt my behavior is a new pain. I could be honorable no more, till I asked you about it. I know not what to deem myself—yesterday "your scholar," but might I be the one you to-night forgave, 'tis a better honor. Mine is but just the thief's request.

Please, sir, hear

"BARABBAS"

> The possibility to pass
> Without a moment's bell
> Into conjecture's presence,
> Is like a face of steel
> That suddenly looks into ours
> With a metallic grin;
> The cordiality of Death
> Who drills his welcome in.

1868
AMHERST

DEAR FRIEND,—Whom my dog understood could not elude others.

I should be so glad to see you, but think it an apparitional pleasure, not to be fulfilled. I am uncertain of Boston.

I had promised to visit my physician for a few days in May, but father objects because he is in the habit of me.

Is it more far to Amherst?

You will find a minute host, but a spacious welcome. . . .

If I still entreat you to teach me, are you much displeased? I will be patient, constant, never reject your knife, and should my slowness goad you, you knew before myself that

> Except the smaller size
> No lives are round.
> These hurry to a sphere

And show and end.
The larger slower grow
And later hang;
The summers of Hesperides
Are long.

1868
AMHERST

DEAR FRIEND,—A letter always feels to me like Immortality because it is the mind alone without corporeal friend. Indebted in our talk to attitude and accent, there seems a spectral power in thought that walks alone. I would like to thank you for your great kindness, but never try to lift the words which I cannot hold.

Should you come to Amherst, I might then succeed, though gratitude is the timid wealth of those who have nothing. I am sure that you speak the truth, because the noble do, but your letters always surprise me.

My life has been too simple and stern to embarrass any. "Seen of angels," scarcely my responsibility.

It is difficult not to be fictitious in so fair a place, but tests' severe repairs are permitted all.

When a little girl I remember hearing that remarkable passage and preferring the "power," not knowing at the time that "kingdom" and "glory" were included.

You noticed my dwelling alone. To an emigrant, country is idle except it be his own. You speak kindly of seeing me; could it please your convenience to come so far as Amherst, I should be very glad, but I do not cross my father's ground to any house or town.

Of our greatest acts we are ignorant. You were not aware that you saved my life. To thank you in person has been since then one of my few requests. . . . You will excuse each that I say, because no one taught me.

August, 1870

DEAR FRIEND,—I will be at home and glad.

I think you said the 15th. The incredible never surprises us, because it is the incredible.

E. DICKINSON

Of his meeting Emily Dickinson in her own home, and of his first impressions of her, Colonel Higginson has told in the pages of The Atlantic.

Withdrawing more and more constantly from accumulated humanity, no thought of the possibility of a lack of congenial occupation ever crossed her mind. During their first interview, indeed, Colonel Higginson asked her "if she never felt any want of employment, not going off the grounds, and rarely seeing a visitor"; to which she replied, "I never thought of conceiving that I could ever have the slightest approach to such a want in all future time."

Among the strong and remarkable things she said to him are several sentences which it seems not irrelevant to insert here:—

"Is it oblivion or absorption when things pass from our minds?"

"Truth is such a rare thing, it is delightful to tell it."

"I find ecstasy in living; the mere sense of living is joy enough."

One or two others Colonel Higginson has called "the very wantonness of over-statement," as,—

"How do most people live without any thoughts? There are many people in the world,—you must have noticed them in the street,—how do they live? How do they get strength to put on their clothes in the morning?"

And this, "a crowning extravaganza,"—

"If I read a book and it makes my whole body so cold no fire can ever warm me, I know that is poetry. If I feel physically as if the top of my head were taken off, I know that is poetry. These are the only ways I know it. Is there any other way?"

After the visit she wrote:—

August, 1870

Enough is so vast a sweetness, I suppose it never occurs, only pathetic counterfeits.

Fabulous to me as the men of the *Revelations* who "shall not hunger any more." Even the possible has its insoluble particle.

After you went, I took Macbeth and turned to "Birnam Wood." Came *twice* "to Dunsinane." I thought and went about my work. . . .

The vein cannot thank the artery, but her solemn indebtedness to him, even the stolidest admit, and so of me who try, whose effort leaves no sound.

You ask great questions accidentally. To answer them would be events. I trust that you are safe.

I ask you to forgive me for all the ignorance I had. I find no nomination sweet as your low opinion.

Speak, if but to blame your obedient child.

You told me of Mrs. Lowell's poems. Would you tell me where I could find them, or are they not for sight? An article of yours, too, perhaps the only one you wrote that I never knew. It was about a "Latch." Are you willing to tell me?[11]

If I ask too much, you could please refuse. Shortness to live has made me bold.

. Abroad is close to-night and I have but to lift my hands to touch the "Heights of Abraham."

DICKINSON

Winter, 1871

To live is so startling, it leaves but little room for other occupations, though friends are, if possible, an event more fair.

I am happy you have the travel you so long desire, and chastened that my master met neither accident nor Death.

Our own possessions, though our own, 'tis well to hoard anew, remembering the dimensions of possibility. I often saw your name in illustrious mention, and envied an occasion so abstinent to me. Thank you for having been to Amherst. Could you come again that would be far better, though the finest wish is the futile one.

When I saw you last, it was mighty summer—now the grass is glass, and the meadow stucco, and "still waters" in the pool where the frog drinks.

These behaviors of the year hurt almost like music, shifting when it ease us most. Thank you for the "lesson." I will study it, though hitherto,—

Menagerie to me
My neighbor be.

YOUR SCHOLAR

---

[11] Perhaps A *Shadow.*

Her father's death (June 16) swept away all her landmarks.
To this friend she wrote:—

July, 1874

The last afternoon that my father lived, though with no premonition, I preferred to be with him, and invented an absence for mother, Vinnie being asleep. He seemed peculiarly pleased, as I oftenest stayed with myself; and remarked, as the afternoon withdrew, he "would like it to not end."

His pleasure almost embarrassed me, and my brother coming, I suggested they walk. Next morning I woke him for the train, and saw him no more.

His heart was pure and terrible, and I think no other like it exists.

I am glad there is Immortality, but would have tested it myself, before intrusting him. Mr. Bowles was with us. With that exception, I saw none. I have wished for you, since my father died, and had you an hour unengrossed, it would be almost priceless. Thank you for each kindness. . . . Your beautiful hymn, was it not prophetic? It has assisted that pause of space which I call "father."

August, 1874

When I think of my father's lonely life and lonelier death, there is this redress,—

> Take all away;
> The only thing worth larceny
> Is left—the Immortality.

My earliest friend wrote me the week before he died, "If I live, I will go to Amherst; if I die, I certainly will."

Is your house deeper off?

YOUR SCHOLAR

DEAR FRIEND,—I find you with dusk, for day is tired, and lays her antediluvian cheek to the hill like a child.

Nature confides now.

I hope you are joyful frequently, these beloved days, and the health of your friend bolder.

I remember her with my blossoms and wish they were hers

> Whose pink career may have a close
> Portentous as our own, who knows?
> To imitate these neighbors fleet,
> In awe and innocence, were meet.

Summer is so kind I had hoped you might come. Since my father's dying, everything sacred enlarged so it was dim to own. When a few years old, I was taken to a funeral which I now know was of peculiar distress, and the clergyman asked, "Is the arm of the Lord shortened, that it cannot save?"

He italicised the "cannot." I mistook the accent for a doubt of Immortality, and not daring to ask, it besets me still, though we know that the mind of the heart must live if its clerical part do not. Would you explain it to me? . . . It comforts an instinct if another have felt it too. I was re-reading your *Decoration*. You may have forgotten it.

June, 1875

DEAR FRIEND,—Mother was paralyzed Tuesday, a year from the evening father died. I thought perhaps you would care.

YOUR SCHOLAR

> A death-blow is a life-blow to some
> Who, till they died, did not alive become;
> Who, had they lived, had died, but when
> They died, vitality begun.

1875

DEAR FRIEND,—The flower was jasmine. I am glad if it pleased your friend. It is next dearest to daphne, except wild-flowers—those are dearer.

I have a friend in Dresden, who thinks the love of the field a misplaced affection—and says he will send me a meadow that is better than summer's. If he does, I will send it to you.

I have read nothing of Tourguéneff's, but thank you for telling me—and will seek him immediately. I did not read Mr. Miller because I could not care about him.

Mrs. Hunt's poems are stronger than any written by women since Mrs. Browning, with the exception of Mrs. Lewes's; but truth like ancestors' brocades can stand alone. You speak of *Men and Women*. That is a broad book.

Bells and Pomegranates I never saw, but have Mrs. Browning's endorsement. While Shakespeare remains, literature is firm.

An insect cannot run away with Achilles's head. Thank you for having written the *Atlantic Essays*. They are a fine joy, though to possess the ingredient for congratulation renders congratulation superfluous.

Dear friend, I trust you as you ask. If I exceed permission, excuse the bleak simplicity that knew no tutor but the north. Would you but guide

DICKINSON?

1875

DEAR FRIEND,—I am sorry your brother is dead. I fear he was dear to you. I should be glad to know you were painlessly grieved.

> Of Heaven above the firmest proof
> We fundamental know—
> Except for its marauding hand
> It had been heaven below.
>
> DICKINSON

*As already shown, Emily had effectively resisted all importunity to publish. Even the eloquent pleading of her long-time friend "*H. H.*" was of no avail; but apparently reinforcement in her decision was sometimes sought:—*

Early in 1876

DEAR FRIEND,—Are you willing to tell me what is right? Mrs. Jackson, of Colorado, was with me a few moments this week, and wished me to write for this.[12] I told her I was unwilling, and she asked me why? I said I was incapable, and she seemed not to believe me and asked me not to decide for a few days. Meantime, she would write to me. She was so sweetly noble, I would regret to estrange her, and if you would be willing to give me a note saying you disapproved it and thought me unfit, she would believe you. I am sorry to flee so often to my safest friend, but hope he permits me.

Acknowledging a photograph, 1876

DEAR FRIEND,—Except your coming I know no gift so great, and in one extent it exceeds that,—it is permanent.

Your face is more joyful when you speak, and I miss an almost arrogant look that at times haunts you, but with that exception, it is so real I could think it you.

---

[12] A circular of the *No Name Series* was enclosed.

Thank you with delight, and please to thank your friend for the lovely suggestion.

I hope she has no suffering now.

Was it Browning's flower that "ailed till evening"? I shall think of your "keeping house" at night when I close the shutter—but to be Mrs. Higginson's guest is the boon of birds.

Judge Lord was with us a few days since, and told me that the joy we most revere we profane in taking. I wish that was wrong.

Mrs. Jackson has written. It was not stories she asked of me. But may I tell her just the same that you don't prefer it? Thank you if I may, for it almost seems sordid to refuse from myself again.

My brother and sister speak of you, and covet your remembrance, and perhaps you will not reject my own to Mrs. Higginson?

> Summer laid her supple glove
> In its sylvan drawer—
> Wheresoe'er, or was she
> The demand of awe?

YOUR SCHOLAR

March, 1876

. . . But two had mentioned the "spring" to me—yourself and the *Revelations.* "I, Jesus, have sent mine angel."

I inferred your touch in the papers on Lowell and Emerson. It is delicate that each mind is itself, like a distinct bird.

I was lonely there was an "or" in that beautiful "I would go to Amherst," though grieved for its cause. I wish your

271

friend had my strength, for I don't care for roving—she perhaps might, though to remain with you is journey.

To abstain from *Daniel Deronda* is hard—you are very kind to be willing. . . . I am glad *Immortality* pleased you. I believed it would. I suppose even God Himself could not withhold that now.

> To disappear enhances,
> The man that runs away
> Is tinctured for an instant
> With Immortality.
>
> But yesterday a vagrant,
> To-day in memory lain
> With superstitious value—
> We tamper with again.
>
> But "never" far as honor
> Withdraws the worthless thing,
> And impotent to cherish
> We hasten to adorn.
>
> Of Death the sternest function
> That just as we discern
> The excellence defies us—
> Securest gathered then
>
> The fruit perverse to plucking,
> But leaning to the sight
> With the ecstatic limit
> Of unobtained delight.

In sending a volume of George Eliot to Mrs. Higginson, Emily wrote, "I am bringing you a little granite book to lean on."

Autumn, 1876

DEAR FRIEND,—Thank you for permission to write Mrs. Higginson. I hope I have not fatigued her—also for thinking of my brother, who is slowly better, and rides for an hour, kind days.

I am glad if I did as you would like. The degradation to displease you, I hope I may never incur.

Often, when troubled by entreaty, that paragraph of yours has saved me—"Such being the majesty of the art you presume to practise, you can at least take time before dishonoring it," and Enobarbus said, "Leave that which leaves itself."

I shall look with joy for the "little book" because it is yours, though I seek you in vain in the magazines where you once wrote. I recently found two papers of yours that were unknown to me, and wondered anew at your withdrawing thought so sought by others.

When flowers annually died and I was a child, I used to read Dr. Hitchcock's book on the *Flowers of North America.* This comforted their absence, assuring me they lived.

YOUR SCHOLAR

1877

Thank you, dear friend, for my "New Year," but did you not confer it? Had your scholar permission to fashion yours, it were perhaps too fair. I always ran home to awe when a child, if anything befell me. He was an awful mother, but I liked him better than none.

There remained this shelter after you left me the other day.

Of your flitting coming it is fair to think, like the bee's coupé, vanishing in music.

> Would you with the bee return,
> What a firm of noon!
> Death obtains the rose,
> But the news of dying goes
> No further than the breeze.

The ear is the last face. We hear after we see, which to tell you first is still my destiny.

Meeting a bird this morning, I began to flee. He saw it and sung.

> Presuming on that lone result,
> His infinite disdain,
> But vanquished him with my defeat—
> 'Twas victory was slain.

I shall read the book.

Thank you for telling me.

After Colonel Higginson had met with a bereavement, in 1877

Dear Friend,—We must be less than Death to be lessened by it, for nothing is irrevocable but ourselves.

I am glad you are better. I had feared to follow you, lest you would rather be lonely, which is the will of sorrow; but the papers had spoken of you with affectionate deference, and to know you were deeply remembered might not too intrude.

To be human is more than to be divine, for when Christ was divine he was uncontented till he had been human.

I remember nothing so strong as to see you. . . .

1877

Dear Friend,—I think of you so wholly that I cannot resist to write again, to ask if you are safe? Danger is not at first, for then we are unconscious, but in the after, slower days.

Do not try to be saved, but let redemption find you, as it certainly will. Love is its own rescue, for we, at our supremest, are but its trembling emblems.

YOUR SCHOLAR

After an interval of silence came this letter, in the same year:—

Must I lose the friend that saved my life without inquiring why? Affection gropes through drifts of awe for his tropic door.

That every bliss we know or guess hourly befall him, is his scholar's prayer.

January, 1878

DEAR FRIEND,—I felt it shelter to speak to you.

My brother and sister are with Mr. Bowles, who is buried this afternoon.

The last song that I heard—that was, since the birds— was, "He leadeth me, he leadeth me; yea, though I walk" —then the voices stooped, the arch was so low.

Summer, 1878

DEAR FRIEND,—When you wrote you would come in November, it would please me it were November then— but the time has moved. You went with the coming of the birds—they will go with your coming, but to see you is so much sweeter than birds, I could excuse the spring.

With the bloom of the flower your friend loved, I have wished for her, but God cannot discontinue Himself.

Mr. Bowles was not willing to die.

When you have lost a friend, Master, you remember you could not begin again, because there was no world. I have thought of you often since the darkness, though we cannot assist another's night.

I have hoped you were saved.

That those have immortality with whom we talked about it, makes it no more mighty but perhaps more sudden. . . .

> How brittle are the piers
> On which our faith doth tread—
> No bridge below doth totter so,
> Yet none hath such a crowd,
>
> It is as old as God—
> Indeed, 'twas built by Him—
> He sent His son to test the plank,
> And he pronounced it firm.

I hope you have been well. I hope your rambles have been sweet, and your reveries spacious.

To have seen Stratford on Avon, and the Dresden Madonna, must be almost peace.

And perhaps you have spoken with George Eliot. Will you "tell me about it"? Will you come in November, and will November come, or is this the hope that opens and shuts, like the eye of the wax doll?

YOUR SCHOLAR

In acknowledgment of his Short Studies of American Authors, 1879

DEAR FRIEND,—Brabantio's gift was not more fair than yours, though I trust without his pathetic inscription, "Which but thou hast already, with all my heart I would keep from thee."

Of Poe, I know too little to think—Hawthorne appalls —entices.

Mrs. Jackson soars to your estimate lawfully as a bird, but of Howells and James, one hesitates. Your relentless music dooms as it redeems.

Remorse for the brevity of a book is a rare emotion, though fair as Lowell's "sweet despair" in the "slipper hymn."

> One thing of it we borrow
> And promise to return,
> The booty and the sorrow
> Its sweetness to have known.
> One thing of it we covet—
> The power to forget,
> The anguish of the avarice
> Defrays the dross of it.

Had I tried before reading your gift to thank you, it had perhaps been possible, but I waited, and now it disables my lips.

Magic, as it electrifies, also makes decrepit. Thank you for thinking of me.

Your Scholar

1880

Dear Friend,—You were once so kind as to say you would advise me. Could I ask it now?

I have promised three hymns to a charity, but without your approval could not give them.

They are short, and I could write them quite plainly, and if you felt it convenient to tell me if they were faithful, I should be very grateful, though if public cares too far fatigue you, please deny

Your Scholar

1880
Dear Friend,—Thank you for the advice. I shall im-
plicitly follow it.

The one who asked me for the lines I had never seen.

He spoke of "a charity." I refused, but did not inquire.
He again earnestly urged, on the ground that in that way
I might "aid unfortunate children." The name of "child"
was a snare to me, and I hesitated, choosing my most rudi-
mentary, and without criterion.

I inquired of you. You can scarcely estimate the opinion
to one utterly guideless. Again thank you.

Your Scholar

Early Summer, 1880
Dear Friend,—I was touchingly reminded of [a child
who had died] this morning by an Indian woman with gay
baskets and a dazzling baby, at the kitchen door. Her little
boy "once died," she said, death to her dispelling him. I
asked her what the baby liked, and she said "to step." The
prairie before the door was gay with flowers of hay, and I
led her in. She argued with the birds, she leaned on clover
walls and they fell, and dropped her. With jargon sweeter
than a bell, she grappled buttercups, and they sank together,
the buttercups the heaviest. What sweetest use of days!
'Twas noting some such scene made Vaughan humbly
say,—

"My days that are at best but dim and hoary."

I think it was Vaughan. . . .

1884

DEAR FRIEND,—May I ask the delight in advance, of
sending you the *Life of Mrs. Cross* by her husband, which
the papers promise for publication?

I feared some other pupil might usurp my privilege.

Emblem is immeasurable—that is why it is better than
fulfilment, which can be drained.

T O *Mr. Perez D. Cowan, Miss Maria Whitney, Mr. Bowles, Mr. F. D. Clark, and Mr. C. H. Clark*

MR. COWAN *graduated at Amherst College in 1866, and "Peter" was Emily Dickinson's especial appellation for this favorite cousin. The first letter was written upon the occasion of his marriage to Miss Margaret Elizabeth Rhea.*

T O *the Rev. Perez D. Cowan*

October 26, 1870

DEAR PETER,—It is indeed sweet news. I am proud of your happiness. To Peter, and Peter's, let me give both hands. Delight has no competitor, so it is always most.

"Maggie" is a warm name.

I shall like to take it.

Home is the definition of God.

EMILY

To the Same

It is long since I knew of you, Peter, and much may have happened to both; but that is the rarest book, which, opened at whatever page, equally enchants us.

I hope that you have power, and as much of peace as in our deep existence may be possible.

To multiply the harbors does not reduce the sea.

We learn, through cousin Montague, that you have lost your sister through that sweeter loss which we call gain.

I am glad she is glad.

Her early pain had seemed to me peculiarly cruel.

Tell her how tenderly we are pleased.

Recall me too to your other sisters, who though they may have mislaid me, I can always find; and include me to your sweet wife. We are daily reminded of you by the clergyman, Mr. Jenkins, whom you strongly resemble.

Thank you for the paper. It is homelike to know where you are.

We can almost hear you announce the text, when the air is clear; and how social if you should preach us a note some Sunday in recess!

EMILY

To the Same
After the death of Mr. Cowan's little daughter Margie
November 8, 1879

Will it comfort my grieved cousin to know that Emily and Vinnie are among the ones this moment thinking of him with peculiar tenderness, and is his sweet wife too faint to remember to Whom her loved one is consigned?

"Come unto me" could not alarm those minute feet— how sweet to remember.

If you feel able, write a few words; if you do not—remember forgetting is a guile unknown to your faithful cousin

EMILY

To the Same

Upon receiving an account of little Margie's life and death
October, 1880

DEAR COUSIN,—The sweet book found me on my pillow, where I was detained, or I should have thanked you immediately.

The little creature must have been priceless—yours and not yours—how hallowed!

It may have been she came to show you Immortality. Her startling little flight would imply she did.

May I remind you what Paul said, or do you think of nothing else, these October nights, without her crib to visit?

The little furniture of loss has lips of dirks to stab us. I hope Heaven is warm, there are so many barefoot ones. I hope it is near—the little tourist was so small. I hope it is not so unlike earth that we shall miss the peculiar form —the mould of the bird. "And with what body do they come?" Then they *do* come! Rejoice! What door? What hour? Run, run, my soul! Illuminate the house!

"Body!" then real,—a face and eyes,—to know that it is them! Paul knew the Man that knew the news, He passed through Bethlehem.

With love for you, and your sweet wife, "whom seeing not, we" trust.

COUSIN EMILY

TO *Miss Maria Whitney*

How well I know her not
Whom not to know has been
A bounty in prospective, now
Next door to mine the pain.

EMILY

The handwriting of this first little stanza sent to Miss Whitney is that of the early middle period, and is too definite to be safely dated; but before the next letter, a long interval seems to have elapsed.

To the Same
1877

Vinnie and her sister thank Miss Whitney for the delicate kindness, and remember her with peculiar love these acuter days. . . .

I fear we think too lightly of the gift of mortality, which, too gigantic to comprehend, certainly cannot be estimated.

E. DICKINSON

To the Same
1878

DEAR FRIEND,—I have thought of you often since the darkness,—though we cannot assist another's night. I have hoped you were saved. That he has received Immortality who so often conferred it, invests it with a more sudden charm. . . .

I hope you have the power of hope, and that every bliss we know or guess hourly befalls you.

E. DICKINSON

To the Same

. . . To relieve the irreparable degrades it.

Brabantio's resignation is the only one—"I here do give thee that with all my heart, which but thou hast already, with all my heart I would keep from thee."

EMILY

To the Same
1878

DEAR FRIEND,—I am constantly more astonished that the body contains the spirit—except for overmastering work it could not be borne.

I shall miss saying to Vinnie when we hear the Northampton bell—as in subtle states of the west we do—"Miss Whitney is going to church," though must not everywhere be church to hearts that have, or have had, a friend?

> Could that sweet darkness where they dwell
> Be once disclosed to us,
> The clamor for their loveliness
> Would burst the loneliness.

I trust you may have the dearest summer possible to loss. One sweet, sweet more, one liquid more, of that Arabian presence!

You spoke very sweetly to both of us, and your sewing and recollecting is a haunting picture, a sweet, spectral protection. Your name is taken as tenderly as the names of our birds, or the flower, for some mysterious cause, sundered from its dew. . . .

In a brief memoir of Parepa, in which she was likened to a rose,—"thornless until she died," some bereaved one

added. To miss him is his only stab, but that he never gave!
A word from you would be sacred.

EMILY

. . . The crucifix requires no glove.

To the Same

Intrusiveness of flowers is brooked by even troubled
hearts.

They enter and then knock—then chide their ruthless
sweetness, and then remain forgiven.

May these molest as fondly!

EMILY

To the Same

Than Heaven more remote,
For Heaven is the root,
But these the flitted seed,
More flown indeed
Than ones that never were,
Or those that hide, and are.

What madness, by their side,
A vision to provide
Of future days
They cannot praise.

My soul, to find them, come,
They cannot call, they're dumb,
Nor prove, nor woo,
But that they have abode
Is absolute as God,
And instant, too.

EMILY

To the Same

The face in evanescence lain
Is more distinct than ours,
And ours, considered for its sake,
As capsules are for flowers.

EMILY

To the Same
1879

DEAR FRIEND,—Your touching suggestion . . . is a tender
permission. . . .

We cannot believe for each other—thought is too sacred
a despot, but I hope that God, in whatever form, is true to
our friend. . . . Consciousness is the only home of which
we *now* know. That sunny adverb had been enough, were
it not foreclosed.

When not inconvenient to your heart, please remember
us, and let us help you carry it, if you grow tired. Though
we are each unknown to ourself and each other, 'tis not
what well conferred it, the dying soldier asks, it is only
the water.

We knew not that we were to live,
Nor when we are to die
Our ignorance our cuirass is;
We wear mortality
As lightly as an option gown
Till asked to take it off.
By His intrusion God is known—
It is the same with life.

EMILY

To the Same
November, 1882
Tuesday

SWEET FRIEND,—Our mother ceased. While we bear her dear form through the wilderness, I am sure you are with us.

EMILY

To the Same
1882

DEAR FRIEND,—The guilt of having sent the note had so much oppressed me that I hardly dared to read the reply, and delayed my heart almost to its stifling, sure you would never receive us again. To come unto our own and our own fail to receive us, is a sere response.

I hope you may forgive us.

All is faint indeed without our vanished mother, who achieved in sweetness what she lost in strength, though grief of wonder at her fate made the winter short, and each night I reach finds my lungs more breathless, seeking what it means.

To the bright east she flies,
Brothers of Paradise
Remit her home,
Without a change of wings,
Or Love's convenient things,
Enticed to come.

Fashioning what she is,
Fathoming what she was,
We deem we dream—
And that dissolves the days
Through which existence strays
Homeless at home.

The sunshine almost speaks, this morning, redoubling the division, and Paul's remark grows graphic, "the *weight* of glory."

I am glad you have an hour for books, those enthralling friends, the immortalities, perhaps, each may pre-receive. "And I saw the Heavens opened."

I hope that nothing pains you except the pang of life, sweeter to bear than to omit.

With love and wonder,

EMILY

To the Same

1883?

DEAR FRIEND;—Is not an absent friend as mysterious as a bulb in the ground, and is not a bulb the most captivating floral form? Must it not have enthralled the Bible, if we may infer from its selection? "The lily of the field!"

I never pass one without being chagrined for Solomon, and so in love with "the lily" anew, that were I sure no one saw me, I might make those advances of which in after life I should repent.

The apple-blossoms were slightly disheartened, yesterday, by a snow-storm, but the birds encouraged them all that they could—and how fortunate that the little ones had come to cheer their damask brethren!

You spoke of coming "with the apple-blossoms"—which occasioned our solicitude.

The ravenousness of fondness is best disclosed by children. . . .

Is there not a sweet wolf within us that demands its food?

I can easily imagine your fondness for the little life so mysteriously committed to your care. The bird that asks our crumb has a plaintive distinction. I rejoice that it was possible for you to be with it, for I think the early spiritual influences about a child are more hallowing than we know. The angel begins in the morning in every human life. How small the furniture of bliss! How scant the heavenly fabric!

> No ladder needs the bird but skies
> To situate its wings,
> Nor any leader's grim baton
> Arraigns it as it sings.
> The implements of bliss are few—
> As Jesus says of *Him*,
> "Come unto me" the moiety
> That wafts the cherubim.
>
> EMILY

To the Same

DEAR FRIEND,—You are like God. We pray to Him, and he answers "No." Then we pray to Him to rescind the "no," and He don't answer at all, yet "Seek and ye shall find" is the boon of faith.

You failed to keep your appointment with the apple-blossoms—the japonica, even, bore an apple to elicit you, but that must be a silver bell which calls the human heart.

I still hope that you live, and in lands of consciousness. It is Commencement now. Pathos is very busy.

The past is not a package one can lay away. I see my father's eyes, and those of Mr. Bowles—those isolated comets. If the future is mighty as the past, what may vista be?

With my foot in a sling from a vicious sprain, and reminded of you almost to tears by the week and its witness, I send this sombre word.

The vane defines the wind.

Where we thought you were, Austin says you are not. How strange to change one's sky, unless one's star go with it, but yours has left an astral wake.

Vinnie gives her hand.

Always with love,

EMILY

To the Same

1883

DEAR FRIEND,—Your sweet self-reprehension makes us look within, which is so wild a place we are soon dismayed, but the seed sown in the lake bears the liquid flower, and so of all your words.

I am glad you accept rest.

Too many disdain it. I am glad you go to the Adirondacks.

To me the name is homelike, for one of my lost went every year with an Indian guide, before the woods were broken. Had you been here it would be sweet, but that, like the peach, is later. With a to-morrow in its cupboard, who would be "an hungered"?

Thank you for thinking of Dick. He is now the horse of association.

Men are picking the grass from father's meadow to lay it away for winter, and it takes them a long time. They bring three horses of their own, but Dick, ever gallant, offers to help, and bears a little machine like a top, which spins the grass away.

It seems very much like a gentleman getting his own supper—for what is his supper winter nights but tumblers of clover?

You speak of "disillusion." That is one of the few subjects on which I am an infidel. Life is so strong a vision, not one of it shall fail.

Not what the stars have done, but what they are to do, is what detains the sky.

We shall watch for the promised words from the Adirondacks, and hope the recess will all be joy. To have been made alive is so chief a thing, all else inevitably adds. Were it not riddled by partings, it were too divine.

I was never certain that mother had died, except while the students were singing. The voices came from another life. . . .

Good-night dear. Excuse me for staying so long. I love to come to you. To one who creates, or consoles, thought, what an obligation!

EMILY

To the Same

1883?

DEAR FRIEND,—Has the journey ceased, or is it still progressing, and has Nature won you away from us, as we feared she would?

Othello is uneasy, but then Othellos always are, they hold such mighty stakes.

Austin brought me the picture of Salvini when he was last in Boston.

The brow is that of Deity—the eyes, those of the lost, but the power lies in the *throat*—pleading, sovereign, savage—the panther and the dove!

Each, how innocent!

I hope you found the mountains cordial—followed your meeting with the lakes with affecting sympathy.

Changelessness is Nature's change.

The plants went into camp last night, their tender armor insufficient for the crafty nights.

That is one of the parting acts of the year, and has an emerald pathos—and Austin hangs bouquets of corn in the piazza's ceiling, also an omen, for Austin believes.

The "golden bowl" breaks soundlessly, but it will not be whole again till another year.

Did you read Emily Brontë's marvellous verse?

> "Though earth and man were gone,
> And suns and universes ceased to be,
> And Thou wert left alone,
> Every existence would exist in Thee."

We are pining to know of you, and Vinnie thinks to see you would be the opening of the burr. . . .

EMILY, with love

To the Same
Probably 1884

DEAR FRIEND,—The little package of Ceylon arrived in fragrant safety, and Caliban's "clust'ring filberds" were not so luscious nor so brown.

Honey in March is blissful as inopportune, and to caress the bee a severe temptation, but was not temptation the first zest?

We shall seek to be frugal with our sweet possessions, though their enticingness quite leads us astray, and shall endow Austin, as we often do, after a parched day.

For how much we thank you.

Dear arrears of tenderness we can never repay till the will's great ores are finally sifted; but bullion is better than minted things, for it has no alloy.

Thinking of you with fresher love, as the Bible boyishly says, "New every morning and fresh every evening,"

EMILY

To the Same
Probably 1884

DEAR FRIEND,—I cannot depict a friend to my mind till I know what he is doing, and three of us want to depict you. I inquire your avocation of Austin, and he says you are "engaged in a great work"! That is momentous but not defining. The thought of you in the great city has a halo of wilderness.

Console us by dispelling it. . . .

Vinnie is happy with her duties, her pussies, and her posies, for the little garden within, though tiny, is triumphant.

There are scarlet carnations, with a witching suggestion, and hyacinths covered with promises which I know they will keep.

How precious to hear you ring at the door, and Vinnie ushering you to those melodious moments of which friends are composed.

This also is fiction.

I fear we shall care very little for the technical resurrection, when to behold the one face that to us comprised it is too much for us, and I dare not think of the voraciousness of that only gaze and its only return.

Remembrance is the great tempter.

EMILY

Emily Dickinson's first letter to the son of her old friend, Mr. Bowles, was written four years after his father's death, and contained a spray of pressed jasmine.

To Mr. Samuel Bowles

1882

DEAR FRIEND,—A tree your father gave me bore this priceless flower.

Would you accept it because of him—

> Who abdicated ambush
> And went the way of dusk,
> And now, against his subtle name,
> There stands an asterisk
> As confident of him as we;
> Impregnable we are—
> The whole of Immortality
> Secreted in a star.

E. DICKINSON

To the Same

1882

DEAR FRIEND,—My mother and sister hoped to see you, and I, to have heard the voice in the house that recalls the strange music of your father's. A little bin of blossoms I designed for your breakfast also went astray.

I hope you are in strength, and that the passengers of peace exalt, not rend, your memory. Heaven may give them rank, it could not give them grandeur, for that they carried with themselves.

With fresh remembrance,

E. DICKINSON

To the Same

August 2, 1882

DEAR FRIEND,—Our friend your father was so beautifully and intimately recalled to-day that it seemed impossible he had experienced the secret of death.

A servant who had been with us a long time, and had often opened the door for him, asked me how to spell "genius" yesterday. I told her and she said no more. To-day she asked me what "genius" meant. I told her none had known.

She said she read in a Catholic paper that Mr. Bowles was "the genius of Hampshire," and thought it might be that past gentleman. His look could not be extinguished to any who had seen him, for "because I live, ye shall live also," was his physiognomy.

I congratulate you upon his immortality, which is a constant stimulus to my household, and upon your noble perpetuation of his cherished *Republican*.

Please remember me tenderly to your mother.

With honor,
EMILY DICKINSON

This is the only letter I have found, written since early girlhood, in which Emily Dickinson signed her name in this way.

About 1882 she wrote of the elder Mr. Bowles to another friend, "I dreamed Saturday night of precious Mr. Bowles. One glance of his would light a world." Upon learning of his son's engagement, Emily sent her unique congratulation:—

October, 1883

DEAR FRIEND,—

The clock strikes one that just struck two—
Some schism in the sum;

A sorcerer from Genesis
Has wrecked the pendulum.
    With warmest congratulation,
                E. DICKINSON

After the birth of Samuel Bowles the Fifth:

                To the Same
                August, 1885

DEAR FRIEND,—I did not know.
God bless you indeed!
Extend to that small hand my own "right hand of fellow-ship," and guide the woman of your heart softly to my own.
I give "his angels charge"—well-remembered angels, whose absence only dims our eyes. The magnanimity I asked, you how freely gave!
If ever of any act of mine you should be in need, let me reply with the laureate, "Speak that I live to hear."
                Vitally,
                E. DICKINSON

                To the Same
                August 19, 1885

DEAR FRIEND,—May I ask a service so sacred as that you will address and mail a note to the friend of my friend Mrs. Jackson? I do not know Mr. Jackson's address, and desire to write him.
That your loved confederate and yourself are in ceaseless peace is my happy faith.
The sweet-peas you hallowed stand in carmine sheaves. Would that you could plunder them.
                Gratefully,
                E. DICKINSON

To the Same
On receiving some flowers
Dear Friends,—Had I not known I was not asleep, I
should have feared I dreamed, so blissful was their beauty,
but day and they demurred. . . .
With joyous thanks,
E. Dickinson

*In the dim and early dawn of a fragrant summer morning
soon after, Emily caused a large cluster of sweet-peas to be
gathered from her dewy, old-fashioned garden, that they
might be put on the very first train to Springfield, taking
the freshness of summer itself to her friends. This note
accompanied them:—*

Dawn and dew my bearers be.
Ever,
Butterfly

*And the old garden still overflows with annual fragrance
and color. Its armies of many-hued hyacinths run riot in
the spring sunshine, while crocuses and daffodils peer above
the fresh grass under the apple-trees; a large magnolia holds
its pink cups toward the blue sky, and scarlet hawthorn
lights a greenly dusky corner.*
*And then the roses, and the hedges of sweet-peas; the
masses of nasturtiums, and the stately procession of hollyhocks, in happy association with huge bushes of lemon
verbena! Still later comes the autumn glory, with salvia and
brilliant zinnias and marigolds and clustering chrysanthe-*

mums, until "ranks of seeds their witness bear," and November folds her brown mantle over sleeping flowers.

This sweet garden, with its whiffs of long ago, needs only borders of box and a sun-dial to be the ideally imagined pleasure-spot of vanished generations. And Emily seems its presiding genius; it is instinct with her presence still, though even before her death years had passed since her footsteps pressed its paths, or her fingers gathered its riches.

In different mood from the cheerful letters to Mr. Bowles are these more sombre ones to Mr. Clark. Begun by association through the death of a mutual friend, they continued to be tinged with the sadness of other and following deaths, until his own, when letters to his brother took their place until almost her own flitting.

T O *Mr. F. D. Clark*

1882

. . . He never spoke of himself, and encroachment I know would have slain him. . . . He was a dusk gem, born of troubled waters, astray in any crest below. Heaven might give him peace, it could not give him grandeur, for that he carried with himself to whatever scene. . . .

> Obtaining but his own extent
> In whatsoever realm,
> 'Twas Christ's own personal expanse
> That bore him from the tomb.

To the Same
Late Autumn, 1882

DEAR FRIEND,—It pains us very much that you have been more ill. We hope you may not be suffering now.

Thank you for speaking so earnestly when our mother died. We have spoken daily of writing you, but have felt unable. The great attempt to save her life had it been successful would have been fatigueless, but failing, strength forsook us.

No verse in the Bible has frightened me so much from a child as "from him that hath not, shall be taken even that he hath." Was it because its dark menace deepened our own door? You speak as if you still missed your mother. I wish we might speak with you. As we bore her dear form through the wilderness, light seemed to have stopped.

Her dying feels to me like many kinds of cold—at times electric, at times benumbing,—then a trackless waste love has never trod. . . .

The letter from the skies, which accompanied yours, was indeed a boon. A letter always seemed to me like Immortality, for is it not the mind alone, without corporeal friend?

I hope you may tell us that you are better.

Thank you for much kindness. The friend anguish reveals is the slowest forgot.

E. DICKINSON

To the Same
March, 1883

DEAR FRIEND,—In these few few weeks of ignorance of you, we trust that you are growing stronger, and drawing near that sweet physician, an approaching spring, for the ear of the heart hears bluebirds already, those enthralling signals. . . . The great confidences of life are first disclosed by their departure, and I feel that I ceaselessly ought to thank you. . . . Our household is scarcely larger than yours —Vinnie and I and two servants composing our simple realm, though my brother is with us often each day. I wish

A Letter always
seemed to me like
Immortality, for is
it not the Mind
alone, without Cor-
poreal friend?
I hope you may
tell us that you
are better.
Thank you for
much kindness.
The friend
Anguish reveals
is the slowest
forgot.
E. Dickinson.

LETTER TO MR. F. D. CLARK, *facsimile*

I could show you the hyacinths that embarrass us by their loveliness, though to cower before a flower is perhaps unwise, but beauty is often timidity—perhaps oftener pain.

A soft "Where is she?" is all that is left of our loved mother, and thank you for all you told us of yours. . . .

Faithfully,

E. DICKINSON

To the Same

1883

DEAR FRIEND,—To thank you is impossible, because your gifts are from the sky, more precious than the birds, because more disembodied. I can only express my rejoiced surprise by the phrase in the Scripture, "And I saw the Heavens opened." . . .

Fathoms are sudden neighbors.

Ignorant till your note that our President's dying had defrauded you, we are grieved anew, and hasten to offer you our sorrow.

We shall make Mrs. Chadbourne's acquaintance in flowers after a few days. "Displeasure" would be a morose word toward a friend so earnest, and we only fear when you delay, that you feel more ill. Allow us to hear the birds for you, should they indeed come.

E. D.

This is the last letter to Mr. Clark, and upon hearing of his farther illness, she wrote his brother:—

T O *Mr. C. H. Clark*

April 18, 1883

DEAR FRIEND,—Would it be possible you would excuse me if I once more inquire for the health of the brother whom association has made sacred?

With the trust that your own is impairless, and that fear for your brother has not too much depressed you, please accept the solicitude of myself and my sister.

E. DICKINSON

To the Same

April 22, 1883

DEAR FRIEND,—The sorrowful tidings of your note almost dissuade reply, lest I for one moment take you from your brother's bedside. I have delayed to tell my sister till I hear again, fearing to newly grieve her, and hoping an encouraging word by another mail.

Please be sure we are with you in sorrowing thought, and take your brother's hand for me, if it is still with you. Perhaps the one has called him of whom we have so often talked during this grieved year.

With sympathy,

E. DICKINSON

To the Same

May 1, 1883

DEAR FRIEND,—The temptation to inquire every morning for your sufferer is almost irresistible, but our own invalid taught us that a sick room is at times too sacred a place for a friend's knock, timid as that is.

I trust this sweet May morning is not without its peace to your brother and you, though the richest peace is of sorrow.

With constant and fervent anxiousness, and the hope of an early word, please be sure we share your suspense.

E. Dickinson

To the Same
May 21, 1883

Dear Friend,—We have much fear, both for your own strength and the health of your brother, having heard nothing since we last asked, many days ago. Will you not, when possible, gives us but a syllable, even a cheering accent, if no more be true? We think of you and your sufferer with intense anxiety, wishing some act or word of ours might be hope or help. The humming-birds and orioles fly by me as I write, and I long to guide their enchanted feet to your brother's chamber.

Excuse me for knocking. Please also excuse me for staying so long. Spring is a strange land when our friends are ill.

With my sister's tenderest alarm, as also my own,

E. Dickinson

To the Same
June 7, 1883

I had, dear friend, the deep hope that I might see your brother before he passed from life, or rather life we know, and can scarcely express the pang I feel at its last denial.

His rare and hallowed kindness had strangely endeared him, and I cannot be comforted not to thank him before he went so far.

I never had met your brother but once. An unforgotten once—to have seen him but once more would have been almost like an interview with my "Heavenly Father" whom he loved and knew. I hope he was able to speak with you in his closing moment. One accent of courage as he took his flight would assist your heart. I am eager to know all you may tell me of those final days. We asked for him every morning, in heart, but feared to disturb you by inquiry aloud. I hope you are not too far exhausted from your "loved employ."

To know of you when possible would console us much, and every circumstance of him we had hoped to see. . . .

E. D.

To the Same
June 16, 1883

DEAR FRIEND,—Thank you for the paper. I felt it almost a bliss of sorrow that the name so long in Heaven on earth, should be on earth in Heaven.

Do you know if either of his sons have his mysterious face or his momentous nature?

The stars are not hereditary. I hope your brother and himself resumed the tie above, so dear to each below. Your bond to your brother reminds me of mine to my sister— early, earnest, indissoluble. Without her life were fear, and Paradise a cowardice, except for her inciting voice.

Should you have any picture of your brother, I should rejoice to see it at some convenient hour—and though we cannot know the last, would you sometime tell me as near the last as your grieved voice is able? . . .

Are you certain there is another life? When over- whelmed to know, I fear that few are sure.

My sister gives her grief with mine. Had we known in time, your brother would have borne our flowers in his mute hand. With tears,

E. DICKINSON

To the Same
July 9, 1883

DEAR FRIEND,—While I thank you immediately for the invaluable gift, I cannot express the bereavement that I am no more to behold it. Believing that we are to have no face in a farther life, makes the look of a friend a boon almost too precious.

The resemblance is faithful—the scholarly gentleness— the noble modesty—the absence of every dross, quite there. What a consoling prize to you, his mate through years of anguish so much sharper to see because endured so willingly.

Chastening would seem unneeded by so supreme a spirit.

I feel great grief for you—I hope his memory may help you, so recently a life. I wish I might say one liquid word to make your sorrow less. Is not the devotion that you gave him an acute balm? Had you not been with him how solitary the will of God!

Thank you for every word of his pure career. I hope it is nearer us than we are aware. Will you not still tell us of yourself and your home—from which this patient guest has flown? I am glad he lies near us—and thank you for the tidings of our other fugitive, whom to know was life. I can scarcely tell you how deeply I cherish your thoughtfulness. To still know of the dead is a great permission, and you have almost enabled that. With the ceaseless sympathy of myself and my sister, and the trust that our sufferer rests,

E. DICKINSON

To the Same

January 4, 1884

DEAR FRIEND,—I have been very ill since early October, and unable to thank you for the sacred kindness, but treasured it each day, and hasten with my first steps, and my fullest gratitude. . . . I never can thank you as I feel. That would be impossible. The effort ends in tears. You seem, by some deep accident, to be the only tie between the Heaven that evanesced, and the Heaven that stays. I hope the winged days that bear you to your brother are not too destitute of song, and wish that we might speak with you of him and of yourself, and of the third member of that sundered trio. Perhaps another spring would call you to Northampton, and memory might invite you here. . . .

With a deep New Year,

Your friend,

E. DICKINSON

Enclosing pressed flowers, February 22, 1884

DEAR FRIEND,—I hoped it might gratify you to meet the little flower which was my final ministry to your brother, and which even in that faint hour, I trust he recognized, though the thronged spirit had not access to words.

These are my first out, and their golden trifles are too full of association to remain unshared.

With faithful thought of yourself and your brother, brothers in bereavement even as myself,

E. DICKINSON

To the Same

April 21, 1884

Never unmindful of your anxiety for your father, dear friend, I refrained from asking, lest even the moment engrossed by reply, might take you from him.

The peril of a parent is a peculiar pang, and one which my sister and myself so long experienced,—oh, would it were longer, for even fear for them were dearer than their absence,—that we cannot resist to offer you our earnest sympathy. I most sincerely trust that the sight is redeemed, so precious to you both, more than vicariously to you— even filially—and that the added fear has not exhausted you beyond the art of spring to cheer.

I have lost, since writing you, another cherished friend, a word of whom I enclose—and how to repair my shattered ranks is a besetting pain. Be sure that my sister and myself never forget your brother, nor his bereaved comrade.

To be certain we were to meet our lost would be a vista of reunion who of us could bear? . . .

Faithfully,

E. DICKINSON

To the Same

April 22, 1884

DEAR FRIEND,—These thoughts disquiet me, and the great friend is gone who could solace them. Do they disturb you?

> The spirit lasts, but in what mode—
> Below, the body speaks,
> But as the spirit furnishes—
> Apart it never talks.
> The music in the violin
> Does not emerge alone

But arm in arm with touch, yet touch
Alone is not a tune.
The spirit lurks within the flesh
Like tides within the sea
That make the water live; estranged
What would the either be?
Does that know now, or does it cease,
That which to this is done,
Resuming at a mutual date
With every future one?
Instinct pursues the adamant
Exacting this reply—
Adversity, if it may be,
Or wild prosperity,
The rumor's gate was shut so tight
Before my mind was sown,
Not even a prognostic's push
Could make a dent thereon.

> With the trust you live,
>
> E. Dickinson

To the Same
January 18, 1885

Dear Friend,—Though no New Year be old, to wish yourself and your honored father a new and happy one is involuntary, and I am sure we are both reminded of that sacred past which has forever hallowed us.

I trust the years which they behold are also new and happy, or is it a joyous expanse of year, without bisecting months—untiring Anno Domini? Had we but one assuring word, but a letter is a joy of earth—it is denied the gods. Vivid in our immortal group we still behold your brother, and never hear Northampton bells without saluting him. . . .

Have you blossoms and books, those solaces of sorrow? That, I would also love to know, and receive for yourself and your father the forgetless sympathy of

Your friend,
E. DICKINSON

To the Same
April 21, 1885

DEAR FRIEND,—The flower for which your brother cared resumes its siren circuit, and choosing a few for his name's sake, I enclose them to you. Perhaps from some far site he overlooks their transit, and smiles at the beatitudes so recently his own. Ephemeral, eternal heart!

I hope you are in health, and that the fragile father has every peace that years possess. . . .

We think of your small mansion with unabated warmth, though is not any mansion vast that contains a father?

That this beloved spring inspirit both yourself and him, is our exceeding wish.

E. DICKINSON

The final letter to Mr. Clark was written a year later, and will be found in the last chapter.

TO *Mr. and Mrs. J. L. Jenkins, Mrs. Hanson Read, Mrs. W. A. Stearns, Mrs. Edward Tuckerman, Mrs. J. S. Cooper, Mrs. A. B. H. Davis, Mrs. H. F. Hills, Mrs. Jameson, Mr. F. F. Emerson, Maggie Maher, Mr. and Mrs. George Montague, Mrs. W. F. Stearns, Mr. J. K. Chickering, Mrs. Joseph Sweetser, Mr. Thomas Niles, Mrs. Carmichael, Dr. and Mrs. Thomas P. Field, Mr. Theodore Holland, "H. H.," Miss Eugenia Hall, Mrs. E. P. Crowell, and Mrs. J. C. Greenough*

THE CHARACTERISTIC *notes in this chapter were, with few exceptions, written to friends in Amherst, accompanying flowers or other dainties, or acknowledging those sent to herself,—not infrequently a sentence of consolation for some pain, or a few words of cheering appreciation for a new happiness.*

The first may be dated as early as 1872; but the largest number are, undoubtedly, to be assigned to the last six or seven years of Emily Dickinson's life.

After her father's death, her retirement from ordinary forms of human intercourse became almost complete; and these notes were the sole link still binding her to the world,—and to only such part of the world as might be represented by those for whom she cared.

Emily's prose style had developed its incisiveness,—like her own thought, it went straight to the essence of things; and while still dressed in language sufficiently to pass in conventional places, it had gradually become divested of everything superfluous.

While the meaning of certain phrases has sometimes puzzled those who received the notes, there is invariably an original, sparkling interpretation for every sentence, clear to any soul possessing even slight accord with hers. Because frequently couched in the form of apparently mysterious oracles, the meaning is sometimes looked for too deeply,—often it is singularly obvious. The remarkable character of these notes seems to have increased as she lived farther and farther away from the years when she had seen and conversed with her friends; and her life was full of thought and occupation during these introspective days. It is impossible to conceive that any sense of personal isolation, or real loneliness of spirit, because of the absence of humanity from her daily life, could have oppressed a nature so richly endowed.

Most of us would require some sudden blow, some fierce crisis, to produce such a result,—a hidden and unusual life like hers. And we love to believe striking and theatrical things of our neighbors; it panders to that romantic element latent in the plainest. But Emily Dickinson's method of living was so simple and natural an outcome of her increasingly shy nature, a development so perfectly in the line of her whole constitution that no far-away and dramatic explanation of her quiet life is necessary to those who are capable of apprehending her.

That sentence alone would reveal the key wherein she wrote with regret for her long-time maid Margaret: "I winced at her loss, for I am in the habit of her, and even a new rolling-pin has an embarrassing element."

Emerson somewhere says, "Now and then a man exquisitely made can live alone"; and Lord Bacon puts the thought with even greater force and directness,—"Whosoever is delighted in Solitude is either a Wilde Beast or a God."

To some natures, introspection is a necessity for expression. "Why should I feel lonely?" exclaimed Thoreau, in his temporary isolation at Walden, "Is not our planet in the Milky Way?" He was, indeed, "no more lonely than the North Star," nor, I believe, was Emily Dickinson, although congenial companionship had, in a sense, been very dear to her.

She has herself written:—

> Never for society
> He shall seek in vain
> Who his own acquaintance
> Cultivates; of men
> Wiser men may weary,
> But the man within
> Never knew satiety,—
> Better entertain
> Than could Border Ballad,
> Or Biscayan Hymn;
> Neither introduction
> Need you—unto him.

Georg Ebers once wrote: "Sheep and geese become restless when separated from the flock; the eagle and lion seek isolation,"—a picturesque and perhaps not less strong presentation of a nearly identical thought.

But although invisible for years, even to life-long friends, Emily never denied herself to children. To them she was always accessible, always delightful, and in their eyes a sort of fairy guardian. Stories are yet told of her roguishly lowering baskets of "goodies" out of her window by a string to little ones waiting below. Mr. MacGregor Jenkins, in a sketch of his recollections of Emily Dickinson,[13] has shown this gracious and womanly side of her nature in a very charming way, quoting a number of her notes to himself and his sister, two members of a quartette of children admitted to her intimacy. Many of Emily Dickinson's daintiest verses are for children,—among them The Sleeping Flowers *and* Out of the Morning.

The notes written during their childhood to Mr. Jenkins and his sister follow, with others to their father and mother:—

1872?

HAPPY "DID" AND MAC,—We can offer you nothing so charming as your own hearts, which we would seek to possess, had we the requisite wiles.

DEAR BOYS,—Please never grow up, which is "far better." Please never "improve"—you are perfect now.

EMILY

LITTLE WOMEN,—Which shall it be, geraniums or tulips?

The butterfly upon the sky, who doesn't know its name,
And hasn't any tax to pay, and hasn't any home,
Is just as high as you and I, and higher, I believe—
So soar away and never sigh, for that's the way to grieve.

---

[13] *The Christian Union*, October 24, 1891.

KATIE "DID" FROM KATIE "DIDN'T"

Will the sweet child who sent me the butterflies, herself a member of the same ethereal nation, accept a rustic kiss, flavored, we trust, with clover?

AMHERST
Christmas, 1874

. . . Atmospherically it was the most beautiful Christmas on record. The hens came to the door with Santa Claus, the pussies washed themselves in the open air without chilling their tongues, and Santa Claus—sweet old gentleman —was even gallanter than usual. Visitors from the chimney were a new dismay, but all of them brought their hands so full and behaved so sweetly, only a churl could have turned them away. And then the ones at the barn were so happy! Maggie gave the hens a check for potatoes, each of the cats had a gilt-edged bone, and the horse had new blankets from Boston.

Do you remember dark-eyed Mr. Dickinson who used to shake your hand when it was so little it had hardly a stem? He, too, had a beautiful gift of roses from a friend away. It was a lovely Christmas. But what made you remember me? Tell me with a kiss—or is it a secret?

EMILY

To a niece of her father's, who had sent for his grave the roses alluded to, she wrote:—

December, 1874

I am sure you must have remembered that father had "become as little children," or you would never have dared send him a Christmas gift, for you know how he frowned upon Santa Claus, and all such prowling gentlemen.

TO *the Rev. J. L. Jenkins and Mrs. Jenkins*

Enclosing some sprays of rowen tied with white ribbon
Autumn, 187–

DEAR MR. AND MRS. PASTOR,—Mrs. Holland pleased us and grieved us, by telling us your triumphs.

We want you to conquer, but we want you to conquer here.

"Marathon" is me. Is there nothing but glow in the new horizon?

You see we keep a jealous heart. That is Love's alloy.

Vinnie is full of wrath, and vicious as Saul toward the Holy Ghost, in whatever form. I heard her declaiming the other night, to a foe that called—and sent Maggie to part them.

Vinnie lives on the hope that you will return. Is it quite fictitious? You are gone too long.

The red leaves take the green leaves' place, and the landscape yields. We go to sleep with the peach in our hands and wake with the stone, but the stone is the pledge of summers to come.

Love for each of you, always, and if there are lands longer than "always," love also for those.

These are sticks of rowen for your stove. It was chopped by bees, and butterflies piled it, Saturday afternoons.

EMILY

To the Same
1875?

. . . There would have been no smile on Amherst's face, had she believed her clergyman's sweet wife to be suffering, but the paper spoke so obligingly, we thought it an accident that endeared, rather than endangered. That sorrow dare to touch the loved is a mournful insult—we are all avenging it all the time, though as Lowell quotes from the stranger "Live—live even to be unkind."

It is hard to think of our "little friend" as a sufferer—we, peculiarly, know how hard, through our suffering mother —but the tiniest ones are the mightiest—the wren will prevail . . .

"Bruised for our iniquities" I had almost feared. Amherst, tell her, suggests her—each of you, my shepherd, and will, while will remains.

EMILY

To the Same

Would you feel more at home with a flower from home in your hand, dear?

To the Same

May the love that occasioned the first Easter shelter a few, this bereaved day.

To the Same
1877?

DEAR FRIEND,—It was pathetic to see your voice, instead of hearing it, for it had grown sweetly familiar in the house, as a bird's.

Father left us in June—you leave us in May. I am glad there will be no April till another year. . . .

Sorrow is unsafe, when it is real sorrow—I am glad so many are counterfeits—guileless because they believe themselves.

Kiss "Diddie" and Mac for us—precious refugees, with

TO *THE REV. AND MRS. J. L. JENKINS · 1878*

love for our brother, whom with yourself, we follow the peculiar distance, "even unto the end."

Perhaps it is "the end" now—I think the *bell* thought so, because it bade us all good-by when you stood in the door.

You concealed that you heard it. Thank you.

EMILY

June, 1878

You deserved a tiding before, dear.

Your little punctualities are generous and precious. . . .

There is a circus here, and farmers' Commencement, and boys and girls from Tripoli, and Governors and swords parade the summer streets. They lean upon the fence that guards the quiet church ground, and jar the grass, now warm and soft as a tropic nest.

Many people call, and wish for you with tears, and Vinnie beats her wings like a maddened bird, whose home has been invaded.

So much has been sorrow, that to fall asleep in Tennyson's verse, seems almost a pillow. "To where beyond these voices there is Peace."

I hope you are each safe. It is homeless without you, and we think of others possessing you with the throe of Othello.

Mother gives her love—Maggie pleads her own. Austin smiles when you mention him. . . .

Daisies and ferns are with us, and he whose meadow they magnify, is always linked with you.

EMILY

TO *Mrs. Hanson Read*

Accompanying flowers for the funeral of her two little boys
December 27, 1873
Vinnie says your martyrs were fond of flowers.
Would these profane their vase?

EMILY

To the Same
Upon a subsequent anniversary
My DEAR MRS. READ,—We have often thought of you
to-day, and almost spoken with you, but thought you might
like to be alone—if one can be alone with so thronged a
Heaven.

E. DICKINSON

TO *Mrs. W. A. Stearns*

Autumn, 1874

Will the dear ones who eased the grieved days spurn the
fading orchard?

EMILY

To the Same
Upon receiving an Easter card, probably 1875
It is possible, dear friend, that the rising of the one we
lost would have engrossed me to the exclusion of Christ's
—but for your lovely admonition.

Sabbath morning was peculiarly dear to my father, and
his unsuspecting last earthly day with his family was that
heavenly one.

Vinnie and I were talking of you as we went to sleep Saturday night, which makes your beautiful gift of to-day almost apparitional.

Please believe how sweetly I thank you.

EMILY

To the Same
1875

What tenements of clover
Are fitting for the bee,
What edifices azure
For butterflies and me—
What residences nimble
Arise and evanesce
Without a rhythmic rumor
Or an assaulting guess.

With love,
E. DICKINSON

To the Same
1875

DEAR FRIEND,—That a pansy is transitive, is its only pang.

This, precluding that, is indeed divine.

Bringing you handfuls in prospective, thank you for the love. Many an angel, with its needle, toils beneath the snow.

With tenderness for your mate,
EMILY

Spring, 1876

DEAR FRIENDS,—Might these be among the fabrics which the Bible designates as beyond rubies?

Certainly they are more accessible to the fingers of your thief

EMILY

When President Stearns died, this stanza came to Mrs. Stearns:—

June 8, 1876

Love's stricken "why"
Is all that love can speak—
Built of but just a syllable
The hugest hearts that break.

EMILY

At the death of Professor Snell, September 18, 1876, Emily sent to his family a beautiful mass of flowers, purple and white; and with them, this single line:—

I had a father once.

T O *Mrs. Stearns*

In response to a box of strawberries received early in March 1877?

DEAR FRIEND,—The little package of nectar mother opened herself, though her hands are frail as a child's.

She could not believe them real till I had hidden one in her mouth, which somewhat convinced her. She asks me to thank you tenderly. The love of her friends is the only remnant of her grieved life, and she clings to it timidly.

I hope you are quite well, and am sure we sometimes think of each other, endeared by that most hallowed thorn, a mutual loss.

With sweet remembrance for your niece, of whom my sister speaks,

EMILY

To the Same
1878

DEAR FRIENDS,—The seraphic shame generosity causes is perhaps its most heavenly result.

To make even Heaven more heavenly, is within the aim of us all.

I was much touched by the little fence dividing the devotions, though devotion should always wear a fence, to pre-empt its claim.

Why the full heart is speechless, is one of the great wherefores.

EMILY, with love

To the Same
1879?

DEAR FRIENDS,—I hope no bolder lover brought you the first pond lilies. The water is deeper than the land. The swimmer never stagnates.

I shall bring you a handful of lotus next, but do not tell the Nile.

He is a jealous brook.

EMILY

To the Same

"A little flower, a faded flower, the gift of one who cared for me."

Please usurp the pronoun.

Emily

The first of the following notes, accompanied with a box of flowers, was an apology for tardy congratulations upon Mrs. Tuckerman's safe return from a long visit in Europe:

TO *Mrs. Edward Tuckerman*

January, 1874

Dear Friend,—I fear my congratulation, like repentance according to Calvin, is too late to be plausible, but might there not be an exception, were the delight or the penitence found to be durable?

Emily

To the Same
March, 1875

Dear Friend,—It was so long my custom to seek you with the birds, they would scarcely feel at home should I do otherwise, though as home itself is far from home since my father died, why should custom tire?

Emily

To the Same, sent with yellow flowers when the country was drenched in rain

May, 1875

I send you inland buttercups as out-door flowers are still at sea.

Emily

To the Same

Accompanying a box of the delicious chocolate caramels she sent her friends at New Year's, with the recipe

Vinnie says the dear friend would like the rule. We have no statutes here, but each does as it will, which is the sweetest jurisprudence.

With it, I enclose Love's "remainder biscuit," somewhat scorched perhaps in baking, but "Love's oven is warm." Forgive the base proportions.

The fairer ones were borne away. The canna was a privilege, the little box a bliss, and the blossoms so real that a fly waylaid them, but I lured him away.

Again receive the love which comes without aspect, and without herald goes.

EMILY

To the Same
About 1877

DEAR FRIEND,—Accept my timid happiness.

No joy can be in vain, but adds to some bright total, whose dwelling is unknown.

The immortality of flowers must enrich our own, and we certainly should resent a redemption that excluded them.

Was not the "breath of fragrance" designed for your cheek solely?

The fear that it was crimsons my own, though to divide its Heaven is Heaven's highest half.

E. DICKINSON

To the Same
June, 1878

Is it that words are suddenly small, or that we are suddenly large, that they cease to suffice us to thank a friend? Perhaps it is chiefly both.

To the Same
July, 1878

Would it be prudent to subject an apparitional interview to a grosser test?

The Bible portentously says "that which is spirit is spirit."

> Go not too near a house of rose,
> The depredation of a breeze
> Or inundation of a dew
> Alarm its walls away;
> Nor try to tie the butterfly,
> Nor climb the bars of ecstasy,
> In insecurity to lie
> Is joy's insuring quality.

E. DICKINSON

To the Same
August, 1878

To see is perhaps never quite the sorcery that it is to surmise, though the obligation to enchantment is always binding.

It is sweet to recall that we need not retrench, as magic is our most frugal meal.

I fear you have much happiness, because you spend so much.

Would adding to it take it away, or is that a penurious question?

To cherish you is intuitive.
As we take Nature, without permission, let us covet you.

To the Same
January, 1879

Your coming is a symptom of summer.
The symptom excels the malady.

To the Same
September, 1879

Should dear Mrs. Tuckerman have no pears like mine,
I should never cease to be harrowed.
Should she, that also would be dismay.
I incur the peril.

EMILY

To the Same
January 5, 1880

DEAR FRIEND,—Your sweetness intimidates.

Had it been a mastiff that guarded Eden, we should
have feared him less than we do the angel.

I read your little letter. It had, like bliss, the minute
length.

It were dearer had you protracted it; but the sparrow
must not propound his crumb.

We shall find the cube of the rainbow,
Of that there is no doubt;
But the arc of a lover's conjecture
Eludes the finding out.

Confidingly,
EMILY

To the Same
March, 1880

The robin is a Gabriel
In humble circumstances,
His dress denotes him socially
Of transport's working classes.
He has the punctuality
Of the New England farmer—
The same oblique integrity,
A vista vastly warmer.
A small but sturdy residence,
A self-denying household,
The guests of perspicacity
Are all that cross his threshold.
As covert as a fugitive,
Cajoling consternation
By ditties to the enemy.
And sylvan punctuation.

EMILY

To the Same
1880

Will the little hands that have brought me so much
tenderness, the sweet hands in which a bird would love to
lie, the fingers that knew no estrangement except the gulf
of down,—will such enfold a daphne?

Almost I trust they will, yet trust is such a shelving
word; part of our treasures are denied us, part of them pro-
visoed, like bequests available far hence, part of them we
partake.

Which, dear, are divinest?

EMILY

To the Same
November, 1880

Thank you, sweet friend, I am quite better.
Were I not, your dainty redemption would save me.
With love and a happy flower,

EMILY

To the Same
1880

Love is done when love's begun,
Sages say.
But have sages known?
Truth adjourn your boon
Without day.

EMILY

To the Same
After Professor Root's death, December, 1880

DEAR FRIEND,—I thought of you, although I never saw
your friend.

Brother of Ophir,
Bright adieu,
Honor the shortest
Route to you.

EMILY

To the Same
New Year's Day, 1881
Saturday

My bird, who is "to-day"?
"Yesterday" was a year ago, and yet

The stem of a departed flower
Has still a silent rank,
The bearer from an emerald court
Of a despatch of pink.

Thank you for the lovely love.

EMILY

To the Same
1881

To find my sweet friend is more difficult than to bless
her, though I trust both are slightly possible this dearest
afternoon.

EMILY

The following little poem-note contained a pressed dandelion tied with scarlet ribbon.

To the Same
November 8, 1881

The dandelion's pallid tube
Astonishes the grass,
And winter instantly becomes
An infinite *Alas.*
The tube uplifts a signal bud,
And then a shouting flower;
The proclamation of the suns
That sepulture is o'er.

Vinnie told me, dear friend, you were speaking of Mr.
Root.

EMILY

To the Same
December, 1881

DEAR FRIEND,—Vinnie asked me if I had any message for you, and while I was picking it, you ran away.

> Not seeing, still we know,
> Not knowing, guess;
> Not guessing, smile and hide
> And half caress,
> And quake and turn away;
> Seraphic fear!
> Is Eden's innuendo
> "If you dare"?

EMILY

To the Same
January, 1882

DEAR FRIEND,—The gray afternoon—the sweet knock, and the ebbing voice of the boys are a pictorial memory; and then the little bins and the purple kernels—'twas like the larder of a doll.

To the inditing heart we wish no sigh had come.

> Sweet pirate of the heart,
> Not pirate of the sea,
> What wrecketh thee?
> Some spice's mutiny—
> Some attar's perfidy?
> Confide in me.

EMILY

To the Same
January, 1883

The presence in life of so sweet an one is of itself fortune—a covert wealth of spirit I shall not disclose.

I have taken all the naughty boys, and Vinnie the navy.
What lovely conceits!

Then the little Smyrna in the dish—how tiny, how affecting—though the heart in the rear *not* tiny. Oh, no, vast
as the sea.

To caress its billows is our liquid aim.

EMILY, with love

To the Same
June, 1883

Sweet foot, that comes when we call it! I can go but a
step a century, now.

> How slow the wind, how slow the sea,
> How late their feathers be!

Lovingly,
EMILY

To the Same
August, 1883

> We wear our sober dresses when we die,
> But summer, frilled as for a holiday,
> Adjourns her sigh.

To the Same
January, 1884

DEAR FRIEND:—

> To try to speak, and miss the way,
> And ask it of the tears,
> Is gratitude's sweet poverty,
> The tatters that he wears.

A better coat, if he possessed,
Would help him to conceal,
Not subjugate, the mutineer
Whose title is "the soul."

EMILY, with love

To the Same
February, 1884

Do "men gather grapes of thorns"?

No, but they do of *roses,* and even the classic fox hushed his innuendo, as we unclasped the little box.

Sherbets untold, and recollection more sparkling than sherbets!

How wondrous is a friend, the gift of neither Heaven nor earth, yet coveted of both!

If the "archangels veil their faces," is not the sacred diffidence on this sweet behalf?

EMILY

To the Same
April, 1884

Be encouraged, sweet friend! How cruel we did not know! But the battles of those we love are often unseen.

"If Thou hadst been here," Mary said, "our brother had not died." Hanging my head and my heart with it, that you sorrowed alone,

Late, but lovingly,
EMILY

To the Same
April, 1885

DEAR FRIEND,—We want you to wake—Easter has come and gone.

Morning without you is a dwindled dawn.

Quickened toward all celestial things by crows I heard this morning, accept a loving caw from a

Nameless friend.

'SELAH'

To the Same
May, 1885

We trust the repairs of the little friend are progressing swiftly, though shall we love her as well, revamped?

Anatomical dishabille is sweet to those who prize us.

A chastened grace is twice a grace. Nay, 'tis a holiness.

With a sweet May day,

EMILY

To the Same
October, 1885

DEAR FRIEND,—I thought of you on your lonely journey, certain the hallowed heroine was gratified, though mute. I trust you return in safety and with closer clutch for that which remains, for dying whets the grasp.

October is a mighty month, for in it little Gilbert died. "Open the door," was his last cry, "the boys are waiting for me." Quite used to his commandment, his little aunt obeyed, and still two years and many days, and he does not return.

Where makes my lark his nest?

But Corinthians' bugle obliterates the birds', so covering your loved heart to keep it from another shot,

Tenderly,

EMILY

TO *Mrs. J. S. Cooper*

June, 1874

Though a stranger, I am unwilling not to thank you personally for the delicate attention to my family.

For the comprehension of suffering, one must one's self have suffered.

E. DICKINSON

To the Same
Later Summer, 1874

DEAR FRIEND,—It was my first impulse to take them to my father, whom I cannot resist the grief to expect.

Thank you.

VINNIE'S SISTER

And to another friend, about the same time, she wrote:—

Should it be possible for me to speak of my father before I behold him, I shall try to do so to you, whom he always remembered.

EMILY

TO *Mrs. F. S. Cooper*

January, 1875

Is it too late to express my sorrow for my grieved friend?

Though the first moment of loss is eternity, other eternities remain

> Though the great waters sleep
> That they are still the deep
> We cannot doubt.
> No vacillating God
> Ignited this abode
> To put it out.

To the Same

On the anniversary of her father's death, June 16, 1875

DEAR FRIEND,—You thought of it.

How dear, how delicate!

With peculiar love,
YOUR STRANGER

To the Same
1875

How can one be fatherless who has a father's friend within confiding reach?

To the Same

"My country, 'tis of thee,"
has always meant the woods to me.
"Sweet land of liberty,"
I trust is your own.

To the Same
After a fire, in 1876

DEAR FRIEND,—I congratulate you.

Disaster endears beyond fortune.

E. DICKINSON

To the Same

The keeper of golden flowers need have no fear of the "Silver Bill."

An Indies in the hand, at all times fortifying, is peculiarly so, perhaps, to-day.

Midas was a rogue.

To the Same

1876

DEAR FRIEND,—Mother thanks you through me, as she does not use her hand for writing. I hope the vicariousness may not impair the fervor.

Mother is very fond of flowers and of recollection, that sweetest flower.

Please accept her happiness, and ours for causing hers.

E. DICKINSON

To the Same

Trusting an April flower may not curtail your February, that month of fleetest sweetness.

E. DICKINSON

To the Same

DEAR FRIEND,—Maggie was taking you a flower as you were going out.

Please accept the design, and bewail the flower, that sank of chagrin last evening.

E. DICKINSON

To the Same

The founders of honey have no names.

To the Same

My family of apparitions is select, though dim.

To the Same

Vinnie suggests these little friends.

Would they be too grovelling? And I add a face from my garden.

Though you met it before, it might not be charmless.

E. DICKINSON

To the Same
1880

Is sickness pathos or infamy?
While you forget to decide, please confirm this trifle.

To the Same
DEAR FRIEND,—I shall deem the little tumblers forever consecrated by the "unseemliness."
With affection,
E. DICKINSON

To the Same
Please accept the progeny of the pinks you so kindly brought mother in winter, with the hope that "wisdom is justified of her children."

To the Same
How strange that Nature does not knock, and yet does not intrude!

To the Same
"Give me thine heart" is too peremptory a courtship for earth, however irresistible in Heaven.

To the Same
DEAR FRIEND,—So valiant is the intimacy between Nature and her children, she addresses them as "comrades in arms."
E. DICKINSON

To the Same
DEAR FRIEND,—Nothing inclusive of a human heart could be "trivial." That appalling boon makes all things paltry but itself.

To thank you would profane you—there are moments when even gratitude is a desecration.

> Go thy great way!
> The stars thou meetest
> Are even as thyself.
> For what are stars but asterisks
> To point a human life?

E. DICKINSON, with love

To the Same

DEAR FRIEND,—In a world too full of beauty for peace, I have met nothing more beautiful.

E. DICKINSON

To the Same
1883?

DEAR FRIEND,—The thoughtfulness was picturesque and the glimpse delightful. The residence of Vinnie's friends could but be fair to me.

And will you, in exchange, accept a view of *my* house, which Nature painted white without consulting me? But Nature is "old-fashioned," perhaps a Puritan.

E. DICKINSON

To the Same

DEAR FRIEND,—It distressed us that you were pained. Are you easier now?

You have sheltered our tears too often that yours should fall unsolaced.

Give us half the thorn—then it will tear you less. To divulge itself is sorrow's right, never its presumption.

Faithfully,
E. DICKINSON

To the Same
1885?

DEAR FRIEND,—Is not the sweet resentment of friends that we are not strong, more inspiriting even than the strength itself?

E. DICKINSON

To Mrs. A. B. H. Davis
and her daughter
On sending flowers and apples

DEAR FRIENDS,—We are snatching our jewels from the frost, and ask you to help us wear them, as also the trinkets more rotund, which serve a baser need.

EMILY

T O *Mrs. Henry Hills*

Christmas, 1878?

With sweet Christmas for the "little brethren and sisters of the mystic tie."

EMILY

To the Same
January, 1879?

Our gentle neighbor must have known that we did not know she was ill, or we should immediately have inquired for her.

EMILY

To the Same
February, 1879

We are much grieved for the sufferings of the little one, which are so artlessly undeserved, and beg her mama to assure her of our tender sympathy.

The odor of the flower might please her, as these little beings are only "on a furlough" from Paradise.

With love for the mama, and sorrow for her weariness,

EMILY

To the Same

February 23, 1879

"Come unto me."

Beloved commandment! The darling obeyed it.

To the Same

February, 1879

The power to console is not within corporeal reach— though its attempt is precious.

To die before it feared to die, may have been a boon.

To the Same

March, 1879

DEAR FRIEND,—The only balmless wound is the departed human life we had learned to need.

For that, even Immortality is a slow solace. All other peace has many roots and will spring again.

With cheer from one who knows.

To the Same

DEAR FRIEND,—The gift was sadly exquisite—were the actual "cross" so divinely adorned, we should covet it.

Thank you for the sacred "flowers"—typical, both of them.

Gethsemane and Cana are still a travelled route.

EMILY

To the Same

Christmas, 1879

DEAR FRIEND,—I think Heaven will not be as good as earth, unless it bring with it that sweet power to remember, which is the staple of Heaven here.

How can we thank each other when omnipotent?

You, who endear our mortal Christmas, will perhaps assure us.

E.

To the Same

1880

We are ignorant of the dear friends, and eager to know how they are, and assure them that we are near them in these grieved hours.

EMILY

To the Same

DEAR FRIEND,—The heavenly flowers were brought to my room.

I had lain awake with the gale and overslept this morning.

That you may wake in Eden, as you enabled me to do, is my happy wish.

EMILY

To the Same

Without the hope of requiting the Sabbath morning blossoms, still sweetly remembered, please allow me to try.

E.

To the Same
With untold thanks, and the little dish, founded while she was here, too late to overtake her, too small for her to sip, but her large heart will excuse.

EMILY, with love

To the Same
Vocal is but one form of remembrance, dear friend— the cherishing that is speechless is equally warm.

To the Same
With Christmas delicacies, 1880
The little annual creatures solicit your regard.

Mrs. Hills often sent dainties from New York, perhaps Florida oranges, confectionery, or hot-house flowers. Upon one of these occasions the reply came:—

1881
Tropics, and dairies, and fairies! Thank the *Arabian Nights.*

EMILY

To the Same
1881
With a kiss and a flower, one of which will endure, I am whom you infer.

To the Same
1882
Only a pond lily that I tilled myself.

To the Same

DEAR FRIENDS,—Even the simplest solace, with a loved aim, has a heavenly quality.

EMILY

To the Same
January, 1883

DEAR FRIEND,—We often say "how beautiful!" But when we mean it, we can mean no more.

A dream personified.

E.

To the Same
With red lilies, Spring, 1883

Persian hues for my dark-eyed neighbor.

T O *Mrs. Jameson*

Many and sweet birthdays to our thoughtful neighbor, whom we have learned to cherish, though ourself unknown.

E. DICKINSON

To the Same

How dare a tear intrude on so sweet a cheek?

Gentlest of neighbors, recall the "sparrows" and the great Logician.

Tenderly,
E. DICKINSON

To the Same

Arthur forgot to set a trap for Santa Claus, but that industrious mouse will excuse him, if he will steal the cakes instead. And Annie.

E. DICKINSON

To ——
1880

DEAR FRIEND,—No "sonnet" had George Eliot. The sweet acclamation of Death is forever bounded.

> There is no trumpet like the tomb—
> The Immortality she gave
> We borrowed at her grave.
> For just one plaudit famishing,
> The might of human love.

Beautiful as it is, its criminal shortness maims it.

T o *Maggie Maher*

Ill with Typhoid Fever at her Home
Autumn, 1880

The missing Maggie is much mourned, and I am going out for "black" to the nearest store.

All are very naughty, and I am naughtiest of all.

The pussies dine on sherry now, and humming-bird cutlets.

The invalid hen took dinner with me, but a hen like Dr. T——'s horse soon drove her away. I am very busy picking up stems and stamens as the hollyhocks leave their clothes around.

What shall I send my weary Maggie? Pillows or fresh brooks?

HER GRIEVED MISTRESS

T o *the Rev. F. F. Emerson*

1880?

A blossom, perhaps, is an introduction, to whom, none can infer.

To the Same

Though tendered by a stranger, the fruit will be forgiven.

Valor in the dark is my Maker's code.

E. DICKINSON

To the Same

Mother congratulates Mr. Emerson on the discovery of the "philosopher's stone." She will never divulge it. It lay just where she thought it did—in making others happy.

E. DICKINSON

To the Same

Any gift but spring seems a counterfeit, but the birds are such sweet neighbors they rebuke us all.

E. DICKINSON

To the Same

Mother was much touched by dear Mrs. Emerson's thoughtfulness, and thanks her exceedingly sweetly. She also asks a remembrance to Mr. Emerson, whom she trusts is well.

Earnestly,
E. DICKINSON

To the Same
1881?

Should Mr. Emerson ever become ill and idle, mother hopes his clergyman will be as delicately thoughtful of him as he has been of her.

Gratefully,
E. DICKINSON

To the Same

DEAR FRIEND,—I step from my pillow to your hand to thank its sacred contents, to hoard, not to partake, for I am still weak.

The little package has lain by my side, not daring to venture, or Vinnie daring to have me—a hallowed denial I shall not forget.

I fear you may need the papers, and ask you to claim them immediately, would you desire them.

I trust you are sharing this most sweet climate with Mrs. Emerson and yourself, than which remembrance only is more Arabian.

Vinnie brings her love, and her sister what gratitude.

EMILY

To ——

DEAR FRIEND,—The little book will be subtly cherished. All we secure of beauty is its evanescence. Thank you for recalling us.

Earnestly,
EMILY

TO *Mr. and Mrs. George Montague*

1881?

DEAR COUSIN,—Thank you for the delightful cake, and the heart adjacent.

EMILY

To the Same

Delicate as bread of flowers. How sweetly we thank you!

To the Same

We trust the dear friend is convalescing.
These loveliest of days are certainly with that design.

EMILY

DEAR COUSIN,—The "Golden Rule" is so lovely, it needs
no police to enforce it.

COUSIN

To the Same

To have "been faithful in a few things" was the delicate
compliment paid one by God. Could I not commend a rarer
candidate for his approval in my loyal Cousin?

To the Same
1881?

Which will I thank—the perpetrator, the propagator, or
the almoner of the delightful bread—or may I compromise
and thank them all?

I for the first time appreciate the exultation of the robin
toward a crumb, though he must be a seductive robin, with
whom I would share my own.

With the hope to requite the loveliness in a future way,

Gratefully,

EMILY

TO *Mrs. W. F. Stearns*

May, 1881

DEAR FRIEND,—I hope you may know with what un-
speakable tenderness we think of you and of your dear
child.

Were it any kingdom but the "Kingdom of Heaven,"
how distant!

But my heart breaks—I can say no more.

E. D.

To the Same
October, 1882

DEAR FRIEND,—Affection wants you to know it is here.
Demand it to the utmost.

Tenderly,
E. DICKINSON

*One friend writes from New York of her regret that many
of Emily's notes to herself have been destroyed. But she
adds: "One little welcome of Emily's to me became a household word; and I can quote it for you, though it should have
the setting of her wide, pure margins, and her most dainty
penmanship. Here it is:—*

"Sweet Mrs. Nellie comes with the robins. Robins have
wings. Mrs. Nellie has wings. A society for the prevention
of wings would be a benefit to us all.

*"It tells its own story, you see, of a flitting visit to the
Grove in the spring, and of her interest in her neighbors
and her information as to their interests, though so invisible
herself."*

TO *Mrs. Joseph Sweetser*

Autumn, 1879?

Aunt Katie and the sultans have left the garden now, and
parting with my own recalls their sweet companionship.

Mine were not, I think, as exuberant as in other years,
—perhaps the Pelham water shocked their stately tastes,—
but cherished avariciously because less numerous. I trust
your garden was willing to die. I do not think that mine was
—it perished with beautiful reluctance, like an evening
star.

I hope you were well since we knew of you, and as
happy as sorrow would allow.

There are sweets of pathos, when sweets of mirth have
passed away.

Mother has had a weary cold, and suffers much from
neuralgia since the changing airs, though I trust is no
feebler than when you were here. She has her little
pleasures as the patient have—the voices of friends, and
devotion of home.

The ravens must "cry," to be ministered to; she need only
sigh. . . . Perhaps it is quite the home it was when you
last beheld it. I hope your few are safe, and your flowers
encouraging.

News of your sultans and yourself would be equally
lovely, when you feel inclined. Blossoms have their leisures.

Lovingly,
EMILY

To the Same
December, 1881

It was the unanimous opinion of the household that Aunt
Katie never wrote so lovely a letter, and that it should be
immediately replied to by each member of the family, from
the geraniums down to the pussies, but unforeseen maligni-
ties prevented. Vinnie lost her sultans too—it was "Guiteau"
year—Presidents and Sultans were alike doomed.

One might possibly come up, having sown itself—if it

should, you shall share—it is an Eastern creature, and does not like this soil. I think its first exuberance was purely accidental. Last was a fatal season. An "envious worm" attacked them; then in early autumn we had midwinter frost. "When God is with us, who shall be against us," but when He is against us, other allies are useless.

We were much amused at your "gardener." You portrayed his treason so wittily it was more effective than loyalty. He knew that flowers had no tongues.

We trust you are safe this Norwegian weather, and "desire your prayers" for another snow-storm, just over our heads, the snows already repealing the fences.

With love for your health, and the promise of sultans, and viziers too, if the monarchs come,

EMILY

To the Same
1884

DEAR AUNT,—Thank you for "considering the lilies."

The Bible must have had us in mind, when it gave that liquid commandment. Were all its advice so enchanting as that, we should probably heed it.

Thank you for promptness, explicitness, sweetness. Your account of the lilies was so fresh I could almost pick them, and the hope to meet them in person, in autumn, through your loving hand, is a fragrant future.

I hope you are well as you deserve, which is a blest circumference, and give my love to each.

Aunt L—— just looked in on us, and I go to make her dish of homestead Charlotte Russe.

Always,
EMILY

To the Same

November, 1884

SWEET AND GRACIOUS AUNT KATIE,—The beloved lilies have come, and my heart is so high it overflows, as this was mother's week, Easter in November.

Father rose in June, and a little more than a year since, those fair words were fulfilled, "and a little child shall lead them"—but boundlessness forbids me. . . .

It is very wrong that you were ill, and whom shall I accuse? The enemy, "eternal, invisible, and full of glory" —but He declares himself a friend! It is sweet you are better.

More beating that brave heart has to do before the emerald recess.

With sorrow for Emma's accident, and love for all who cherish you, including the roses, your velvet allies.

Tenderly,

EMILY

To the Same

Cousin T—— and Cousin O—— little thought when they were paying their antiquated respects to Aunt Katie that they were defrauding Emily of that last moment—but they needed it most—new moments will grow.

When I found it beyond my power to see you, I designed to write you, immediately, but the Lords came as you went, and Judge Lord was my father's closest friend, so I shared my moments with them till they left us last Monday; then seeing directly after, the death of your loved Dr. A——, I felt you might like to be alone—though Death is perhaps an intimate friend, not an enemy. Beloved Shakespeare says, "He that is robbed and smiles, steals something from the thief." . . .

Maggie said you asked should you "eat the flower." Please consult the bees—they are the only authority on Etruscan matters. Vinnie said the sherry I sent you was brandy—a vital misapprehension. Please also forgive it. I did not intend to be so base to the aunt who showed me the first mignonette, and listened with me to the great wheel, from Uncle Underwood's "study," and won me in "divers other ways" too lovely to mention. Of all this we will talk when you come again.

> Meanwhile accept your
> TRIFLING NIECE

To the Same
1885

Aunt Katie's rose had many thorns, but it is still a rose, and has borne the extremities of a flower with ethereal patience—and every deference to her is so sweetly deserved, we do not call it courtesy, but only recognition. It is sweeter that noon should be fair, than that morning should, because noon is the latest, and yet your morning had its dew you would not exchange. Thank you for telling us of your triumphs.

"Peace hath her victories, no less than War."

Thank you for speaking so tenderly of our latest lost. We had hoped the persuasions of the spring, added to our own, might delay his going, but they came too late. "I met," said he in his last note, "a crocus and a snowdrop in my yesterday's walk," but the sweet beings outlived him. I thought the churchyard Tarrytown, when I was a child, but now I trust 'tis Trans—

In this place of shafts, I hope you may remain unharmed.

I congratulate you upon your children, and themselves upon you.

To have had such daughters is sanctity—to have had such a mother, divine. To still have her—but tears forbid me. My own is in the grave. "So loved her that he died for her," says the explaining Jesus.

With love,
YOUR EMILY

To the Same

Aunt Katie never forgets to be lovely, and the sweet clusters of yesterday only perpetuate a heart warm so many years.

Tropic, indeed, a memory that adheres so long. They were still vivid and fragrant when they reached my fingers, and were the wrist that bears them bolder, it would give reply. As it is, only a kiss and a gratitude, and every grace of being, from your loving niece. "I give his angels charge!"

Should I say his flowers, for qualified as saints they are. Vinnie's and my transport.

To the Same

DEAR AUNT,—I have found and give it in love, but reluctant to entrust anything so sacred to my father as my grandfather's Bible to a public messenger, will wait till Mr. Howard comes, whom Mrs. Nellie tells us is due this week. Thank you for loving my father and mother. I hope they are with the Source of love. You did not tell me of your health—I trust because confirmed. Thank you too for sorrow, the one you truly knew.

With Vinnie's affection, in haste and fondness,

EMILY

TO *Professor J. K. Chickering*

Autumn, 1882

DEAR FRIEND,—I do not know the depth of my indebtedness. Sorrow, benighted with fathoms, cannot find its mind.
Thank you for assisting us.
We were timidly grateful.

E. DICKINSON

To the Same

DEAR FRIEND,—Thank you for being willing to see me, but may I defer so rare a pleasure till you come again? Grief is a sable introduction, but a vital one, and I deem that I knew you long since through your shielding thought.

I hope you may have an electrical absence, as life never loses its startlingness, however assailed. "Seen of angels" only, an enthralling aim.

Thank you for the kindness, the fervor of a stranger the latest forgot.

E. DICKINSON

To the Same

DEAR FRIEND,—I had hoped to see you, but have no grace to talk, and my own words so chill and burn me that the temperature of other minds is too new an awe.

We shun it ere it comes,
Afraid of joy,
Then sue it to delay,
And lest it fly
Beguile it more and more.

353

> May not this be,
> Old suitor Heaven,
> Like our dismay at thee?

Earnestly,
E. Dickinson

To the Same
1885

Dear Friend,—The Amherst heart is plain and whole and permanent and warm.

In childhood I never sowed a seed unless it was perennial —and that is why my garden lasts.

We dare not trust ourselves to know that you indeed have left us.

The fiction is sufficient pain. To know you better as you flee, may be our recompense.

I hope that you are well, and nothing mars your peace but its divinity—for ecstasy is peril.

With earnest recollection,
E. Dickinson

To the Same

How charming the magnanimity which conferring a favor on others, by some mirage of valor considers itself receiving one!

Of such is the kingdom of knights!

E. Dickinson

It is hard for many persons to believe, even now, that Emily Dickinson had nothing to do with the Saxe Holm stories, and certainly some of their incidental poetry bears strong evidence of her unique touch. The little mystery of those remarkable tales was so carefully guarded that after a time people lost interest in surmising, and are now content to accept them as they are. The No Name *series of Roberts Brothers was not so long a secret, and in the volume of its verse,* A Masque of Poets, *appeared, probably through the efforts of her old friend* "H. H.," *Emily Dickinson's* Success, *afterward the opening poem in the first of her published volumes. However obtained, it formed the beginning of an occasional and pleasant correspondence between herself and Mr. Niles, always the genial, helpful, and generous friend of writers. She often sent him poems, which, contrary to her usual custom, she had named herself.*

TO *Mr. Thomas Niles*

1880?

DEAR FRIEND,—I bring you a chill gift—*My Cricket*[14] and *The Snow*.[15] A base return, indeed, for the delightful book which I infer from you, but an earnest one.

To the Same
1883?

Thank you, Mr. Niles.

I am very grateful for the mistake. I should think it irreparable deprivation to know no farther of her here, with the impregnable chances.

The kind but incredible opinion of "H. H." and yourself I would like to deserve.

Would you accept a pebble I think I gave to her, though I am not sure.

With thanks,
E. DICKINSON

[14] *Poems*, Second Series, page 167.
[15] *Poems*, Second Series, page 174.

The "pebble" was that wonderful stanza,

> How happy is the little stone
> That rambles in the road alone,
> And doesn't care about careers,
> And exigencies never fears;
> Whose coat of elemental brown
> A passing universe put on;
> And independent as the sun,
> Associates, or glows alone,
> Fulfilling absolute decree
> In casual simplicity.

To the Same, 1885

DEAR FRIEND,—Thank you for the kindness.

I am glad if the bird seemed true to you.

Please efface the others, and receive these three, which are more like him—*A Thunder Storm,*[16] *A Humming Bird,*[17] and *A Country Burial.*[18]

The life of Marian Evans had much I never knew— a doom of fruit without the bloom, like the Niger fig:—

> Her losses make our gains ashamed—
> She bore life's empty pack
> As gallantly as if the East
> Were swinging at her back.
> Life's empty pack is heaviest,
> As every porter knows—
> In vain to punish honey,
> It only sweeter grows.

[16] Poems, Second Series, page 158.
[17] *ibid.*, p. 130.
[18] *ibid.*, p. 207.

T O *Mrs. Carmichael*

1882?

. . . I fear Vinnie gave my message as John Alden did the one from Miles Standish, which resulted delightfully for John, but not as well for his friend.

Had you seen the delighted crowd that gathered round the box—did you ever see a crowd of three?—you would have felt requited. Your presenting smile was alone wanting.

"Dear Mrs. Carmichael," said one; "The one that never forgets," said another; and a tear or two in the eyes of the third, and the reception was over. Can you guess which the third was?

The candy was enchanting, and is closeted in a deep pail, pending Vinnie's division, and the little box, like Heaven and mice, far too high to find.

Failure be my witness that I have sought them faithfully.

We often think of your evening circle—Mr. Skeel presiding at the piano, and Mrs. Skeel and yourself taking mutual lessons.

I am studying music now with the jays, and find them charming artists.

Vinnie and Gilbert have pretty battles on the pussy question, and you are needed for umpire, oftener than you think.

"Weren't you chasing pussy?" said Vinnie to Gilbert. "No, she was chasing herself."

"But wasn't she running pretty fast?" said pussy's Nemesis. "Well, some slow and some fast," said the beguiling villain.

With the little kiss he gave me last, and a pair of my own, and love for Mr. and Mrs. Skeel,

Warmly,
EMILY

To the Same
1884?

LOVED MRS. CARMICHAEL AND MRS. SKEEL,—I heard long since at school that Diogenes went to sea in a tub. Though I did not believe it, it is credible now.

Against the peril of ocean steamers I am sweetly provided, and am sure you had my safety in mind, in your lovely gifts.

I have taken the passengers from the hold—passengers of honey—and the deck of silk is just promenaded by a bold fly, greedy for its sweets. The little tub with the surcingle I shall keep till the birds, filling it then with nectars, in Mrs. Skeel's sweet honor.

Will each of the lovely friends present my thanks to the other, as Vinnie's correspondence with them is too impressive for what dear Dickens calls "the likes of me" to invade.

Their sweet intercession with Santa Claus in my behalf, I shall long remember.

Always,
EMILY

To the Same
1885?

My consoleless Vinnie convinces me of the misfortune of having known dear Mrs. Carmichael, whom "to name is to praise," for indeed, were we both intelligent mourners, I

358

fear delight would close; but the "fair uncertainty" aids me, which is denied Vinnie.

Of her noble loss it is needless to speak—that is incalculable.

Of her sweet power to us when we were overwhelmed, that, too, shall be mute. She has "borne our grief and carried our sorrow," that is the criterion. . . .

Let me hope she is well to-day, and sheltered by every love she deserves, which were indeed countless.

We congratulate sweet Mrs. Skeel on her beloved booty, and ask a remembrance in her prayer for those of us bereaved.

> Lovingly,
> EMILY

TO *Dr. and Mrs. Field*

Who had sent flowers
1884?

Expulsion from Eden grows indistinct in the presence of flowers so blissful, and with no disrespect to Genesis, Paradise remains.

Beaconsfield says "the time has now come when it must be decided forever, who possesses the great gates to India."

I think it must be my neighbor.

> With delicate gratitude,
> E. DICKINSON

To the Same
1885

I was much chagrined by the delayed flower—please accept its apology.

> E. DICKINSON

To the Same
1885

Should you not have this flower, the first of spring with me, I should regret not sending it. Your azaleas are still vivid, though the frailer flowers are flitted away.

E. DICKINSON

To ——

I send a violet, for L——. I should have sent a stem, but was overtaken by snowdrifts. I regret deeply not to add a butterfly, but have lost my hat, which precludes my catching one.

To —— ——, *with flowers*

With the leave of the bluebirds, without whose approval we do nothing.

E. DICKINSON

T O *Mr. Theodore Holland*

1885

DEAR SIR,—Your request to "remain sincerely" mine demands investigation, and if after synopsis of your career all should seem correct, I am tersely yours. I shall try to wear the unmerited honor with becoming volume.

Commend me to your kindred, for whom, although a stranger, I entertain esteem.

I approve the paint—a study of the Soudan, I take it, but the Scripture assures us our hearts are all Dongola.

E. DICKINSON

To —— ——
1885

. . . If you saw a bullet hit a bird, and he told you he wasn't shot, you might weep at his courtesy, but you would certainly doubt his word. Thomas's faith in anatomy was stronger than his faith in faith. . . . Vesuvius don't talk— Ætna don't. One of them said a syllable, a thousand years ago, and Pompeii heard it and hid forever. She couldn't look the world in the face afterward, I suppose. Bashful Pompeii! . . .

To ——

DEAR FRIEND,—I thank you with wonder. Should you ask me my comprehension of a starlight night, awe were my only reply, and so of the mighty book. It stills, incites, infatuates, blesses and blames in one. Like human affection, we dare not touch it, yet flee, what else remains?

But excuse me—I know but little. Please tell me how it might seem to you.

How vast is the chastisement of beauty, given us by our Maker! A word is inundation, when it comes from the sea.

Peter took the marine walk at the great risk.

E. DICKINSON

What book may be thus described is, unhappily, not known, as I have been unable to discover even to whom the note was written.

A severe disappointment in the preparation of these volumes is the fact that Emily's letters to "H. H." cannot be found.

Entertained delightfully during the summer of 1893 *at Mr. Jackson's lovely home in Colorado Springs, I was very happy to learn that these letters had certainly not been destroyed. During the months before her death Mrs. Jackson had herself arranged her mass of papers, letters, and manuscripts, each marked for its fate; and Emily's letters were especially reserved in a package apart, as unique and too valuable to share the fate of much other correspondence. But though careful search has been most kindly made by her family, the letters still remain in hiding, and the inference is that they must have been accidentally destroyed in flames intended for other things.*

Among Emily's own papers I have found this draft of a letter to Mrs. Jackson, discarded on account of a number of substituted words; and I give it just as it is, with both erasures and substitutes, as an interesting study of her afterthoughts:—

TO *"H. H."*

March, 1885

DEAR FRIEND,—To reproach my own foot in behalf of yours is involuntary, and finding meagre[19] solace in "whom He loveth He chasteneth," your valor[20] astounds me. It was only a small wasp, said the French physician repairing the sting, but the strength to perish is sometimes withheld— though who but you can[21] tell a foot.

> Take all away from me
> But leave me ecstasy,
> And I am richer then
> Than all my fellow-men.
> Is it becoming me
> To dwell so wealthily,
> When at my very door
> Are those possessing more,
> In abject[22] poverty?

[19] Myself little.
[20] Prowess.
[21] Could.
[22] Boundless.

That you glance at[23] Japan as [24] you breakfast, not in the least surprises me, thronged[25] only with music, like the decks[26] of birds.

Thank you for hoping I am well. Who could be ill in March, that month of proclamation? Sleighbells and jays contend in my matinée, and the north surrenders instead of the south, a reverse of bugles.

Pity me, however, I have finished *Ramona*. Would that like Shakespeare it were just published!

Knew I how to pray, to intercede for your foot were intuitive, but I am but a pagan.

Of God we ask one favor, that we may be forgiven. For what, He is presumed to know. The crime, from us, is hidden.

> Immured the whole of life
> Within a magic prison,
> We reprimand the happiness
> That too competes with Heaven.

May I once more know, and that you are saved?

Yours,
E. DICKINSON

After Mrs. Jackson's death, August 12, 1885, Emily wrote of her:—

Helen of Troy will die, but Helen of Colorado, never. Dear friend, can you walk, were the last words that I wrote her.

---

[23] Compass.
[24] Before.
[25] Clogged.
[26] Wheels.

Dear friend, I can fly—
Her immortal reply.

To ——

SWEET FRIENDS,—I send a message by a mouth that cannot speak.

The ecstasy to guess
Were a receipted bliss
If grace could talk.

With love.

To ——

. . . What a hazard an accent is! When I think of the hearts it has scuttled or sunk, I almost fear to lift my hand to so much as a punctuation.

TO *Mrs. E. P. Crowell*

When about to sail for Europe
March 2, 1885

Is it too late to touch you, dear?
We this moment knew
Love marine and love terrene,
Love celestial too.

I give his angels charge.

EMILY

TO *Miss Eugenia Hall*

1885?

Let me thank the little cousin in flowers, which, without lips, have language.

Somewhat cousin,
EMILY

To the Same

DEAR "GENIE,"—The lovely flower you sent me is like a little vase of spice, and fills the hall with cinnamon.

You must have skilful hands to make such sweet carnations. Perhaps your doll taught you. I know that dolls are sometimes wise. Robins are my dolls. I am glad you love the blossoms so well. I hope you love birds, too. It is economical. It saves going to Heaven.

Lovingly,
EMILY

To the Same, with a Wedding Gift, October 20, 1885

Will the sweet cousin who is about to make the Etruscan experiment, accept a smile which will last a life, if ripened in the sun?

COUSIN EMILY

TO *Mrs. J. C. Greenough*

Three notes were sent at different times, with flowers

Lest any bee should boast.

Trusting the happy flower will meet you at the door where spring will soon be knocking, we challenge your "come in."

EMILY

The flower keeps its appointment—should the heart be tardy?

When Memory rings her bell, let all the thoughts run in.

EMILY

TO *Mrs. Greenough*

After her Mother's Death, October, 1885

DEAR FRIEND,—I had the luxury of a mother a month longer than you, for my own mother died in November, but the anguish also was granted me to see the first snow upon her grave the following day, which, dear friend, you were spared.

But Remembrance engulfs me, and I must cease.

I wish I could speak a word of courage, though that love has already done. Who could be motherless who has a mother's grave within confiding reach?

Let me enclose the tenderness born of bereavement.

To have had a mother—how mighty!

EMILY

T O *Mrs. Todd, Mrs. Tuckerman, the Misses* ——, *Mr. Clark, and Mrs. Currier*

From the many notes sent me by Emily Dickinson during the last four years of her life, it was a difficult matter to select those best fitted for publication. But the first one available was probably this response to a small panel which I had painted for her,—a group of Indian pipes, those weird white flowers of shade and silence:—

T O *Mrs. Todd*

Winter, 1882

Dear Friend,—That without suspecting it you should send me the preferred flower of life, seems almost supernatural, and the sweet glee that I felt at meeting it I could confide to none. I still cherish the clutch with which I bore it from the ground when a wondering child, an unearthly booty, and maturity only enhances mystery, never decreases it. To duplicate the vision is even more amazing, for God's unique capacity is too surprising to surprise. I know not how to thank you. We do not thank the rainbow, although its trophy is a snare.

To give delight is hallowed—perhaps the toil of angels, whose avocations are concealed.

I trust that you are well, and the quaint little girl with the deep eyes, every day more fathomless.

With joy,

E. DICKINSON

A few days later came another, enclosing that brilliant, meteoric flash in words, her "humming-bird," printed in the second volume of the Poems:—

To the Same

DEAR FRIEND,—I cannot make an Indian pipe, but please accept a humming-bird,—

> A route of evanescence
> With a revolving wheel;
> A resonance of emerald,
> A rush of cochineal;
> And every blossom on the bush
> Adjusts its tumbled head,—
> The mail from Tunis, probably,
> An easy morning's ride.

When, after her death, the great mass of Emily Dickinson's verses had been collated and an appropriate drawing for the cover was desired, there seemed a peculiar fitness in this ethereal flower; and the design was cut from the little panel which stood so long in her room.

Many of her most beautiful verses came to me, in the following years; and one autumn day this:—

1884

How martial the apology of nature! We die, said the
deathless of Thermopylæ, in obedience to law.

> Not sickness stains the brave,
> Nor any dart,
> Nor doubt of scenes to come,
> But an adjourning heart.

*After I had sent her a painting of the gorgeous blossoms
of the trumpet vine, which, on first seeing, she had called
"the Soudan," she wrote:—*

March 21, 1885

DEAR FRIEND,—Nature forgot. The circus reminded her.
Thanks for the Ethiopian face.
The Orient is in the west.
"You knew, oh Egypt," said the entangled Antony.

And later,—

September, 1885

Why should we censure Othello, when the criterion
Lover says, "Thou shalt have no other gods before me"?

*Music had always charm for Emily Dickinson. Frequently,
when I had been singing, or playing upon the piano at her
request, a dainty note would come in to me, with a glass of
wine, or a rare rose; in one instance a cream whip, with the
single line, "Whom He loveth He chasteneth,"—of which
the application might have been taken in various ways.*

*I can never forget the twilight seclusion of the old draw-
ing-room, the square piano in its corner, the ancient ma-*

369

hogany furniture, and Emily just outside the door, her dress a spot of white in the dim hall. With the waning afternoon, I would play one thing and another, or sing melodies which often sounded too light and modern and sunshiny for surroundings so like a dreamy corner of the past. At first it seemed to me as if a visitor from another world had alighted for a time, wishing, for some inscrutable reason, to be entertained on a foreign planet. Later, it became not only entirely natural, but so much a habit that I should have missed my solitary recitals quite as much as my often invisible auditor.

Other notes to me, having especial reference to particular persons or occasions, are not of sufficient general interest to be given here.

As her unique life drew toward its close, she became, for the last two years, a semi-invalid,—she who had always rejoiced in strength and bravery enough for her own need, and that of all her friends.

Only a handful of notes remains, written during the final weeks while Emily brightened the old house with her airy, yet forceful and brilliant personality, for, even ill, she was a pervasive presence.

Upon the death of Professor Tuckerman, March 15, 1886, she wrote:—

T O *Mrs. Tuckerman*

DEAR ONE,—"Eye hath not seen nor ear heard." What a recompense! The enthusiasm of God at the reception of His sons! How ecstatic! How infinite! Says the blissful voice, not yet a voice, but a vision, "I will not let thee go, except I bless thee."

EMILY

Sometime during this month, also, she wrote her cousins:—

TO *the Misses ——*

March, 1886

I scarcely know where to begin, but love is always a safe place. I have twice been very sick, dears, with a little recess of convalescence, then to be more sick, and have lain in my bed since November, many years, for me, stirring as the arbutus does, a pink and russet hope; but that we will leave with our pillow. When your dear hearts are quite convenient, tell us of their contents, the fabric cared for most, not a fondness wanting.

Do you keep musk, as you used to, like Mrs. Morene of Mexico? Or cassia carnations so big they split their fringes of berry? Was your winter a tender shelter—perhaps like Keats's bird, "and hops and hops in little journeys"?

Are you reading and well, and the W ——s near and warm? When you see Mrs. French and Dan give them a tear from us.

Vinnie would have written, but could not leave my side. Maggie gives her love. Mine more sweetly still.

EMILY

TO *Mr. C. H. Clark*

April 5, 1886

DEAR FRIEND,—Are you living and well, and your father in peace, and the home in —— Street without effacing change? I received your very kind message, I think in November, since which I have been very ill, and begin to roam in my room a little, an hour at a time.

Do you, as time steals on, know anything of the W—— whom Mr. —— so loved, and of whom he said with a smile, "Should he find a gold watch in the street he would not pick it up, so unsullied was he"? . . .

My sister gives her faithful remembrance to yourself and your father, the brother so cherished never once forgot.

You will recall the flower sacred to your brother.

No sloth has memory.

E. D<small>ICKINSON</small>

T O Mrs. Currier

April 10, 1886

. . . Mr. Hunt was tinning a post this morning, and told us L—— didn't feel quite as well as usual, and I haven't felt quite as well as usual since the chestnuts were ripe, though it wasn't the chestnuts' fault, but the crocuses are so martial and the daffodils to the second joint, let us join hands and recover.

"I do remember an apothecary," said that sweeter robin than Shakespeare, was a loved paragraph which has lain on my pillow all winter, but perhaps Shakespeare has been "up street" oftener than I have, this winter.

Would father's youngest sister believe that in the "Shire town" where he and Blackstone went to school, a man was hung yesterday, for the murder of a man by the name of Dickinson, and that Miss M—— was poisoned by a strolling juggler to be tried in the Supreme Court next week?

Don't you think fumigation ceased when father died?

Poor, romantic Miss M——! But perhaps a *Police Gazette* was better for you than an essay.

I hope you are both stronger, and ask a word of gain with these ecstatic days. I give my anxious love, and Vinnie's faithfulness with mine.

Y<small>OUR</small> E<small>MILY</small>

TO *Mr. C. H. Clark*

April 15, 1886

Thank you, dear friend, I am better. The velocity of the ill, however, is like that of the snail. I am glad of your father's tranquillity, and of your own courage. Fear makes us all martial.

I could hardly have thought it possible that the scholarly stranger to whom my father introduced me, could have mentioned my friend, almost itself a vision, or have still left a legend to relate his name. With the exception of —— . . . your name alone remains.

"Going home," was he not an aborigine of the sky?

The last time he came in life I was with my lilies and heliotropes. Said my sister to me, "The gentleman with the deep voice wants to see you, Emily"—hearing him ask of the servant.

"Where did you come from?" I said, for he spoke like an apparition. "I stepped from my pulpit to the train," was his simple reply; and, when I asked, "how long?"— "twenty years," said he, with inscrutable roguery.

But the loved voice has ceased; and to some one who heard him "going home" it was sweet to speak. . . . Thank you for each circumstance, and tell me all you love to say. . . .

Excuse me for the voice, this moment immortal.

E. DICKINSON

This letter, in her bold, clear, detached hand (to an accustomed eye slightly less firm than usual), is the last one, so far as known, which Emily Dickinson wrote. Afterward, she continued to be delicate, though hardly alarmingly so; but just before the fifteenth of May, 1886, she sent two words to her cousins, freighted with startling import,—

LITTLE COUSINS,—Called back.

EMILY

Almost immediately she fell asleep, and never woke again to earthly sunshine.

In the quiet of leafy Amherst, in the old brick mansion behind its hedges and pines, she lived and wrote, and there she

> "Ascended, from our vision
> To countenances new."

We can be only grateful that she was moved to crystallize in words her thronging visions of blossom, and bird, and "blue, beloved air,"—of "life, death, and that vast forever" which was her nearest companion.

This is hardly the place to speak in detail of Emily Dickinson's verses, their electrical quality, or their impressive effect upon the public, four years after her death. They are pervaded by a singular cadence of hidden rhythmical music, which becomes sympathetically familiar upon intimate acquaintance.

Dr. Holmes somewhere says that rhymes "are iron fetters: it is dragging a chain and a ball to march under their encumbrance"; and if in Emily Dickinson's work there is frequently no rhyme where rhyme should be, a subtle something, welcome and satisfying, takes its place. An orchid among every-day, sweet-smelling flowers, strangeness and irregularity seem but to enhance her fascination.

A striking characteristic of her verse is its epigrammatic quality; terseness and vigor predominate, rather than feminine grace and smoothness. Homely experiences which all recognize, but few record, were to her texts for profound generalization. When the unmeaning mass of much modern poetry is compared with Emily Dickinson's swift revelations, the operation suggests comparing distilled water with richest Burgundy. And as such water is no less insipid if served in cut-glass flagons, so we cannot care in what kind of bottle has been stored for years the condensed sweetness of tropic suns.

The eighteenth of May, 1886, Emily Dickinson was carried lovingly over the threshold she had not passed beyond in years.

> "She went as softly as the dew
> From a familiar flower.
> Not like the dew did she return
> At the accustomed hour."

To the few who gathered, that sunny afternoon, her friend, fellow-poet, and "master" read Emily Brontë's noble Last Lines, *with their lofty voicing of an unchangeable belief in the soul's immortality,—"a favorite," as Colonel Higginson so fitly said, "with our friend, who has now put on that Immortality which she seemed never to have laid off."*

She had lived in voluntary retirement from outside eyes; and now, in the sweet May sunshine, tender hands bore her through meadows starry with daisies into a silence and seclusion but little deeper.

INDEX

"Aborigine of the sky," 373
Accent, a hazard, 364
Accidents, funny, 131
Adams, Miss, 18, 21, 22, 23-24
Adams, Mrs., sons' death, 202
Adder's tongue, 33
Adirondacks, 290, 291
Aetna "don't talk," 361
Alden, John, 357
Alexandria Bay, 152
Amherst, notes to friends in, 310; sole link with the world, 311
Amherst Academy, 22, 30-31, 51-52, 106
Amherst College, levees at, 90; students in the war, 224
Amherst heart, 354
Anatomical dishabille, 332
Angels, 179
Anthon, Mrs., 104; letters to, 121, 122, 123
Apparitions, family of, 335
Apple blossoms, 288
April, 316, 335
Arabia in the eyes, 192
Arabian Nights, 59, 61, 186, 341
"Arabian presence," 284
Arbutus, trailing, 33, 108, 143, 157
Atlantic Monthly, The, 105, 252, 254
Aurora Leigh, 200
Autumn, 79, 80-81, 149, 187
"Awakening" in the church, 234

Baltimore Convention (1852), 90
Barabbas, 262
Beaconsfield, 359
Beauty, world too full of, 337; evanescence all we secure of, 345; chastisement of, 361
Bedouin guest, 213
Bee, 133; "blossoms belong to," 145
Bee's prong, 145
Bees "only authority on Etruscan matters," 351
Beecher, H. W., 46
Belchertown, Mass., 87, 95
Bell and Everett party, 198
Bellatrix, 4
Belle of Amherst, 7
Bells, chime of, 224
Bereavement, "tenderness born of," 429
Berlin for her eyes, 219
Bertini's music-book, 10
Betelgeux, 4
Bible, grandfather's, 352
Bird, "spacious," 142; "the new," 154
Bird song, 69
Birds, 160, 161, 190; "the boundless," 52; "in plush teams," 227; "sweet neighbors," 344; love for, 365
"Black Fanny," 86
Blood-root, 33
Blossom, note compared to a, 186

Blossoms, cheer from, 111; belong to the bee, 145; "have their leisures," 348
Blueberry, 164
Bluebirds, 218, 223
Bobolinks, 142
Boltwood, Lucius, 64
Books, love for, 229; "joggle the mind," 254
Boston, 66; visit to, 18-19, 21-22
Bowdoin, Mr. E. G., 113
Bowles, Mr. and Mrs. Samuel, letters to, 158-192
Bowles, Samuel, death of, 188; picture of, with Gov. Bross and Mr. Colfax, 251; "genius of Hampshire," 295
Bowles, Samuel, jr., 293; letters to, 294-298
Brabantio's gift, 276
Bread, learning to make, 13; "twin loaves, born," 39
Brevoort House, 163
Bridal gift, 155
Briggs, Gov., 28
Brontë, 180
Brontë, Bramwell, 237
Brontë, Charlotte, 113, 156, 236
Brontë, Charlotte, 113, 156, "marvellous verse," 292; "*Last Lines*," 375
Brooks, 176, 178
Bross, Gov., picture of, 251
Browne, Sir Thomas, 253
Browning, Robert, 180, 249, 253; "made a new poem," 205; *Pippa Passes*, 257; *Bells and Pomegranates*, 269; *Men and Women*, 269
Browning, Mrs., 200, 253, 259; grave of, 173; poems by, 269; *Bells and Pomegranates*, 269
Bumblebees, 160
Bunker Hill, 19, 117
Byron, 106

CALLED BACK, "a haunting story," 251
Campbell, Miss, 24
Cana and Gethsemane, 339
Cannon, given by Gen. Burnside in memory of Adjt. Stearns, 224
Carlo, 161, 162, 173, 174
Carmichael, Mrs., letters, 357-359
Cashmere confederate, 192
Cattle-show, 79, 134
Centennial at Concord, 236
Cephas and Apollos, 178
Chadbourne, Mrs., 301
Charnel steps, 205
Chestnut-tree in blossom, 258
Chickering, Prof. J. K., letters to, 353, 354
Children, 278, 288-289, 313
China, the ship, 172
Chinese writing-master, 19, 20
Cholera anticipated, 68
Christmas, 24, 156, 314, 315, 340
Christmas presents, 16, 157
Circumference, 257
Circumstance, 254
Circus, 142
Clark, C. H., letters to, 302, 371
Clark, J. D., letters to, 298
Clark, Col. W. S., 204
Climbing fern, 105
Clovers, 174
Cold, taking, account of, 35, 36
Colds, "make one carnal," 39

Colfax, Schuyler, picture of, 251

Colton, Rev. A. M., 29

Commencement, 21, 95, 142, 173, 289, 317

Compositions, 7-8, 31

Conductor, railway, 74

Congress, 99

Conservatory, description of, 293

Consolation, 339

Convalescence, slow, 373

Conway, Hugh, 251

Cooper, Mrs. J. S., letters to, 333

Cowan, Mr., letters to, 280-282

"Cricket on the hearth," 86

Crickets, 68, 79, 119, 120

Crocuses, "stud many mounds," 144

Crowell, Mrs. E. P., 264

Crows, "quickened by," 332

"Currer Bell," 113

Currier, Mrs., letter to, 372

Daisies, 144, 150

Daisy, 140, 182

Dandelion, 52, 169, 238; pressed, 328

Daniel Deronda, 272

Daphne, 269, 326

David, 142, 191

Davis, Jefferson, capture of, 126

Death, 141, 143, 147, 149, 150, 151, 155, 180; of friend, 43; "dainty, democratic," 150; of aunt, 196; of mother, "many kinds of cold," 299; "an intimate friend," 250; "in obedience to law," 369

Decoration, 268

Departure reduced to a science, 235

De Quincey, 232

Dick, the horse of association, 290

Dickens, Charles, 102

Dickinson, Edward, in Congress, 55, 100; in Baltimore convention (1852), 90; directing firemen, 92; and New London R. R., 96; death of, 235, 236, 267

Dickinson, Mrs. Edward, paralyzed, 268; death of, 247-248

Dickinson, Emily, spiritual guard, xviii; varying moods, xviii; change of style, xviii; epigrammatic power early foreshadowed, xviii; did not address envelopes in later years, xix; disliked theology current in her girlhood, xx; no irreverence in her writings, xx; biblical quotation, xxi; complete retirement from even village social life, xxii; passionate love of, and intimacy with, Nature, xxii; fondness for March, xxii; intellectual brilliancy at seventeen, 31; handwriting, 34, 53; Mrs. Ford's recollections of her, 104-109; wood-lore, 105; wit and humor, 106; personal appearance, 107-108; gardening, 108; under treatment of the eyes, 124; aversion to society, 158; urged to publish, 225-226, 270, 277-278; as to portrait, 256; verbal portrait, 256; declined to mould her verse, 258; isolation a necessity,

311-312; accessible to children, 313; death, 374; funeral, 375,

—— Letters, reason for publishing, xvii; arrangement explained, xvii; difficulties in chronological arrangement, xix; punctuation, dashes used for, xix; acknowledgement of those sent, xxii

—— Poems, Dr. Holland on, 108; her view in writing, 159; not named by herself, 163; design for cover of the volume, 368; electrical quality of, 374; epigrammatic quality of, 374

—— included in the Letters, *see below, under* Poems

Dickinson, Miss Lavinia, 104, 124; letters to, 125, 126, 127, 196

Dickinson, Misses, 244

Dickinson, Samuel Fowler, 138

Dickinson, William A., letters to, 55-103

Diogenes, 358

Disaster endears, 334

Disraeli, 246

Distinguished, deciding to be, 194

Dolls "sometimes wise," 365

Dongola, 360

Dream, about rye-field sold, 56-57

Drought, "gorgeous," 152

Dwight, Rev. E. S., 98, 101, 103

Echo song, 69

Eden, 189; mastiff guarding, 325; expulsion from, 359

Education, finishing an, 5

Elijah, 125

Eliot, George, 225, 276, 343, 357; death of, 241; Cross's Life of, 251, 279; poems by, 269

Ellen Middleton, 67

Emerson, Rev. F. F., letters to, 343-345

Emerson, R. W., 105, 106; Life of, by Dr. Holmes, 251

"Emilie," name spelled, 3

Endicott School, 71

Enobarbus, 273

Ephesus, "moving to," 251

Epicurean, Moore's, 33

Eternity, 20, 248

Etruscan experiment, marriage an, 365

Euclid, satisfaction in finishing, 59

Evangeline, 33

Eve, 17

Examinations, dread of, 10, 30; at Mt. Holyoke, 24, 25, 30

Eyes, first trouble with, 261

Faith of the fathers, 162

Fast Day, 66

February, 140; "that month of fleetest sweetness," 335

Field, Dr. T. P. and Mrs., 359

Fire in Amherst (1852), 92; (1879), 240; Phoenix row (1881), 243

Fiske, Prof. N. W., 245

Flood, law of, 185

Flower "that never will in other climate grow," 157

Flowers, 112, 126; preserved from Jack Frost, 14; love for spring, 33; wild, driven to a distance from Mt. Holyoke Sem., 33; coaxing the fading to wait, 80; sent in her stead, 112; blooming of, ascribed to her influence, 126; dreaming of picking, 133; gathering, in heaven, 133; of frost on window, 162; in the conservatory, 213; sent with notes, 310; "qualified as saints," 352

Flowers of North America, Hitchcock's, 273

Fly, "a precious," 195

Ford, Mrs. Gordon L., 252; letters to, 109-112, 118-121

Forest Leaves, 106

Forget-me-not, 119

Fowler, Emily, *see* Ford, Mrs. G. L.

Fowler, Prof. W. C., 104

Franking privilege, 99

Friend, how wondrous, 331

Friends, 133, 134, 137, 141, 159, 160, 173, 174, 176; love for, 228

Frink, Mr., 92

Frogs, 123, 124

Fruit, 76, 77

Fumigation, ceasing, 372

GABRIEL, 192; "morning call from," 241

Garden, 11, 14, 81, 133, 137, 143, 146, 149, 150, 161, 165; Emily's old-fashioned, 297-298; "perished with beautiful reluctance," 348

Gems abscond, 187

Genesis, 241

Genius, 145

Gentian, "a greedy flower," 144

Geometry, satisfaction in finishing, 59

Geranium, like a sultana, 165

Geraniums, 173

German, studying, 16

Germania Band, 101

Gethsemane and Cana, 339

Gibraltar lights, 147

"Give me thine heart," 336

God, "the Great Eclipse," xx; "jealous," xxi; presence in solitude, 34, 35

Golden Rule needs no police, 346

Gratitude "a desecration," 337

Grave of Bonaparte, 12

Green and gold, "immortal colors," 162

Greenough, Mrs. J. C., letters to, 365, 366

Grief "a sable introduction," 353

Grout, Austin, 73

Grout, Jennie, 83

"Guiteau year," 348

Gulf of down, 326

"H. H.," *see* Jackson, Mrs.

Hall, Miss, letters to, 364, 365

Harper's Magazine, 199

Harvard Law School, 55

Haven, Prof. Joseph, 65, 90, 100

Haven, Mrs. Joseph, 65

Hawthorne, death of, 261; "appalls, entices," 277

Hay, the second, 160

Heart, an "appalling boon," 336; "the Amherst," 354

Heaven, 48, 133, 135, 139, 141, 153, 160, 178

Heights of Abraham, 266

Heliotrope, yellow, 161

Higginson, Col. T. W., 252, 256, 257, 258, 260, 375; interview with, 264, 265; letters to, 252-279; *Atlantic Essays,* 269; on Emerson and Lowell, 271

Higginson, Mrs., 272, 273; to be the guest of, "the boon of birds," 271

Hills, Mrs. Henry, letters to, 338

Hippodrome, 97

Hitchcock, President, 6; *Flowers of North America,* 273

Hitchcock, Mrs. E., death of, 208

Holland, Annie, marriage of, 155

Holland, Dr. J. G., 96, 108; letters to, 129-157; death of, 153, 246

Holland Mrs. J. G., 100, 129; letters to, 129-157

Holland, Mr. Theodore, 360

Hollyhock, 121

Holmes, Dr. O. W., 105-106; *Life of Emerson,* 251; "Rhymes are iron fetters," 374

Home, 174; absence from, 24; missed at, 27; return to, 27, 28, 29; kept at, by illness, 32, 33; unwillingness to leave, 54; fondness for, 60, 61; brother dearer than, 73, 74; "a holy thing," 75; "bright and shining," 78; away from (verse), 148

Homesickness at school, 30, 33

Honeysuckle, 172

Horse of association, 290

House-cleaning, pestilence preferred to, 143

Household tasks, 13, 40

Household work, dislike for, 42

Housekeeping, "a prickly art," 250

Howells, W. D., 277

Howland, William, 115

Hunt, Helen, *see* Jackson, Mrs.

Humming-bird poem, 368

Humming-birds, 165

Humphrey, Pres. Heman, 131

Humphrey, Mr. Leonard, 22, 42, 43

"Ik Marvel," 66

Illness, first serious, 249

Imagination, 8, 9, 11, 59

Immortality, 99, 131, 155, 179, 191, 260, 268; "a slow solace," 339

Immortality, 272

India, gates to, 359

Indian pipes, 220, 238, 367; on binding of *Poems,* 368

Indies in the hand, 334

Insanity, 124

Invisibility to friends, 324, 353

Ivy, 190

Jackson, Mr., 296, 361, 362

Jackson, Mrs. ("H. H."), 106, 269, 270, 277, 355; desires E. D. to publish, 270, 271; letters to, 361, 362, 363, 364; death of, 363

James, Henry, 277

Jameson, Mrs., 342

Jane Eyre, 113

Jasmine, 213, 293; next dearest to daphne except wild-flowers, 269

Jays, 140, 222; "studying music with," 357

Jenkins, Rev. and Mrs. J. L., letters to, 315-317

Jenkins, Mr. MacGregor, article by, 313; letters to, 313
John Alden, 357
John Gilpin, 162
Judgment Day, 134
July, Fourth of, 238, 239
June, 96, 141, 181, 215, 235, 267, 316, 350
Juneating apple, 164
Junius, 184

KATIE, Aunt, 347, 350, 351, 352
Keats, 253
Keats's bird, 371
Kemble, Fanny, 194
Kingman, Martha, 83

LADY'S-SLIPPERS, yellow, 105
Lancers Quickstep, 12
Last letter, Emily Dickinson's, 373
Lathrop, G. P., poem, 247
Legislature, 231
Leontodon, 52
Letter, a life-warrant or death-warrant, 245
Letters, union, 151
Lilies of the field, 162, 288, 349
Lind, Jenny, 65; at Northampton, 68-70
Liver-leaf, 33
Locofoco, 57
Logician, the great, 342
Longfellow, H. W., 33, 105
Lord, Judge, 271, 350
Loss of friends, first moment eternity, 333
Lowell, J. R., 105, 106, 277; *Winter*, 218
Lowell, Mrs., poems of, 265

Lyon, Mary, 25, 26, 56, 57; kindness to pupils, 27; against valentines, 61

MADONNA, 181; Dresden, 276
Maggie, little, wilting, 223; "folding her tent," 226; death, 226
Maher, Maggie, letter to, 343
Maiden and Married Life of Mary Powell, 138
Maiden, weep no more, 12
Maplewood Institute, 107
March, 140, 292; flowers in, 121; infinite, 223; "that month of proclamation," xxii, 363
Margaret, 125, 147
Marian Erle, 226; dim pallet, 246
Marriage of Mrs. Holland's daughter, 155; of Mr. Cowan, 280; of Miss Hall, 365
Masque of Poets, A, 355
Mastiff "guarding Eden," 325
May, 179, 202, 205, 262, 302, 316, 375
Memory, 172; tropic, 352; rings her bell, 365
Menagerie, 56
Mexican War, 57
Middlemarch, 235
Miller, Joaquin, 269
Montague, Fanny, 106
Montague, Mr. and Mrs. George, letters to, 345, 346
Montague, Mass., 87
Moth in the work-basket, 47
Mother, death of, 299, 366; "to have had a," 366
Motherwell, William, 106
Mount Auburn, 19

Mt. Holyoke Seminary, before entering, 17, 18; entering, 24; order of exercises, 25, 26; domestic work, 26; letters from, 24, 31, 55, 57, 59, 62; attachment to, 30; homesickness at, 30, 32, 33; textbooks, 30; examinations, 24, 30; recalled from, 32; studies, 34; cousins at, 39; menagerie visited by pupils, 56; bill of fare, 58, 59

Mount Vernon, visit to, 136

Moving, 138, 139

Museum, 97; Chinese, 19, 20

Music, 9, 10, 12, 14, 369; her study of, 9, 10, 12, 14; of winds, 82

Music teachers, 11

Myra, death of, 205

Mystery, "maturity enhances," 367

NATURE, xxii, 63, 190; love of, 105, 151, 179; "neither knocks nor intrudes," 336; intimacy with, 336; old-fashioned, perhaps a Puritan, 337; "apology of," 369; "forgot—the circus reminded her," 369

Nest, perennial, 180; emerald, 184

New London trip, 95, 96, 97

New Year's presents, 24; resolutions, 15; greetings, 135, 162

New York Times, 223

Niger fig, 356

Nile, the, 143; "is a jealous brook," 321

Niles, Mr. Thomas, 355; letters to, 355-356

Nims, Seth, 57

Noah, "docile, but somewhat sceptic," 210; "would have liked mother," 218

No Name Series, 355

Northampton, Jenny Lind, 68-70

Norway, "of the year," 147

Norwottock, Mount, 105

November, 147

Numidian haunts, 187

OBSERVER, 84

October, 220, 246, 332

"Old Amos," 92

Opium-eating Chinese, 19

Orion, 4

"Othello is uneasy," 291; the throe of, 317; why censure? 369

PALMER, railroad from, 96

Paradise, 339; "superfluous," 141; remains, 359

Parepa, 284

Park, Prof. E. A., 85

Parker, Theodore, 162

Parting, 154, 155

Pathos, sweets of, 348

Pelham, 125, 173

Pelham hills, 189

Pelham water, 348

Perdition, sermon on, 134

"Peter," Cousin, 140

Peter the Great, 97

Philadelphia, 135, 136

Philosopher's stone, 344

Photograph requested, 256

Piano wished for, 6

Pines "sing tunes," 161

Pinks, 165; progeny of, 336

Pittsfield, 107

Plants, 7, 14, 16, 126

Plato, 5, 79

Poe, E. A., 277

Poems, "Success," 355; "My cricket," 355; "The snow," 355; "A pebble," 355; "A thunder storm," 356; "A humming-bird," 356, 368; "A country burial," 356

—— included in the letters, indexed by first lines:—

"A death-blow is a life-blow to some," 268

"A feather from the whippoorwill," 184

"A route of evanescence," 368

"A word left careless on a page," 233

"As if I asked a common alms," 256

"As summer into autumn slips," 187

"Awake, ye muses nine, sing me a strain divine," 113

"Away from home are some and I," 148

"Before he comes," 174

"Best gains must have the losses' test," 260

"Brother of Ophir," 327

"Could that sweet darkness where they dwell," 284

"Count not that far that can be had," 143

"Each that we lose takes part of us," 248

"Except the smaller size," 262

"Faith is a fine invention," 167

"Go not too near a house of rose," 324

Poems, indexed by first lines— (*continued*)

"Go slow, my soul, to feed thyself," 223

"Go thy great way," 337

"God made no act without a cause," 221

"Her breast is fit for pearls," 180

"Her losses make our gains ashamed," 356

"How brittle are the piers," 276

"How happy is the little stone," 356

"How much of Source escapes with thee," 156

"How slow the wind, how slow the sea," 330

"How well I know her not," 283

"I cannot see my soul, but know 'tis there," 229

"I have no life but this," 185

"I stole them from a bee," 177

"I'll send the feather from my hat," 180

"If recollecting were forgetting," 182

"If she had been the mistletoe," 176

"Immured the whole of life," 363

"Is it too late to touch you, dear," 364

"It is not dying hurts us so," 211

"Just once—oh! least request!" 184

"Last to adhere," 188

"Love is done when love's begun," 327

Poems, indexed by first lines—
(*continued*)

"Love's stricken 'why'," 320

"Menagerie to me," 266

"Nature and God, I neither knew," 179

"Never for society," 312

"No ladder needs the bird but skies," 289

"No wilderness can be," 181

"Not all die early, dying young," 148

"Not 'Revelation' 'tis that waits," 260

"Not seeing, still we know," 329

"Not sickness stains the brave," 369

"Obtaining but his own extent," 298

"Of Heaven above the firmest proof," 270

"One thing of it we borrow," 277

"Perhaps you think me stooping!" 177

"Presuming on that lone result," 274

"Publication is the auction," 226

"*Sic transit gloria mundi*," 115

"So glad we are, a stranger'd deem," 175

"*Speech* is a prank of Parliament," 177

"Summer laid her supple glove," 271

"Sweet pirate of the heart," 329

"Take all away," 267

"Take all away from me," 362

Poems, indexed by first lines—
(*continued*)

"Teach him, when he makes the names," 164

"Than Heaven more remote," 285

"The butterfly upon the sky, who doesn't know its name," 313

"The clock strikes one that just struck two," 295

"The dandelion's pallid tube," 328

"The ecstasy to guess," 364

"The face in evanescence lain," 286

"The going from a world we know," 250

"The juggler's hat her country is," 177

"The longest day that God appoints," 216

"The loss of sickness—was it loss?" 176

"The most triumphant bird," 234

"The only news I know," 261

"The possibility to pass," 262

"The robin is a Gabriel," 326

"The show is not the show," xxi

"The spirit lasts, but in what mode," 307

"The stem of a departed flower," 328

"The zeros taught us phosphorus," 167

"There are two ripenings, one of sight," 122

"There is no frigate like a book," 229

Poems, indexed by first lines—
(*continued*)
"There is no trumpet like the tomb," 343
" 'They have not chosen me,' he said," 182
"This is the place they hoped before," 228
"This was in the white of the year," 214
"Though my destiny be fustian," 149
"Though the great waters sleep," 333
"To disappear enhances," 272
"To this world she returned," 127
"To try to speak and miss the way," 330
"Trusty as the stars," 238
"Truth is as old as God," 135
"We know not that we were to live," 286
"We never know how high we are," xxi
"We never know we go— when we are going," 244
"We send the wave to find the wave," 233
"We shall find the cube of the rainbow," 325
"We shun it ere it comes," 353
"We wear our sober dresses when we die," 330
"We'll pass without a parting," 128
"What tenements of clover," 319
"While asters," 175
"Who abdicated ambush," 294

Poems, indexed by first lines—
(*continued*)
"Whose pink career may have a close," 268
"Would you with the bee return," 274
Pompeii, 239, 361
Portrait, verbal, 256
Postage, reduced to five cents, 4
Potomac, 136
Prescott, Harriet, 254
Princess, Tennyson's, 33
Publishing, foreign as "firmament to fin," 255; urged upon her, 225, 226, 270, 277, 278
Punctuation, dangers in, 364; dashes used for, xix, 39

QUICK and the dead, the, 166

RAILROAD, Amherst and Belchertown, 73, 87, 95, 96
Ramona, 363
Ravens, Elijah's, 125
Read, Mrs. Hanson, letters to, 318
Reading, 33
Remembrance, 161; "the staple of Heaven," 340; vocal, but one form, 341; "engulfs," 366
Resurrection, 160, 185
Revelation of St John, 253, 265, 271
Revival in the church, 234
Rhea, Miss, 280
Robert, 163, 166, 171
Roberts Brothers, 355
Robins, 172, 205, 216, 233; "my dolls," 365
Root, Prof. Elihu, death of, 327
Rose, 178

Roses, 133, 180; "of a steadfast summer," 149

Rowen, 160; "chopped by bees and piled by butterflies," 315

Rubinstein, reminds of "polar nights," 228

Ruskin, 253

St. Augustine, 157

Salvini, T., portrait of, 291

Sanborn, F. B., lecture by, 249

Sand, George, 200

Sanderson, Frederick M., 204

Santa Claus, 314, 315

Saxe Holm stories, 354

Sea "is ordained," the, 192

September, 144, 253

Sermon, death and judgment, 134

Shakespeare, 107, 372; Club, 107

Shrine, a homely, 181

Sickness unwelcome, 40; "is it patho or infamy?" 336

Silver Bill, 334

Skeel, Mr. and Mrs., 357, 358

Smith, Alexander, 95

Smith, Prof. H. B., 62

Snakes, 37

Snell, Prof., death of, 320

Snow, in spring, 88; "repealing the fences," 349

Socrates, 5, 79

Soldier, 174

Soldiers, 164

Solomon, "chagrined for," 288

Sorrow, 153, 154, 155, 156, 188

Soudan, 360, 369

South Hadley, 33, 39, 55, 58; danger of attack on, 57

Sparrow, 180, 190, 191

Spofford, A. R., 106

Spofford, H. M., 106

Spring, 52, 118, 143, 170, 200, 234, 249, 265, 271, 275

Springfield, 97, 129, 130, 136, 166, 171

Standish, Miles, 357

Star-gazing, 4

Stearns, Adjutant Frazer, 170, 202; death of, at Newbern, 204

Stearns, George, 157

Stearns, Pres., death of, 237, 320

Stearns, Mrs. W. A., letters to, 318, 319, 320, 321, 322

Stearns, William French, gave college church, 224

Stearns, Mrs. W. F., letter to, 346, 347

Steelyard, fraudulent, 146

"Step a century, can go but a," 330

Stratford-on-Avon, 276

Strong, Mrs. A. P., letters to, 1-54

Studies, 7, 16, 23, 30, 34, 59

Suffering, comprehended only by sufferers, 333

Sultans, 347, 348

Summer, 123, 125, 149, 150, 160, 164, 179, 187, 188, 203, 218, 240, 260, 297

Sunderland, Mass., 87, 105

Sunrise, 38

Sunset, very remarkable, 77-78

"Sweet despair," 277

Sweet pea, 152

Sweet williams, 165

Tarrytown, churchyard a, 351

Taylor, Mr., 21

Tears, unavailing, 32

Temptation, 41
Tennyson, 33
Thanksgiving, 27, 28, 29, 30, 83, 84, 127
Theophilus, 184
Thermopylæ, deathless of, 369
Thunder-shower, 89
Time, salt on the tail of, 6-7; fleetness of, 9, 14; value of, 20
Todd, Mrs. David P., 367
Tourguéneff, 269
Trillium, pink and white, 105
Trumbull, Mr., 78
Truth, eternity of (Verse), 135
Tuckerman, Prof. Edward, death of, 370
Tuckerman, Mrs. Edward, letters to, 322-332, 370
Tupper, M. F., 33
Turnpike, variegated, 195
Twins and Hearts, The, 33
Tyler, Mr., 6
Tyler, Prof. W. S., 90, 96
Tyrian dye, 175

Uncle Tom's Cabin, 102
Underwood, Uncle, 351
"Untiring Anno Domini," 308

Vaill, Rev. Joseph, 151, 173
Valentines, 61-62, 113, 115
Valor in the dark, 344
Vanderbilt, Mrs., 127
Vaughan, Henry, 278
Vesuvius "don't talk," 361
Village life very democratic," xix
Violet, yellow, 33; "sucking her way," 121; with "the mother's eyes," 124; in November, 137; estates of, 180

War, "an oblique place," 260
Warner, Prof. Aaron, 29
Warner, D., 87
Warner's hotel, Northampton, 69
Washington, George, tomb of, 136
Washington, D. C., visit to, 100, 101, 135, 136
Weather, Norwegian, 349
Webster, Daniel, 27, 90
Webster, Dr. J. W., 67
Welcome home, 29
Whig Convention, 90
Whig feelings, 6
Whippoorwill, 125, 184
Whitman, Miss, 58, 60, 61, 62
Whitman, Walt, 254
Whitney, Miss Maria, letters to, 283-293
Whittier, J. G., 105
Wilson, John, Christopher North, 232
Winds, orchestra of, 82
Winter, 161, 164; an infinite *Alas!*, 328
Winter, Lowell's, 218
Witch-hazel, 143; tinsel fringe, 238
Woodbridge, Miss, 23
Woods, the, 160
Work "a bleak redeemer," 188-189
World "to be burned up," 94

Xerxes, 228

Zeros, 201, 203; taught us phosphorus, 167
Zinnia, 150
Zones "a caprice," 186

A CATALOG OF SELECTED
DOVER BOOKS
IN ALL FIELDS OF INTEREST

A CATALOG OF SELECTED DOVER
BOOKS IN ALL FIELDS OF INTEREST

CONCERNING THE SPIRITUAL IN ART, Wassily Kandinsky. Pioneering work by father of abstract art. Thoughts on color theory, nature of art. Analysis of earlier masters. 12 illustrations. 80pp. of text. 5⅜ x 8½.   23411-8

ANIMALS: 1,419 Copyright-Free Illustrations of Mammals, Birds, Fish, Insects, etc., Jim Harter (ed.). Clear wood engravings present, in extremely lifelike poses, over 1,000 species of animals. One of the most extensive pictorial sourcebooks of its kind. Captions. Index. 284pp. 9 x 12.   23766-4

CELTIC ART: The Methods of Construction, George Bain. Simple geometric techniques for making Celtic interlacements, spirals, Kells-type initials, animals, humans, etc. Over 500 illustrations. 160pp. 9 x 12. (Available in U.S. only.)   22923-8

AN ATLAS OF ANATOMY FOR ARTISTS, Fritz Schider. Most thorough reference work on art anatomy in the world. Hundreds of illustrations, including selections from works by Vesalius, Leonardo, Goya, Ingres, Michelangelo, others. 593 illustrations. 192pp. 7⅛ x 10¼.   20241-0

CELTIC HAND STROKE-BY-STROKE (Irish Half-Uncial from "The Book of Kells"): An Arthur Baker Calligraphy Manual, Arthur Baker. Complete guide to creating each letter of the alphabet in distinctive Celtic manner. Covers hand position, strokes, pens, inks, paper, more. Illustrated. 48pp. 8¼ x 11.   24336-2

EASY ORIGAMI, John Montroll. Charming collection of 32 projects (hat, cup, pelican, piano, swan, many more) specially designed for the novice origami hobbyist. Clearly illustrated easy-to-follow instructions insure that even beginning papercrafters will achieve successful results. 48pp. 8¼ x 11.   27298-2

THE COMPLETE BOOK OF BIRDHOUSE CONSTRUCTION FOR WOODWORKERS, Scott D. Campbell. Detailed instructions, illustrations, tables. Also data on bird habitat and instinct patterns. Bibliography. 3 tables. 63 illustrations in 15 figures. 48pp. 5¼ x 8½.   24407-5

BLOOMINGDALE'S ILLUSTRATED 1886 CATALOG: Fashions, Dry Goods and Housewares, Bloomingdale Brothers. Famed merchants' extremely rare catalog depicting about 1,700 products: clothing, housewares, firearms, dry goods, jewelry, more. Invaluable for dating, identifying vintage items. Also, copyright-free graphics for artists, designers. Co-published with Henry Ford Museum & Greenfield Village. 160pp. 8¼ x 11.   25780-0

HISTORIC COSTUME IN PICTURES, Braun & Schneider. Over 1,450 costumed figures in clearly detailed engravings–from dawn of civilization to end of 19th century. Captions. Many folk costumes. 256pp. 8⅜ x 11¾.   23150-X

CATALOG OF DOVER BOOKS

STICKLEY CRAFTSMAN FURNITURE CATALOGS, Gustav Stickley and L. & J. G. Stickley. Beautiful, functional furniture in two authentic catalogs from 1910. 594 illustrations, including 277 photos, show settles, rockers, armchairs, reclining chairs, bookcases, desks, tables. 183pp. 6½ x 9¼. 23838-5

AMERICAN LOCOMOTIVES IN HISTORIC PHOTOGRAPHS: 1858 to 1949, Ron Ziel (ed.). A rare collection of 126 meticulously detailed official photographs, called "builder portraits," of American locomotives that majestically chronicle the rise of steam locomotive power in America. Introduction. Detailed captions. xi+ 129pp. 9 x 12. 27393-8

AMERICA'S LIGHTHOUSES: An Illustrated History, Francis Ross Holland, Jr. Delightfully written, profusely illustrated fact-filled survey of over 200 American lighthouses since 1716. History, anecdotes, technological advances, more. 240pp. 8 x 10¾. 25576-X

TOWARDS A NEW ARCHITECTURE, Le Corbusier. Pioneering manifesto by founder of "International School." Technical and aesthetic theories, views of industry, economics, relation of form to function, "mass-production split" and much more. Profusely illustrated. 320pp. 6⅛ x 9¼. (Available in U.S. only.) 25023-7

HOW THE OTHER HALF LIVES, Jacob Riis. Famous journalistic record, exposing poverty and degradation of New York slums around 1900, by major social reformer. 100 striking and influential photographs. 233pp. 10 x 7⅞. 22012-5

FRUIT KEY AND TWIG KEY TO TREES AND SHRUBS, William M. Harlow. One of the handiest and most widely used identification aids. Fruit key covers 120 deciduous and evergreen species; twig key 160 deciduous species. Easily used. Over 300 photographs. 126pp. 5⅜ x 8½. 20511-8

COMMON BIRD SONGS, Dr. Donald J. Borror. Songs of 60 most common U.S. birds: robins, sparrows, cardinals, bluejays, finches, more–arranged in order of increasing complexity. Up to 9 variations of songs of each species.
Cassette and manual 99911-4

ORCHIDS AS HOUSE PLANTS, Rebecca Tyson Northen. Grow cattleyas and many other kinds of orchids–in a window, in a case, or under artificial light. 63 illustrations. 148pp. 5⅜ x 8½. 23261-1

MONSTER MAZES, Dave Phillips. Masterful mazes at four levels of difficulty. Avoid deadly perils and evil creatures to find magical treasures. Solutions for all 32 exciting illustrated puzzles. 48pp. 8¼ x 11. 26005-4

MOZART'S DON GIOVANNI (DOVER OPERA LIBRETTO SERIES), Wolfgang Amadeus Mozart. Introduced and translated by Ellen H. Bleiler. Standard Italian libretto, with complete English translation. Convenient and thoroughly portable–an ideal companion for reading along with a recording or the performance itself. Introduction. List of characters. Plot summary. 121pp. 5¼ x 8½. 24944-1

TECHNICAL MANUAL AND DICTIONARY OF CLASSICAL BALLET, Gail Grant. Defines, explains, comments on steps, movements, poses and concepts. 15-page pictorial section. Basic book for student, viewer. 127pp. 5⅜ x 8½. 21843-0

THE CLARINET AND CLARINET PLAYING, David Pino. Lively, comprehensive work features suggestions about technique, musicianship, and musical interpretation, as well as guidelines for teaching, making your own reeds, and preparing for public performance. Includes an intriguing look at clarinet history. "A godsend," *The Clarinet,* Journal of the International Clarinet Society. Appendixes. 7 illus. 320pp. 5⅜ x 8½. 40270-3

HOLLYWOOD GLAMOR PORTRAITS, John Kobal (ed.). 145 photos from 1926-49. Harlow, Gable, Bogart, Bacall; 94 stars in all. Full background on photographers, technical aspects. 160pp. 8⅜ x 11¼. 23352-9

THE ANNOTATED CASEY AT THE BAT: A Collection of Ballads about the Mighty Casey/Third, Revised Edition, Martin Gardner (ed.). Amusing sequels and parodies of one of America's best-loved poems: Casey's Revenge, Why Casey Whiffed, Casey's Sister at the Bat, others. 256pp. 5⅜ x 8½. 28598-7

THE RAVEN AND OTHER FAVORITE POEMS, Edgar Allan Poe. Over 40 of the author's most memorable poems: "The Bells," "Ulalume," "Israfel," "To Helen," "The Conqueror Worm," "Eldorado," "Annabel Lee," many more. Alphabetic lists of titles and first lines. 64pp. $5\frac{3}{16}$ x 8¼. 26685-0

PERSONAL MEMOIRS OF U. S. GRANT, Ulysses Simpson Grant. Intelligent, deeply moving firsthand account of Civil War campaigns, considered by many the finest military memoirs ever written. Includes letters, historic photographs, maps and more. 528pp. 6⅛ x 9¼. 28587-1

ANCIENT EGYPTIAN MATERIALS AND INDUSTRIES, A. Lucas and J. Harris. Fascinating, comprehensive, thoroughly documented text describes this ancient civilization's vast resources and the processes that incorporated them in daily life, including the use of animal products, building materials, cosmetics, perfumes and incense, fibers, glazed ware, glass and its manufacture, materials used in the mummification process, and much more. 544pp. 6⅛ x 9¼. (Available in U.S. only.) 40446-3

RUSSIAN STORIES/RUSSKIE RASSKAZY: A Dual-Language Book, edited by Gleb Struve. Twelve tales by such masters as Chekhov, Tolstoy, Dostoevsky, Pushkin, others. Excellent word-for-word English translations on facing pages, plus teaching and study aids, Russian/English vocabulary, biographical/critical introductions, more. 416pp. 5⅜ x 8½. 26244-8

PHILADELPHIA THEN AND NOW: 60 Sites Photographed in the Past and Present, Kenneth Finkel and Susan Oyama. Rare photographs of City Hall, Logan Square, Independence Hall, Betsy Ross House, other landmarks juxtaposed with contemporary views. Captures changing face of historic city. Introduction. Captions. 128pp. 8¼ x 11. 25790-8

AIA ARCHITECTURAL GUIDE TO NASSAU AND SUFFOLK COUNTIES, LONG ISLAND, The American Institute of Architects, Long Island Chapter, and the Society for the Preservation of Long Island Antiquities. Comprehensive, well-researched and generously illustrated volume brings to life over three centuries of Long Island's great architectural heritage. More than 240 photographs with authoritative, extensively detailed captions. 176pp. 8¼ x 11. 26946-9

NORTH AMERICAN INDIAN LIFE: Customs and Traditions of 23 Tribes, Elsie Clews Parsons (ed.). 27 fictionalized essays by noted anthropologists examine religion, customs, government, additional facets of life among the Winnebago, Crow, Zuni, Eskimo, other tribes. 480pp. 6⅛ x 9¼. 27377-6

FRANK LLOYD WRIGHT'S DANA HOUSE, Donald Hoffmann. Pictorial essay of residential masterpiece with over 160 interior and exterior photos, plans, elevations, sketches and studies. 128pp. 9¼ x 10¾. 29120-0

THE MALE AND FEMALE FIGURE IN MOTION: 60 Classic Photographic Sequences, Eadweard Muybridge. 60 true-action photographs of men and women walking, running, climbing, bending, turning, etc., reproduced from rare 19th-century masterpiece. vi + 121pp. 9 x 12. 24745-7

1001 QUESTIONS ANSWERED ABOUT THE SEASHORE, N. J. Berrill and Jacquelyn Berrill. Queries answered about dolphins, sea snails, sponges, starfish, fishes, shore birds, many others. Covers appearance, breeding, growth, feeding, much more. 305pp. 5¼ x 8¼. 23366-9

ATTRACTING BIRDS TO YOUR YARD, William J. Weber. Easy-to-follow guide offers advice on how to attract the greatest diversity of birds: birdhouses, feeders, water and waterers, much more. 96pp. 5³⁄₁₆ x 8¼. 28927-3

MEDICINAL AND OTHER USES OF NORTH AMERICAN PLANTS: A Historical Survey with Special Reference to the Eastern Indian Tribes, Charlotte Erichsen-Brown. Chronological historical citations document 500 years of usage of plants, trees, shrubs native to eastern Canada, northeastern U.S. Also complete identifying information. 343 illustrations. 544pp. 6½ x 9¼. 25951-X

STORYBOOK MAZES, Dave Phillips. 23 stories and mazes on two-page spreads: Wizard of Oz, Treasure Island, Robin Hood, etc. Solutions. 64pp. 8¼ x 11. 23628-5

AMERICAN NEGRO SONGS: 230 Folk Songs and Spirituals, Religious and Secular, John W. Work. This authoritative study traces the African influences of songs sung and played by black Americans at work, in church, and as entertainment. The author discusses the lyric significance of such songs as "Swing Low, Sweet Chariot," "John Henry," and others and offers the words and music for 230 songs. Bibliography. Index of Song Titles. 272pp. 6½ x 9¼. 40271-1

MOVIE-STAR PORTRAITS OF THE FORTIES, John Kobal (ed.). 163 glamor, studio photos of 106 stars of the 1940s: Rita Hayworth, Ava Gardner, Marlon Brando, Clark Gable, many more. 176pp. 8⅜ x 11¼. 23546-7

BENCHLEY LOST AND FOUND, Robert Benchley. Finest humor from early 30s, about pet peeves, child psychologists, post office and others. Mostly unavailable elsewhere. 73 illustrations by Peter Arno and others. 183pp. 5⅜ x 8½. 22410-4

YEKL and THE IMPORTED BRIDEGROOM AND OTHER STORIES OF YIDDISH NEW YORK, Abraham Cahan. Film Hester Street based on *Yekl* (1896). Novel, other stories among first about Jewish immigrants on N.Y.'s East Side. 240pp. 5⅜ x 8½. 22427-9

SELECTED POEMS, Walt Whitman. Generous sampling from *Leaves of Grass.* Twenty-four poems include "I Hear America Singing," "Song of the Open Road," "I Sing the Body Electric," "When Lilacs Last in the Dooryard Bloom'd," "O Captain! My Captain!"—all reprinted from an authoritative edition. Lists of titles and first lines. 128pp. 5³⁄₁₆ x 8¼. 26878-0

THE BEST TALES OF HOFFMANN, E. T. A. Hoffmann. 10 of Hoffmann's most important stories: "Nutcracker and the King of Mice," "The Golden Flowerpot," etc. 458pp. 5⅜ x 8½. 21793-0

FROM FETISH TO GOD IN ANCIENT EGYPT, E. A. Wallis Budge. Rich detailed survey of Egyptian conception of "God" and gods, magic, cult of animals, Osiris, more. Also, superb English translations of hymns and legends. 240 illustrations. 545pp. 5⅜ x 8½. 25803-3

FRENCH STORIES/CONTES FRANÇAIS: A Dual-Language Book, Wallace Fowlie. Ten stories by French masters, Voltaire to Camus: "Micromegas" by Voltaire; "The Atheist's Mass" by Balzac; "Minuet" by de Maupassant; "The Guest" by Camus, six more. Excellent English translations on facing pages. Also French-English vocabulary list, exercises, more. 352pp. 5⅜ x 8½. 26443-2

CHICAGO AT THE TURN OF THE CENTURY IN PHOTOGRAPHS: 122 Historic Views from the Collections of the Chicago Historical Society, Larry A. Viskochil. Rare large-format prints offer detailed views of City Hall, State Street, the Loop, Hull House, Union Station, many other landmarks, circa 1904-1913. Introduction. Captions. Maps. 144pp. 9⅜ x 12¼. 24656-6

OLD BROOKLYN IN EARLY PHOTOGRAPHS, 1865-1929, William Lee Younger. Luna Park, Gravesend race track, construction of Grand Army Plaza, moving of Hotel Brighton, etc. 157 previously unpublished photographs. 165pp. 8⅞ x 11¾. 23587-4

THE MYTHS OF THE NORTH AMERICAN INDIANS, Lewis Spence. Rich anthology of the myths and legends of the Algonquins, Iroquois, Pawnees and Sioux, prefaced by an extensive historical and ethnological commentary. 36 illustrations. 480pp. 5⅜ x 8½. 25967-6

AN ENCYCLOPEDIA OF BATTLES: Accounts of Over 1,560 Battles from 1479 B.C. to the Present, David Eggenberger. Essential details of every major battle in recorded history from the first battle of Megiddo in 1479 B.C. to Grenada in 1984. List of Battle Maps. New Appendix covering the years 1967-1984. Index. 99 illustrations. 544pp. 6½ x 9¼. 24913-1

SAILING ALONE AROUND THE WORLD, Captain Joshua Slocum. First man to sail around the world, alone, in small boat. One of great feats of seamanship told in delightful manner. 67 illustrations. 294pp. 5⅜ x 8½. 20326-3

ANARCHISM AND OTHER ESSAYS, Emma Goldman. Powerful, penetrating, prophetic essays on direct action, role of minorities, prison reform, puritan hypocrisy, violence, etc. 271pp. 5⅜ x 8½. 22484-8

MYTHS OF THE HINDUS AND BUDDHISTS, Ananda K. Coomaraswamy and Sister Nivedita. Great stories of the epics; deeds of Krishna, Shiva, taken from puranas, Vedas, folk tales; etc. 32 illustrations. 400pp. 5⅜ x 8½. 21759-0

THE TRAUMA OF BIRTH, Otto Rank. Rank's controversial thesis that anxiety neurosis is caused by profound psychological trauma which occurs at birth. 256pp. 5⅜ x 8½. 27974-X

A THEOLOGICO-POLITICAL TREATISE, Benedict Spinoza. Also contains unfinished Political Treatise. Great classic on religious liberty, theory of government on common consent. R. Elwes translation. Total of 421pp. 5⅜ x 8½. 20249-6

MY BONDAGE AND MY FREEDOM, Frederick Douglass. Born a slave, Douglass became outspoken force in antislavery movement. The best of Douglass' autobiographies. Graphic description of slave life. 464pp. 5⅜ x 8½.   22457-0

FOLLOWING THE EQUATOR: A Journey Around the World, Mark Twain. Fascinating humorous account of 1897 voyage to Hawaii, Australia, India, New Zealand, etc. Ironic, bemused reports on peoples, customs, climate, flora and fauna, politics, much more. 197 illustrations. 720pp. 5⅜ x 8½.   26113-1

THE PEOPLE CALLED SHAKERS, Edward D. Andrews. Definitive study of Shakers: origins, beliefs, practices, dances, social organization, furniture and crafts, etc. 33 illustrations. 351pp. 5⅜ x 8½.   21081-2

THE MYTHS OF GREECE AND ROME, H. A. Guerber. A classic of mythology, generously illustrated, long prized for its simple, graphic, accurate retelling of the principal myths of Greece and Rome, and for its commentary on their origins and significance. With 64 illustrations by Michelangelo, Raphael, Titian, Rubens, Canova, Bernini and others. 480pp. 5⅜ x 8½.   27584-1

PSYCHOLOGY OF MUSIC, Carl E. Seashore. Classic work discusses music as a medium from psychological viewpoint. Clear treatment of physical acoustics, auditory apparatus, sound perception, development of musical skills, nature of musical feeling, host of other topics. 88 figures. 408pp. 5⅜ x 8½.   21851-1

THE PHILOSOPHY OF HISTORY, Georg W. Hegel. Great classic of Western thought develops concept that history is not chance but rational process, the evolution of freedom. 457pp. 5⅜ x 8½.   20112-0

THE BOOK OF TEA, Kakuzo Okakura. Minor classic of the Orient: entertaining, charming explanation, interpretation of traditional Japanese culture in terms of tea ceremony. 94pp. 5⅜ x 8½.   20070-1

LIFE IN ANCIENT EGYPT, Adolf Erman. Fullest, most thorough, detailed older account with much not in more recent books, domestic life, religion, magic, medicine, commerce, much more. Many illustrations reproduce tomb paintings, carvings, hieroglyphs, etc. 597pp. 5⅜ x 8½.   22632-8

SUNDIALS, Their Theory and Construction, Albert Waugh. Far and away the best, most thorough coverage of ideas, mathematics concerned, types, construction, adjusting anywhere. Simple, nontechnical treatment allows even children to build several of these dials. Over 100 illustrations. 230pp. 5⅜ x 8½.   22947-5

THEORETICAL HYDRODYNAMICS, L. M. Milne-Thomson. Classic exposition of the mathematical theory of fluid motion, applicable to both hydrodynamics and aerodynamics. Over 600 exercises. 768pp. 6⅛ x 9¼.   68970-0

SONGS OF EXPERIENCE: Facsimile Reproduction with 26 Plates in Full Color, William Blake. 26 full-color plates from a rare 1826 edition. Includes "The Tyger," "London," "Holy Thursday," and other poems. Printed text of poems. 48pp. 5¼ x 7.
24636-1

OLD-TIME VIGNETTES IN FULL COLOR, Carol Belanger Grafton (ed.). Over 390 charming, often sentimental illustrations, selected from archives of Victorian graphics—pretty women posing, children playing, food, flowers, kittens and puppies, smiling cherubs, birds and butterflies, much more. All copyright-free. 48pp. 9¼ x 12¼.
27269-9

PERSPECTIVE FOR ARTISTS, Rex Vicat Cole. Depth, perspective of sky and sea, shadows, much more, not usually covered. 391 diagrams, 81 reproductions of drawings and paintings. 279pp. 5⅜ x 8½. 22487-2

DRAWING THE LIVING FIGURE, Joseph Sheppard. Innovative approach to artistic anatomy focuses on specifics of surface anatomy, rather than muscles and bones. Over 170 drawings of live models in front, back and side views, and in widely varying poses. Accompanying diagrams. 177 illustrations. Introduction. Index. 144pp. 8⅜ x11¼. 26723-7

GOTHIC AND OLD ENGLISH ALPHABETS: 100 Complete Fonts, Dan X. Solo. Add power, elegance to posters, signs, other graphics with 100 stunning copyright-free alphabets: Blackstone, Dolbey, Germania, 97 more–including many lower-case, numerals, punctuation marks. 104pp. 8⅛ x 11. 24695-7

HOW TO DO BEADWORK, Mary White. Fundamental book on craft from simple projects to five-bead chains and woven works. 106 illustrations. 142pp. 5⅜ x 8. 20697-1

THE BOOK OF WOOD CARVING, Charles Marshall Sayers. Finest book for beginners discusses fundamentals and offers 34 designs. "Absolutely first rate . . . well thought out and well executed."–E. J. Tangerman. 118pp. 7¾ x 10⅝. 23654-4

ILLUSTRATED CATALOG OF CIVIL WAR MILITARY GOODS: Union Army Weapons, Insignia, Uniform Accessories, and Other Equipment, Schuyler, Hartley, and Graham. Rare, profusely illustrated 1846 catalog includes Union Army uniform and dress regulations, arms and ammunition, coats, insignia, flags, swords, rifles, etc. 226 illustrations. 160pp. 9 x 12. 24939-5

WOMEN'S FASHIONS OF THE EARLY 1900s: An Unabridged Republication of "New York Fashions, 1909," National Cloak & Suit Co. Rare catalog of mail-order fashions documents women's and children's clothing styles shortly after the turn of the century. Captions offer full descriptions, prices. Invaluable resource for fashion, costume historians. Approximately 725 illustrations. 128pp. 8⅜ x 11¼. 27276-1

THE 1912 AND 1915 GUSTAV STICKLEY FURNITURE CATALOGS, Gustav Stickley. With over 200 detailed illustrations and descriptions, these two catalogs are essential reading and reference materials and identification guides for Stickley furniture. Captions cite materials, dimensions and prices. 112pp. 6½ x 9¼. 26676-1

EARLY AMERICAN LOCOMOTIVES, John H. White, Jr. Finest locomotive engravings from early 19th century: historical (1804–74), main-line (after 1870), special, foreign, etc. 147 plates. 142pp. 11⅜ x 8¼. 22772-3

THE TALL SHIPS OF TODAY IN PHOTOGRAPHS, Frank O. Braynard. Lavishly illustrated tribute to nearly 100 majestic contemporary sailing vessels: Amerigo Vespucci, Clearwater, Constitution, Eagle, Mayflower, Sea Cloud, Victory, many more. Authoritative captions provide statistics, background on each ship. 190 black-and-white photographs and illustrations. Introduction. 128pp. 8⅞ x 11¾. 27163-3

LITTLE BOOK OF EARLY AMERICAN CRAFTS AND TRADES, Peter Stockham (ed.). 1807 children's book explains crafts and trades: baker, hatter, cooper, potter, and many others. 23 copperplate illustrations. 140pp. 4⅝ x 6.   23336-7

VICTORIAN FASHIONS AND COSTUMES FROM HARPER'S BAZAR, 1867–1898, Stella Blum (ed.). Day costumes, evening wear, sports clothes, shoes, hats, other accessories in over 1,000 detailed engravings. 320pp. 9⅜ x 12¼. 22990-4

GUSTAV STICKLEY, THE CRAFTSMAN, Mary Ann Smith. Superb study surveys broad scope of Stickley's achievement, especially in architecture. Design philosophy, rise and fall of the Craftsman empire, descriptions and floor plans for many Craftsman houses, more. 86 black-and-white halftones. 31 line illustrations. Introduction 208pp. 6½ x 9¼.   27210-9

THE LONG ISLAND RAIL ROAD IN EARLY PHOTOGRAPHS, Ron Ziel. Over 220 rare photos, informative text document origin (1844) and development of rail service on Long Island. Vintage views of early trains, locomotives, stations, passengers, crews, much more. Captions. 8⅞ x 11¾.   26301-0

VOYAGE OF THE LIBERDADE, Joshua Slocum. Great 19th-century mariner's thrilling, first-hand account of the wreck of his ship off South America, the 35-foot boat he built from the wreckage, and its remarkable voyage home. 128pp. 5⅜ x 8½.
40022-0

TEN BOOKS ON ARCHITECTURE, Vitruvius. The most important book ever written on architecture. Early Roman aesthetics, technology, classical orders, site selection, all other aspects. Morgan translation. 331pp. 5⅜ x 8½.   20645-9

THE HUMAN FIGURE IN MOTION, Eadweard Muybridge. More than 4,500 stopped-action photos, in action series, showing undraped men, women, children jumping, lying down, throwing, sitting, wrestling, carrying, etc. 390pp. 7⅞ x 10⅝.
20204-6 Clothbd.

TREES OF THE EASTERN AND CENTRAL UNITED STATES AND CANADA, William M. Harlow. Best one-volume guide to 140 trees. Full descriptions, woodlore, range, etc. Over 600 illustrations. Handy size. 288pp. 4½ x 6⅜.   20395-6

SONGS OF WESTERN BIRDS, Dr. Donald J. Borror. Complete song and call repertoire of 60 western species, including flycatchers, juncoes, cactus wrens, many more–includes fully illustrated booklet.   Cassette and manual 99913-0

GROWING AND USING HERBS AND SPICES, Milo Miloradovich. Versatile handbook provides all the information needed for cultivation and use of all the herbs and spices available in North America. 4 illustrations. Index. Glossary. 236pp. 5⅜ x 8½.
25058-X

BIG BOOK OF MAZES AND LABYRINTHS, Walter Shepherd. 50 mazes and labyrinths in all–classical, solid, ripple, and more–in one great volume. Perfect inexpensive puzzler for clever youngsters. Full solutions. 112pp. 8⅛ x 11.   22951-3

PIANO TUNING, J. Cree Fischer. Clearest, best book for beginner, amateur. Simple repairs, raising dropped notes, tuning by easy method of flattened fifths. No previous skills needed. 4 illustrations. 201pp. 5⅜ x 8½. 23267-0

HINTS TO SINGERS, Lillian Nordica. Selecting the right teacher, developing confidence, overcoming stage fright, and many other important skills receive thoughtful discussion in this indispensible guide, written by a world-famous diva of four decades' experience. 96pp. 5⅜ x 8½. 40094-8

THE COMPLETE NONSENSE OF EDWARD LEAR, Edward Lear. All nonsense limericks, zany alphabets, Owl and Pussycat, songs, nonsense botany, etc., illustrated by Lear. Total of 320pp. 5⅜ x 8½. (Available in U.S. only.) 20167-8

VICTORIAN PARLOUR POETRY: An Annotated Anthology, Michael R. Turner. 117 gems by Longfellow, Tennyson, Browning, many lesser-known poets. "The Village Blacksmith," "Curfew Must Not Ring Tonight," "Only a Baby Small," dozens more, often difficult to find elsewhere. Index of poets, titles, first lines. xxiii + 325pp. 5⅝ x 8¼. 27044-0

DUBLINERS, James Joyce. Fifteen stories offer vivid, tightly focused observations of the lives of Dublin's poorer classes. At least one, "The Dead," is considered a masterpiece. Reprinted complete and unabridged from standard edition. 160pp. 5³⁄₁₆ x 8¼. 26870-5

GREAT WEIRD TALES: 14 Stories by Lovecraft, Blackwood, Machen and Others, S. T. Joshi (ed.). 14 spellbinding tales, including "The Sin Eater," by Fiona McLeod, "The Eye Above the Mantel," by Frank Belknap Long, as well as renowned works by R. H. Barlow, Lord Dunsany, Arthur Machen, W. C. Morrow and eight other masters of the genre. 256pp. 5⅜ x 8½. (Available in U.S. only.) 40436-6

THE BOOK OF THE SACRED MAGIC OF ABRAMELIN THE MAGE, translated by S. MacGregor Mathers. Medieval manuscript of ceremonial magic. Basic document in Aleister Crowley, Golden Dawn groups. 268pp. 5⅜ x 8½. 23211-5

NEW RUSSIAN-ENGLISH AND ENGLISH-RUSSIAN DICTIONARY, M. A. O'Brien. This is a remarkably handy Russian dictionary, containing a surprising amount of information, including over 70,000 entries. 366pp. 4½ x 6⅛. 20208-9

HISTORIC HOMES OF THE AMERICAN PRESIDENTS, Second, Revised Edition, Irvin Haas. A traveler's guide to American Presidential homes, most open to the public, depicting and describing homes occupied by every American President from George Washington to George Bush. With visiting hours, admission charges, travel routes. 175 photographs. Index. 160pp. 8¼ x 11. 26751-2

NEW YORK IN THE FORTIES, Andreas Feininger. 162 brilliant photographs by the well-known photographer, formerly with *Life* magazine. Commuters, shoppers, Times Square at night, much else from city at its peak. Captions by John von Hartz. 181pp. 9¼ x 10¾. 23585-8

INDIAN SIGN LANGUAGE, William Tomkins. Over 525 signs developed by Sioux and other tribes. Written instructions and diagrams. Also 290 pictographs. 111pp. 6⅛ x 9¼. 22029-X

THE STORY OF THE TITANIC AS TOLD BY ITS SURVIVORS, Jack Winocour (ed.). What it was really like. Panic, despair, shocking inefficiency, and a little heroism. More thrilling than any fictional account. 26 illustrations. 320pp. 5⅜ x 8½.
20610-6

FAIRY AND FOLK TALES OF THE IRISH PEASANTRY, William Butler Yeats (ed.). Treasury of 64 tales from the twilight world of Celtic myth and legend: "The Soul Cages," "The Kildare Pooka," "King O'Toole and his Goose," many more. Introduction and Notes by W. B. Yeats. 352pp. 5⅜ x 8½.
26941-8

BUDDHIST MAHAYANA TEXTS, E. B. Cowell and others (eds.). Superb, accurate translations of basic documents in Mahayana Buddhism, highly important in history of religions. The Buddha-karita of Asvaghosha, Larger Sukhavativyuha, more. 448pp. 5⅜ x 8½.
25552-2

ONE TWO THREE . . . INFINITY: Facts and Speculations of Science, George Gamow. Great physicist's fascinating, readable overview of contemporary science: number theory, relativity, fourth dimension, entropy, genes, atomic structure, much more. 128 illustrations. Index. 352pp. 5⅜ x 8½.
25664-2

EXPERIMENTATION AND MEASUREMENT, W. J. Youden. Introductory manual explains laws of measurement in simple terms and offers tips for achieving accuracy and minimizing errors. Mathematics of measurement, use of instruments, experimenting with machines. 1994 edition. Foreword. Preface. Introduction. Epilogue. Selected Readings. Glossary. Index. Tables and figures. 128pp. 5⅜ x 8½.   40451-X

DALÍ ON MODERN ART: The Cuckolds of Antiquated Modern Art, Salvador Dalí. Influential painter skewers modern art and its practitioners. Outrageous evaluations of Picasso, Cézanne, Turner, more. 15 renderings of paintings discussed. 44 calligraphic decorations by Dalí. 96pp. 5⅜ x 8½. (Available in U.S. only.)   29220-7

ANTIQUE PLAYING CARDS: A Pictorial History, Henry René D'Allemagne. Over 900 elaborate, decorative images from rare playing cards (14th–20th centuries): Bacchus, death, dancing dogs, hunting scenes, royal coats of arms, players cheating, much more. 96pp. 9¼ x 12¼.
29265-7

MAKING FURNITURE MASTERPIECES: 30 Projects with Measured Drawings, Franklin H. Gottshall. Step-by-step instructions, illustrations for constructing handsome, useful pieces, among them a Sheraton desk, Chippendale chair, Spanish desk, Queen Anne table and a William and Mary dressing mirror. 224pp. 8⅛ x 11¼.
29338-6

THE FOSSIL BOOK: A Record of Prehistoric Life, Patricia V. Rich et al. Profusely illustrated definitive guide covers everything from single-celled organisms and dinosaurs to birds and mammals and the interplay between climate and man. Over 1,500 illustrations. 760pp. 7½ x 10⅛.
29371-8

Paperbound unless otherwise indicated. Available at your book dealer, online at **www.doverpublications.com**, or by writing to Dept. GI, Dover Publications, Inc., 31 East 2nd Street, Mineola, NY 11501. For current price information or for free catalogues (please indicate field of interest), write to Dover Publications or log on to **www.doverpublications.com** and see every Dover book in print. Dover publishes more than 500 books each year on science, elementary and advanced mathematics, biology, music, art, literary history, social sciences, and other areas.